W9-BKJ-952

THE
MOBILE
PROFESSORS

378.12
B877m

If one of the nation's scarcest resources . . . manpower capable of teaching at the college level . . . is to be effectively utilized, we must gain a better understanding of . . .

THE MOBILE PROFESSORS

DAVID G. BROWN

AMERICAN COUNCIL ON EDUCATION

© 1967 by American Council on Education
1785 Massachusetts Avenue, N.W.
Washington, D.C. 20036

Library of Congress Card No. 67-21046

Printed in the United States of America

Acknowledgments

Thanks are due—

to the 2,000 college presidents and 13,000 college faculty members who gave unselfishly of their time in answering our questionnaires;

to Dr. Jay Tontz who has ever so capably and willingly acted as my research assistant for these eighteen months and who has contributed in innumerable ways to the quality of this study;

to Mr. Thomas Weiss who acted in the same capacity and with equal ability and spirit during the final three months;

to Mr. Carven Angel, Mr. Ron Bone, Mr. Heathcote Wales, and Mr. Marshall Casse who have also served as research assistants;

to my wife who assisted in the management of the coding and provided valuable insights throughout the study;

to Mrs. Carolyn Geller and Mr. E. N. Schroeder of the Duke University Computing Laboratory who spent months of their time devising ingenius ways to meet particularized requests for data;

to the U.S. Department of Labor, Office of Manpower, Automation and Training and my capable contract supervisor, Mr. Morton Levine, for providing the financial assistance that made this study possible;

and to the more than 200 students of the academic labor market with whom I have discussed, either in person or through correspondence, matters of mutual concern.

April 1967   David G. Brown

Contents

List of Tables

1

An Economic Analysis
of the Academic Labor Market

From *The Academic Man* to *Academic Women,* recent studies have involved virtually all aspects of the academic institution. Paul Lazarsfeld and Wagner Thielens have studied *The Academic Mind.* The organizational structure and systems of authority of the nation's best universities have been reported by Theodore Caplow and Reece McGee in *The Academic Marketplace.* These studies, however, have been conducted by sociologists from a sociological perspective. The present analysis adds the perspective of an economist. Herein the analytical tools of economics are applied to the behavior of job-changing professors to accomplish twin objectives—the formulation of policy recommendations to enable a more efficient allocation of professorial talent, and the development of a wage-employment theory that is not confined to blue collar markets.

The policy objective is pursued first by answering a series of primarily descriptive questions:

1. How do college teachers learn about jobs? What is the relative importance of tips from friends and former graduate instructors, want ads in newspapers and professional journals, unannounced letters to possible employers, and chance? Are there significant differences in the ways different persons locate jobs by geographic region, years of experience, type of hiring school, prestige of hiring school, scholarly discipline, extent of education, prestige of educating school, or demographic characteristics?

I

2. What formal procedures have been developed to facilitate college teacher placement? Who offers formal placement services? How are these agencies organized and administered? Are there certain groups of professors that are dissatisfied with existing placement procedures? How can the services and techniques of the present agencies be improved? What would be the "ideal placement service"? How could the practical problems that would be encountered in developing this ideal be overcome?

3. Why do college teachers choose particular jobs? How important are salary differentials and other factors in job choice? What roles do friends, climate, work load, physical and research facilities, rank, and administration play in the job-switch and job-choice decisions? Are there significant differences in why professors choose jobs by geographic region, years of experience, types of experience, types of hiring school, scholarly discipline, extent of education, prestige of educating school, or demographic characteristics?

The answers to these questions provide the background for improving the flow of information about candidates and jobs, supplementing the data available about the opportunities in college teaching to students choosing a career, and increasing the opportunity for professors currently committed to a teaching career to find personally satisfying assignments without leaving teaching behind to enter business or government. My intent is to suggest policies for improving the market mechanisms so that one of the nation's most vital resources, college teachers, may be allocated efficiently. Many of the suggested policies demand initiative from government officials; others must be implemented by individual colleges and individual professors.

I also extend wage-employment theory, especially those portions of the theory most applicable to professional workers. Although universities do not adhere to the revenue-minus-cost maximization principle, they nevertheless can be considered "firms." They are akin to a corporation. They exist to fulfill the demands of the consumer for their final product, educational services. Institutions are multiproduct firms supplying college education to undergraduates, teachers to the nation's schools, refresher institutes on specialized topics to persons too busy to attend college full time, consultation services to government and business, and programs in the performing arts to the public. Universities and colleges, like other firms, combine resources to produce products; they convert input to output. Institutions of higher learning face resource markets for capital and labor where the supply of goods and services are rationed to the buyers who offer the highest prices. One of the most vital resource markets faced by these institutions is the market for faculty, the so-called academic labor market. Here supply (college teachers) meets the demand for teaching, research, and administrative services.

Academic labor markets serve the tremendously important role of allocating a resource (qualified manpower) which is not only scarce but vital to the social production function.[1] If professors are poorly placed, the quality of education will suffer. So also will the standard of living and the quality of life.[2] Almost each individual professor is a scarce resource whose optimal placement is severely restricted and whose marginal product would be conspicuous by its absence.

Both in importance and structure, the market for college teachers is representative of an entire specie of professional white collar labor markets. Little is known about this specie though it represents an increasing portion of our work force. Wage and employment theories have grown from the study of blue collar workers. White collar markets function differently. Theories require modification. The present study will suggest some of these modifications, revisions applicable not only to professors but to most professional occupations. Toward developing a theory of white collar labor markets, three groups of questions are posed:

1. What are the sources of imperfection in academic labor markets? Is there one academic labor market, or are there many divided markets? If the markets are divided, in what ways do they differ and what are the determinants of these differences? To what extent is labor homogeneous and substitutable? How free are the flows of in-

---

[1] For statements of the importance of education in the social production function see, for example, Harold M. Groves, *Education and Economic Growth* (Washington: National Education Association, 1961), and Theodore W. Schultz, "Investment in Human Capital," *American Economic Review*, LI, No. 1 (March 1961), 1–16.

[2] Edward Denison has demonstrated that increased education increased the quality of labor input, and increased knowledge increased the output per unit of input: *The Sources of Economic Growth in the United States and the Alternatives Before Us* ("Supplementary Paper No. 13"; Washington: The Committee for Economic Development, 1962).

formation within markets? Do individual employers and employees act in economically rational ways? How conscious is decision-making?

2. *What are the shapes of the demand and supply functions?* Is the quantity demanded of labor an inverse function of price? To what extent is hiring constrained by the heterogeneity of academic positions? Is the demand for labor affected by largely noneconomic factors such as a preference for not hiring women? To what extent is supply influenced by economic considerations? How much is the availability of supply determined by the matching resources that a given institution of higher education can supply its faculty? How substitutable are capital and labor in the higher education production function?

3. *How is the theory of blue collar labor markets applicable to professional markets?* Where the theory is not applicable, what extensions can be proposed?

Methodology

The publishing of this study represents the climax of a number of events. In the fall of 1962, under the sponsorship of the University Research Council and the Business Foundation of the University of North Carolina, I spent two months visiting eighteen southeastern universities gleaning the thoughts and experiences of over one hundred social scientists who had recently moved to their new jobs, and the men, mostly department chairmen, who had employed them. From the interviews and relevant literature a number of hypotheses were framed and then tested against the experience of those whom I had interviewed. The next year, 1963, was devoted to analyzing the results of the pilot project as presented in *The Market for College Teachers: An Economic Analysis of Career Patterns Among Southeastern Social Scientists.*[3]

In Fall 1964, I spent a day interviewing each of the directors of fifteen organizations involved in placing college teachers[4] and sum-

---

[3] Chapel Hill, N.C.: University of North Carolina Press, 1965.

[4] Teacher Placement Office at the University of Illinois, the College Placement Office at the University of Michigan, Office of Academic Placement at Columbia University, the New York City Professional Placement Office of the New York State Bureau of Employment Security, American Nurses' Association, American Chemical Society, American College Bureau, College and Specialist Bureau, Southern Baptist Convention, Board of Education of the Methodist

marized their operations in *Placement Services for College Teachers*.[5]

Commencing the study reported here, the twelve months of 1964 were spent resurveying the literature, discussing a list of over five hundred hypotheses with more than 170 educational administrators and researchers, designing and pretesting (n = 300) a questionnaire (a copy appears as appendix C), and developing a mailing list.

During the same period a second questionnaire was framed and sent to all heads of two-year and four-year institutions of higher education (1,891 of them) as listed in the 1963–64 *Education Directory*.[6] These college presidents were asked to list all *full-time* faculty newly appointed in 1963–64 (mostly for the academic year 1964–65), excluding faculty in schools of medicine, law, theology, dentistry, nursing, and pharmacy. As indicated in table 1 of the Methodological Appendix (appendix A), over 95 percent of the heads of four-year institutions of higher education returned completed forms.[7] Because the institutions not responding are randomly distributed according to control, location, and type, bias from nonresponse is unlikely.

In early 1965 printed questionnaires were mailed to 10,312 of the 28,700 persons listed by the heads of institutions.[8] This sample inten-

---

Church, Convention Placement Service Headquarters at the U.S. Employment Service, Department of English at the University of North Carolina, Department of History at the University of Wisconsin, Cooperative Bureau for Teachers, and the American Association of University Women.

[5] A report to the Office of Manpower, Automation and Training, U.S. Department of Labor, 1965.

[6] *Education Directory 1963–1964, Part 3: Higher Education*, prepared by Theresa Birch Wilkins, Division of Higher Education, Office of Education ("OE–50000–64"; Washington: Government Printing Office, 1964). Reasoning that these are more trade schools than colleges, self-contained schools of optometry, art institutes, commerce schools, and other special schools were not contacted. These schools are mostly those classified as "V" or "other" in the *Education Directory*.

[7] Ninety-two percent of the heads of two-year institutions responded. The statistics cited subsequently, except where otherwise stated, relate only to four-year institutions.

[8] The 10,312 excludes those persons later found to have been listed incorrectly (e.g., part-time faculty). The method used to select the 10,312 is explained in the Methodological Appendix. The 28,700 includes an estimate of the number who would have been named by the presidents who did not respond. The estimate is made from information on the enrollments in nonresponding schools as a portion of total student enrollment and is based on the assumption that the student-faculty ratios are the same in the responding versus the nonresponding schools.

tionally excluded not only part-time faculty and not only doctors, lawyers, pharmacists, nurses, and theologians, but also faculty who were: (1) teaching at their graduate school while working on a degree, (2) on active military duty, (3) unsalaried members of a religious order, and (4) not teaching any degree-credit hours. After three follow-ups spanning a three-month period, 73.9 percent returned usable questionnaires—an excellent response as the six-page form takes about an hour to complete. The respondents were, in general, representative of the sample when stratified by the size, region, stature, type, and control of the institution, and the candidate's discipline. The results of this research are analyzed in a report to the U.S. Department of Labor, *Academic Labor Markets*.[9] *The Mobile Professors* is a much condensed and rewritten version of *Academic Labor Markets*.

In chapters 2 and 3 of this book, general behavior in academic labor markets is discussed. Here topics such as mobility, turnover, and the balance of supply and demand are covered. Chapter 4 seeks to identify the boundaries of submarkets within the total academic labor market. The importance of balkanizations by discipline, region, quality of the institution, religion, sex, education, and type of employer is discussed. The market mechanism and channels of communication are discussed in chapter 5. Chapter 6 considers the reasons why professors choose certain jobs. And in chapter 7 implications for the nation, the individual, the employer, and the body of economic theory are contemplated.

Digression on the Boundary of the Academic Labor Market

Though colleges and universities are the only producers of persons with advanced degrees, they are not the only consumers. Persons holding advanced degrees, the usual qualification for college teaching, have developed mental facilities useful in the production of

[9] A report to the Office of Manpower, Automation and Training, U.S. Department of Labor, 1965. Reports covering special facets of the academic labor market have also been prepared: David G. Brown and Jay L. Tontz, *The Mobility of Academic Scientists*, A Report to the U.S. National Science Foundation, 1966; and David G. Brown, *The Instructor Exchange: Staffing Junior Colleges*, A Report by the Center for Research, Development, and Training in Occupational Education at North Carolina State University, for the U.S. Department of Health, Education, and Welfare under the Administration of the Division of Adult and Vocational Research, 1966.

many types of commodities. Private enterprise seeks advanced degree holders to discover new and better products, to analyze the best methods of marketing them, and to apply linear programming techniques to distribution and inventory control. The larger business firms also hire trained political scientists to write speeches, psychologists to analyze factory mores, economists to project the state of the economy, humanists to bring "culture" to their top executives. Governments require trained minds to structure data gathering, to plan area development or redevelopment, to evaluate research proposals, to frame tax cuts, to judge the safety of new drugs, and to pursue innumerable other vital roles.

> The role of the professor in society has become enormously enlarged, and the university is no longer the only force influencing him. He has a new role in government and a new value to industry. The universities themselves are increasingly competing for his services. He can pick and choose, indeed, among careers and roles.[10]

The National Science Foundation maintains a manpower registry which lists virtually all persons working as professional scientists. Institutions of higher education are only the third most important employer of trained scientists; colleges and universities employ only 19 percent of this group. Government employs 20 percent, and business and industry, the largest employer, accounts for 42 percent of the hiring.[11]

Institutions of higher education are a more dominant force in markets for nonscientists. Although general statistics are not available on the stock in nonscientific disciplines, the National Education Association (NEA) regularly publishes data on the flow. In 1961–63, 46.7 percent of all new doctorates entered college teaching. Only 38.1 percent were known to move to noneducation jobs, and 11.1 percent became teachers at the primary and secondary levels. Almost without exception, the doctorates from scientific fields were more likely to accept employment outside higher education than either the doctorates in the humanities or in the social sciences. For example in English, history, foreign languages, and philosophy, over 80 percent

[10] As quoted in "Cal Professors Turn Up Flaws," *The Wall Street Journal,* June 3, 1965, p. 10.

[11] National Science Foundation, *American Science Manpower,* A Report of the National Register of Scientific and Technical Personnel, 1962 (Washington: Government Printing Office, 1964), p. 21.

of those receiving doctorates accepted appointments at colleges and universities, compared to 40 percent and less in the biological sciences, psychology, physics, geology, and chemistry.[12] Weighted averages computed from the NEA data show that 31 percent of natural scientists, 66 percent of social scientists, and 70 percent of the humanities doctorates enter college teaching.

When the definition of graduate-trained personnel is broadened from "doctorates only" to include master's degree holders as well, nonacademic employers are seen as a greater force in the market. The major employers of holders of master's degrees are primary and secondary educational institutions, since 45 percent of all second-level degrees are in education. Another 16 percent of all master's degrees granted are in the applied disciplines of engineering and business administration, so that even if all of those receiving master's degrees in the traditional "academic" disciplines were to enter college teaching, they would represent only 40 percent of all degree recipients.[13] In fact, a smaller percentage of M.A.'s than Ph.D.'s enter college teaching, for the Ph.D. is more important in academic employment. An analysis of academic and nonacademic scientists according to the highest degree received shows that 52 percent of those employed by educational institutions hold Ph.D.'s, but only 23 percent of the scientists employed outside academia are so qualified.[14]

Since the market for graduate-trained personnel extends beyond the confines of academic institutions and into the world of business and government, a full discussion of the market for college faculty should include an examination of all types of employers of persons who might be qualified to teach at the college level. But a market may be defined in terms of the characteristics of the demanders, instead of the suppliers. There is a market for graduate-trained personnel, but there is also a market for college teachers. The two do not coincide. As a practical solution to a problem of semantics, herein the term, "the academic labor market," applies to something less than all

[12] *Teacher Supply and Demand in Universities, Colleges, and Junior Colleges, 1961–1962 and 1962–1963* ("Higher Education Series, Research Report 1963–R3"; Washington: National Education Association, 1963), p. 53.

[13] U.S. Office of Education, *Earned Degrees Conferred, 1959–60: Bachelor's and Higher Degrees,* by Wayne E. Tolliver ("OE–54013–60, Circular 687"; Washington: Government Printing Office, 1962), p. 5.

[14] National Science Foundation, *American Science Manpower,* p. 14.

types of jobs which graduate-trained personnel may, and often do, fill. Specifically the academic labor market refers to *the market for college teachers,* excluding all noncollegiate employers arbitrarily. Since this study is most directly concerned with the welfare of the system of higher education, this more limiting and narrow definition seems justified.

2

Shortage and Solutions

Faculty scarcity is well documented. The rapid rise in college enrollments, the increased demands for research that specialized society places upon its educational institutions, and the increasingly generous lures placed before potential faculty members by business and government employers who need their specialized skills have combined to create what many have called a "staffing crisis."

The Shortage

There are many indicators of the present and impending shortage. In a 1960 study of over five hundred private liberal arts colleges, Earl F. McGrath found that 68 percent of the schools had difficulty obtaining "properly qualified teachers."[1] Howard D. Marshall, studying faculty mobility in the fields of chemistry, economics, and English in the 1960's, observed a level of turnover that implies strong excess demand in all fields.[2] The U.S. Office of Education (USOE) has repeatedly issued heavily documented warnings about the shortage of college teachers.[3] Another Cassandra, the biennial survey of the National Education Association, warns that 49.5 percent of the universities and colleges report inability to fill their faculty positions "even by lowering their standards." When asked about

[1] *The Quantity and Quality of College Teachers* (New York: Teachers' College Press, 1961)

[2] *The Mobility of College Faculties* (New York: Pageant Press, Inc., 1964).

[3] See, for example, U.S. Office of Education, *The Biennial Survey of Education in the United States* (Washington: Government Printing Office).

the future, 77.5 percent foresee even greater shortage ahead.[4] Most predictions lament that the shortage will grow worse before it lessens. Richard C. Porter, applying the Harrod growth framework, foresees continuing shortages through the 1970's.[5] Summarizing the three most widely discussed projections, Harold Wolozin concludes that general shortages will prevail for the next decade, at least.[6]

Experts disagree upon whether there would be a shortage today if all faculty were properly utilized; that is, if academic institutions were better managed and advantage were taken of already available faculty-economizing technology. Experts also disagree on the present magnitude of the shortage and upon when the shortage will end.[7] But it is a rare person who argues that, given present production

[4] *Teacher Supply and Demand in Universities, Colleges, and Junior Colleges, 1961–62 and 1962–63,* p. 24.

[5] "A Growth Model Forecast of Faculty Size and Salaries in United States Higher Education," *Review of Economics and Statistics,* XLVII, No. 2 (May 1965), 191–7.

[6] "How Serious is the Faculty Shortage?" *Challenge,* XIII, No. 5 (June 1965), 4–8. The projections discussed are: (1) Bernard Berelson's *Graduate Education in the United States* (New York: McGraw-Hill Book Co., Inc., 1960), (2) U.S. Office of Education's "Ten-Year Objectives," and (3) National Education Association's 1959–60 survey of teacher supply and demand.

[7] Recent literature on the projections and problems of faculty supply and demand falls into two broad classifications. The first group—represented by Ray Maul ("Look at the New College Teacher," *The Educational Record,* XLVI. No. 3 [Summer 1965], 259–66, and the NEA biennial survey of teacher supply and demand); the Carnegie Foundation for the Advancement of Teaching (*Annual Report, 1963–64*); John Chase ("The Numbers Game in Graduate Education," *Journal of Higher Education,* XXXV [March 1964], 138–43); J. W. Nason ("Is There a Balm in Gilead?" *Liberal Education,* LI [March 1965], 5–12) and James F. Rogers, *Staffing American Colleges and Universities* ["OE–53028"; Washington: Government Printing Office, 1967]—sees an immediate and continuing critical shortage of qualified staff and pleas for dynamic corrective action. The second group—represented by Bernard Berelson (*Graduate Education in the United States;* Harold Wolozin (*Challenge,* XIII); Richard Porter (*Review of Economics and Statistics,* XLVII, No. 2); Allan Cartter ("New Look at the Supply of College Teachers," *The Educational Record,* XLVI, No. 3 [Summer 1965], 267–77, and "The Supply and Demand of College Teachers," a paper read before the American Statistical Association Meetings, September 8, 1965); and Robert Farrell (Cartter and Farrell, "Higher Education in the Last Third of the Century," *The Educational Record,* XLVI, No. 2 [Spring 1965], 119–28)—proposes that current shortages are not overly critical and that dire shortages are not likely to develop in the foreseeable future.

Much of the work up to now has been impressionistic. Where rigorous models have been developed, the lack of information has necessitated the assumption

functions and present supplies, there is not still a shortage today.

The rapid rise in faculty salaries over the past five years signals the shortage. In spite of the fact that the Ph.D. output of our graduate schools rose more rapidly (by 47 percent) than enrollments (by 33 percent), academic salaries skyrocketed 21 percent, compared to only a 13 percent increase in the manufacturing wage level.[8] The rise in salaries has been common to all disciplines as has the shortage.

It would be wrong to imply, however, that all types of professors have been in equally short supply. In table 1, 23 disciplines are ordered by scarcity.[9] Electrical engineers are most scarce; French professors least scarce. The rationale for this ordering is: Reasoning that when employers are unable to attract faculty at the going rate they will raise salaries and offer generally more attractive terms to the specialists in shortest supply; high salaries, large salary increases, and generous starting rounds signal tight markets. Many unfilled positions in a discipline and rapid expansion in the number of positions are also signs of tightness. A less direct but still important influence upon shortage is the extent of competition from nonacademic employers.

To measure relative scarcity in 23 disciplines, seven factors—each either a cause or a result of excess demand—were selected for study:

---

of critical ratios on the basis of a priori reasoning. Since small changes in assumptions have been shown to cause large variations in conclusions, it is extremely important to extend these rigorous models with more realistic assumptions as more data become available. A valuable model is suggested in a recent dissertation by Jay L. Tontz ("An Inquiry into the Concepts of Supply and Demand in a Labor Market," University of North Carolina, 1966).

[8] This figure is computed from data contained in: U.S. Office of Education, *Trends in Higher Education Planning and Management Data, 1957–58 to 1959–60*, by W. Robert Bokelman and Louis A. D'Amico ("OE–53010"; Washington: Government Printing Office, 1961); U.S. Office of Education, *Higher Education Planning and Management Data, 1960–61* (Washington: Government Printing Office, 1962); U.S. Office of Education, *Higher Education Salaries, 1961–62*, by W. Robert Bokelman and Louis A. D'Amico ("OE–53013–62, Circular 683"; Washington: Government Printing Office, 1963); *Higher Education Salaries, 1962–63*, by W. Robert Bokelman and Louis A. D'Amico ("OE–53013–63, Circular 712"; Washington: Government Printing Office, 1964); *Higher Education Salaries, 1963–64*, by Louis D'Amico ("OE–53013–64, Circular 759"; Washington: Government Printing Office, 1965); and U.S. Department of Labor, *Manpower Report to the President and a Report on Manpower, Resources, Utilization, and Training* (Washington: Government Printing Office, 1965).

[9] The method of computation is explained in appendix A, pp. 187–91.

1 | **Measures of Shortage in 23 Disciplines**[a]

Discipline (in order of overall shortage)	Shortage Index	Rank of Discipline by Various Measures						
		Mean Salary, New Ph.D.'s	Salaries of New Ph.D.'s vs. Assistant Professor	Hire In Rank, New Ph.D.'s	Percentage of New Ph.D.'s Entering Academia	Fields with Most Rapid Expansion	Mean Salary, Full Professor	Unfilled Positions Divided by Total Positions
Electrical engineering	1	1	1	1	(b)	3	6	6
Educational service and administration[c]	2	2	2	3	(b)	8	1	(b)
Mechanical engineering	3	3	3	7	(b)	2	4	8
Mathematics	4	6	5	15	7	1	10	2
Physics	5	8	11	14	2	4	7	1
Economics	6	5	6	6	9	15	9	7
Civil engineering	7	4	10	5	(b)	12	8	12
Chemistry	8	14	15	12	1	7	12	5
Counseling and guidance[c]	9	7	4	2	(b)	11	23	11
Clinical psychology	10	13	19	18	3	6	2	(b)
Sociology	11	15	16	4	11	16	11	3
Art	12	9	8	16	8	9	17	16
Secondary education	13	10	9	10	(b)	14	21	(b)
Political science	14	16	20	19	12	10	3	10
Earth science and geology	15	19	18	13	4	13	5	20
General biology	16	17	13	9	5	23	22	4
Biochemistry	17	12	23	8	(b)	5	14	19
Physical education and health	18	11	12	11	13	18	18	17
Music	19	18	7	20	10	22	19	18
General zoology	20	20	22	17	6	20	15	15
English and literature	21	21	14	21	15	17	16	13
History	22	23	17	22	14	19	13	14
French	23	22	21	23	(b)	21	20	9

[a] The rank of "1" means that excess demand is greatest in that discipline.
[b] Information unavailable.
[c] Teachers of.
Source: survey data.

1. Starting salaries to newly graduated Ph.D.'s,
2. Extent of salary increase,
3. Salaries paid to full professors in 1962–63,
4. Academic rank of newly graduated Ph.D.'s,
5. Unfilled positions as a percentage of all positions,
6. Percentage of newly graduated Ph.D.'s entering college teaching,
7. Expansion demand as a percentage of all hiring.

Each of the 23 disciplines was ranked against other disciplines on *each* factor, making seven lists. Then, for each discipline, the seven ranks were totaled. The list in table 1 is the ordering of the disciplines according to their overall rank.

Adjustments to Labor Shortage

When jobs go begging, when the features offered fail to attract needed staff, a college must make adjustments—either plan less ambitiously, or accept less qualified staff, or offer more attractive jobs. Each strategy has several facets. Each is pursued.

INCREASED SALARY

Colleges may outbid competitive employers with better salaries. And they do. As a result, academic salaries are higher in the areas of greatest scarcity. In shortage disciplines, such as electrical engineering and mathematics, emerging graduate students with Ph.D.'s attract significantly higher salaries than in surplus disciplines, such as history and French.[10] Similarly, Ph.D.'s are paid more than non-Ph.D.'s, experienced professors more than inexperienced, and publishing scholars more than those without publications.

INCREASE RANK

Colleges also divert faculty from competitive employers by offering better ranks. As a result, rank is cheapest for the most scarce. In the shortage disciplines (first eight disciplines in table 1), only 18 per-

[10] Spearman's rank correlation coefficient between "scarcity" and "annual income" is significant, whether scarcity is measured by "percentage of vacancies" or by the "rate of expansion." Scarcity cannot be measured by the Shortage Index, as detailed in table 1, because salary level is a component of the index.

cent of the emerging Ph.D.'s must settle at the academic rank of instructor, compared to 41 percent in the surplus disciplines (last eight in table 1). The average man in a shortage discipline is two and one-half years younger when he gains the highest rank of full professor.

Another result is the cheapening of rank in the poorer schools. The best universities (top 10 percent of schools[11]) hire 16 percent of their new *Ph.D.*-qualified faculty at the lowly rank of instructor and only 28 percent as associate and full professors. Unable to match dollars, stature, and visibility, the least prestigious colleges (the bottom 20 percent) are able to hire only one-half as many (eight percent) as instructors and must offer the senior rank to 40 percent of the PhD.'s they hire.

INCREASE JOB ATTRACTIVENESS

Higher salary and higher rank are two aspects of more attractive jobs. But there are many others. In the long run, a college may make its jobs more attractive by raising its stature in the eyes of scholars, pursuing a more selective admissions policy, developing a better library and more adequate laboratory facilities, nurturing cooperative relationships with neighboring institutions, financing more secretarial service and better teaching-research assistance, building a luxurious faculty club, improving the local school system, ad infinitum. More immediate, though less impressive, results may come from improving the "appearance" of the status quo: for example, by distributing a "chamber of commerce" type brochure extolling the advantages of the community, arranging campus and community tours at the time of on-campus interviews, and providing information on housing and fringe benefits.

Even though resource constraints may prohibit granting these same considerations to all, special considerations may be granted to the hardest-to-recruit faculty: for example, promised additions to the

[11] To indicate significant variations between different employers within the academic labor market, the institutions whose newly hired faculty form the basis of this study were ranked into five categories hereafter termed "top 20 percent" (with a further refinement "top 10 percent" as here), "20 to 40 percent," "40 to 60 percent," "60 to 80 percent," and "bottom 20 percent." The criteria used in this ranking are explained in appendix B. The number of schools in each category and the number of faculty employed by schools in each group are detailed in table 72. When reference is made to the "Prestige Index," the citation is to this ranking system.

library in his field, purchases of desired laboratory equipment, rental of a university-owned house, special secretarial assistance, better course assignments, a lower teaching load, or the payment of moving expenses. Colleges are doing just this. In the eight shortage disciplines the new recruit is asked to teach only nine hours, compared to over eleven in the eight surplus disciplines. Market pressures force colleges to pay a part or all of moving expenses for 27 percent of the specialists in shortage disciplines, which is 50 percent higher than the 18 percent for surplus disciplines.[12] Similarly, colleges pay the moving expenses for 43 percent of the "researchers," who are in short supply, but only for 16 percent of the "teachers."[13]

Thus, in both areas where data are available, evidence supports the hypothesis that institutions of higher learning are adjusting to manpower shortage by granting special dispensations to those persons in greatest shortage. It seems reasonable to expect that the same people are receiving incremental adjustments in some of the less measurable aspects of net advantage.

EXTEND RECRUITMENT

The potential rewards from recruitment are great. Because the communications systems in academia do not provide for the free flow of information, there are many candidates actively seeking new positions who are unaware of a given vacancy. By sending notices of vacancy to more sources of supply, additional candidates may thus be located.

The publicizing of a vacancy can actually bring persons into the market who had not considered changing jobs. In the college teaching profession where overt job-seeking is condemned and many professors prefer to remain at the fringes of the market, job availability is a particularly important lure. At the fringes of labor supply are

[12] Of the institutions that pay at least part of moving expenses, about one-third ask the candidate to share the burden.

[13] Another pressure influencing whether the institution pays moving expenses is need. When moving expenses are likely to be high, the institution is more likely to share in the expense. For example, institutions pay for the moves of those "married with children" five times as frequently as those "single." Of those who move over 1,000 miles, 17 percent have their expenses paid, compared to only seven percent moving less than 50 miles. Persons moving to full professorships have their way paid 25 percent of the time, contrasted to only 11 percent for instructors.

many individuals who want to teach in college but who feel they are not qualified. They may be able to work only part time and believe that no part-time teaching jobs are available. They may be high school teachers with a master's degree who never have seriously assessed their qualifications for college teaching.[14]

After a candidate is located, recruitment may increase the likelihood that he will accept the offer that is extended. An employer may place a job in a more favorable light by paying for a trip to the campus. When a candidate learns more about the less measurable qualities of a job, such as congeniality of colleagues, he may consider them more heavily in his decision.

Jobs often seek candidates. Over one-fourth of all newly hired professors do not in any way seek their jobs. Recruitment is common. The marginal costs of recruitment are less, at least in most cases, than the benefits derived from an extension of the hunt on the part of the employer.

LOWER HIRING STANDARDS

Academic manpower is not homogeneous. Some professors are more productive and more prestigious than others. By lowering hiring standards, it is possible to increase the number of candidates available to an institution without changing the rate of remuneration. Faced with the necessity of placing teachers in front of already admitted students, colleges with limited funds find that quality deterioration is a "solution" to their problem. To quote a recent study:

> Because of the strong urge to staff the classrooms, even at the cost of desired quality, employing officials in all types of universities and colleges have been forced to condone the acceptance of many candidates with severely limited preparation.[15]

Quality deterioration is expeditious in that it is relatively inconspicuous, both to students and to fellow faculty members. Moreover

[14] See Frank G. Lankard, "The Selection of Faculty Members," in *Problems of Faculty Personnel,* edited by John Dale Russell (Proceedings of the Institute for Administrative Officers of Higher Institutions, 1964); also Eugene W. Dils, Eleanor F. Dolan, and Richard G. Axt, "What Sources and Techniques Should Be Utilized in the Recruitment of College Teachers, and What Methods of Retention Should Be Employed?" *Current Issues in Higher Education* (Washington: National Education Association, 1958), pp. 183–91.

[15] National Education Association, *Teacher Supply and Demand,* p. 24.

it is more politic to pay the last man hired more by employing a man of lower quality at the same salary than by employing a man of the same quality at a higher salary.[16]

The pressures for quality deterioration are strongest in the least prosperous and least prestigious institutions. Whereas the best universities command the trademark of academic respectability (the Ph.D. degree) in 71 percent of those they hire, the comparable figure for the poorest institutions is only 32 percent. As shown in table 2, the poorer institutions must overload their faculties with less qualified appointees at the instructor rank.

2

Characteristics of New Faculty, by Quality of Schools

QUALITY OF SCHOOL[a]	PERCENTAGE WITH PH.D.'s[b]*	PERCENTAGE HIRED AS INSTRUCTORS*	PERCENTAGE HIRED DIRECTLY FROM GRADUATE SCHOOL	PERCENTAGE HIRED FROM PRIMARY AND SECONDARY SCHOOLS*
Top 20 percent	71	30	36	3
20 to 40 percent	54	36	44	6
40 to 60 percent	53	36	41	8
60 to 80 percent	40	40	39	12
Bottom 20 percent	32	46	44	16

[a] Institutions are rated by the Prestige Index explained in appendix B (see table 72 for details).
[b] The percentage of Ph.D.'s on the faculty is one of the variables used to calculate the Prestige Index. Therefore, it is not surprising to learn that "prestige" and "percent with Ph.D.'s" are positively related. What is surprising is the strength of the relationship.
* Means that differences are statistically significant by a chi-square test at the .05 level.
Source: survey data.

The greatest compromises must be made in scarcity disciplines. In all disciplines the poorer schools draw fewer Ph.D.'s than the good

[16] Lowering of hiring standards is a common method of increasing supply as predicted by Reder and as cited by Lester, McCormick, and Palmer. It is often cheaper for a firm to lower the quality of the labor force hired than to raise wage rates, especially if the supply of labor at the previous quality is inelastic as it is in the short run in academic labor markets. Melvin W. Reder, "The Theory of Occupational Wage Differentials," *American Economic Review*, XLV (December 1955), 833–53. Gladys L. Palmer, *Labor Mobility in Six Cities* (New York: Social Science Research Council, 1954), pp. 99–100. Brian McCormick, "Labor Hiring Policies and Monopolistic Competition Theory," *Quarterly Journal of Economics*, LXXIII (November 1959), 607–18. Richard A. Lester, *Adjustments to Labor Shortages* (Princeton, N.J.: Industrial Relations Section, Princeton University, 1955), pp. 52–5.

ones. But in the areas of manpower surplus such as history and English the disparity is not nearly as large as in fields such as mathematics and physics. In the eight surplus disciplines the poor schools contract 56 percent as many Ph.D.'s as the good ones, but in the eight shortage disciplines the poorer schools hire only 36 percent as many Ph.D.'s (see table 3). In scarcity areas, which tend to coincide with the areas where the research degree is more essential (for example, physics as opposed to English), the top schools continue to insist on the doctorate whereas the poorer schools compromise. In the poorer schools, the result is that the percentage of Ph.D.'s is as high in the humanities (where Ph.D.'s are plentiful but less necessary) as in the sciences.

3|

Percentage of Doctorates Hired by Top Schools
versus Bottom Schools, by Extent of Shortage

	PERCENTAGE OF DOCTORATES		RATIO OF (2) TO (1)*
SCARCITY	(1) Top 20 Percent Schools	(2) Bottom 20 Percent Schools	
8 shortage disciplines	87	31	.36
7 in-between disciplines	75	31	.41
8 surplus disciplines	55	31	.56

* Means differences are significant by a chi-square test at the .05 level.
Note: Shortage Index is detailed in table 1; Prestige Index in table 2.
Source: survey data.

Regardless of discipline, there is a noticeable tendency to be less particular as the days approach September. Recruiters who ask for a Ph.D. in November accept a "near Ph.D." in January, a good M.A. holder in March, any M.A. in June and, if the position is still unfilled in the late days of August, a candidate for the M.A. degree is sought eagerly. Whereas nearly one-half of all newly hired faculty hold Ph.D.'s, of those hired in late summer and early fall only one-fourth have their doctorate (see table 4). In the months immediately prior to the opening of the school, institutions seem more willing to raid teaching staff from lower eschelon schools, to hire retired professors, to accept one-year appointees, to negotiate part-time positions

4 |

Quality of Newly Hired Faculty, by Month Contracted

Characteristics of Candidates	Percentage of August-September Hires	Percentage of All Hires
Holders of doctorate*	26	46
Teaching in higher education last year*	20	32
Teaching in primary or secondary education last year*	16	10
1-year appointment*	50	15
Retired	2	1

* Means differences are significant by a chi-square test at the .05 level.
Source: survey data.

and, in general, to hire from the nontraditional pools of labor that are not drawn on so heavily during the earlier part of the season.[17]

UTILIZE AVAILABLE STAFF

Even if staff is not available to produce the desired output if the traditional methods of production are used, by altering the production function it may be possible to employ less faculty without sacrificing output: for example, faculty may be economized by registering more students per class, by employing mechanical devices such as television, by hiring more grading and secretarial assistance, by turning over some routine committee work to student government and to professional administrators, and by encouraging more independent student work. Methods of teaching may be altered so as to economize faculty time: for example, using video-tape lectures or assigning ten term papers throughout the semester, reading only one or two of them. The aim of most of these labor-saving innovations is to reduce the faculty-student ratio without jeopardizing the quality of teaching and of research.

At first it would seem that many schools are adopting these technological innovations and are thereby bringing about the needed re-

[17] The better schools seemingly avoid the late summer panic by either hiring earlier in the season or by delaying the hire for another year. Of all August-September contracts 38 percent are negotiated with the bottom 20 percent schools, another 29 percent with the 60 to 80 percent schools, and only 7 percent with the top 20 percent schools.

duction in the demand for faculty. In spite of these innovations however, faculty is not being economized. During the last decade the faculty-student ratio has remained relatively constant. The economies in staff might have resulted in a decreased need for faculty but have resulted instead in more time to give individual attention to students and more time for faculty research.

The adjustments which are made relate to changing the *nature* of the need for staff rather than the size of the need. Production functions are altered. Instead of substituting capital for labor, plentiful labor is substituted for scarce labor—non-Ph.D.'s for Ph.D.'s, neophytes for veterans, and humanists for scientists.

LIMIT OUTPUT

A college may decide, for instance, to admit fewer students or to limit the production of special services and research. A firm may consciously admit that the resources needed for production are simply not available at a reasonable price and may limit its output accordingly. The enrollment quotas and planned rates of expansion that virtually all institutions profess are conspicuous evidence that output restriction is a frequent response to the problem of faculty shortage. Unfortunately, without a full-scale study well beyond the scope of the present one, it is not possible to indicate the exact extent to which demand for faculty is limited by such decisions or, congruently, to estimate how much greater the shortage would be if the institutions were to respond to all the legitimate demands placed upon them. Unquestionably the demand for college faculty would be somewhat larger if the constraint of the limited availability of qualified faculty did not bind.

Summary

Increased demands upon the nation's institutions of higher learning have heightened faculty shortages, especially in the fields where the opportunities for graduate-trained specialists outside academia are expanding most rapidly. Colleges are responding to these shortages in many ways, the character of the response being determined largely by the size, stature, financial strength of the institution, and by the extent of the shortage. Lower quality schools more often must sweeten their bargains by offering higher salaries and rank to less qualified recruits. In disciplines where specialists are very scarce even the better schools find they must enhance their offers with paid on-campus interviews, contributions to moving costs, lower teaching loads, higher ranks, or relaxed quality criteria.

3

Academic Musical Chairs

Tom Weissmuller had been an assistant professor at Great Lakes State University for four years when he decided it was time to move. The public health department was growing stale for him: several top men had left and the big name in his particular field was in Washington with the government. He was near completion of his work on a fairly large state-financed project which had resulted in a book and several journal articles under his name, although he had received only a short credit line in the main project report. But the research money was gradually drying up: GLSU wasn't receiving the latest major project grants it had been seeking. And Weissmuller had developed into something of an expert in a small segment of the field, requiring the use of the library of a nearby private university to get the necessary volumes for his work.

Weissmuller had come to GLSU largely for the money and because it was convenient. At 29, it was his first academic job. He was a midwestern boy, born, bred, and educated, and GLSU was only 350 miles and one state boundary away from where he had done his graduate work. He had had three possibilities in other areas of the country, but the starting salaries were not as high, and he wanted to get established in familiar surroundings. The GLSU position had allowed him to save a little money and do some rather extensive research for such a new man. The results of the latter had won a compliment or two from several colleagues at a recent professional convention in Chicago, giving him the idea that he might be able to initiate a little bargaining at some other schools.

His department chairman would sense his restlessness, if not now, certainly when he began to receive offers and other departments started making inquiries into his record. He would probably be offered a promotion to associate professor with an accompanying raise in salary and, who could tell, it might be his best offer. But there were other things to think about—his possibility for future professional advancement, his potential salary over the long run, and the satisfaction of opening up new paths of knowledge in the specialized area he had fenced off for himself. Then too there were the potential offers from nonacademic firms and government agencies which might come with increased recognition of his work. He needed a change of scenery.

At the same time, Weissmuller dreaded the problems attached to a move. In the past four years he had become very familiar with the laboratory facilities and the library, both at GLSU and at the neighboring institution. He knew where things could be found when needed. He had his own arrangements in the public health building along with a carrel in the library. To supplement the shortcomings of the school, he had built up quite a sizable library in his specialty which belonged to the department and could not be moved.

There were the personal friends, both in the department and in town. He, himself, had developed close professional friendships with fellow project workers. His wife was a member of several civic groups and had even dragged him into one of them. Fortunately though, the children were not yet in school, a consideration which made Weissmuller all the more eager to leave at this time. There were no problems with the house; he had rented from the university, knowing ahead of time he did not want to settle permanently.

The right offer came a few months later. He handed his resignation to his department chairman effective the following June, and the Weissmuller family prepared to embark for a new home at a booming young university on the West Coast.

Extent of Mobility

The Weissmuller story is typical of a pattern among college teachers today. The first appointment, usually at a school other than the one awarding the Ph.D., is only temporary. A man may move three or four times before settling down in a school to live out his career. Some never do settle down.

Job-switching, mostly voluntary, is the rule. The idea of working one's way up in a single institution, without seriously considering jobs at other schools, is foreign to faculties. Except for a few professors who are asked to leave and a few professors deeply entrenched by tenure and other ties, each year every professor voluntarily considers possible new jobs. Because loyalty to discipline transcends loyalty to school and because teaching-research skills are readily transferable among schools, mobility is accepted and approved by the profession.

As shown in table 5, between the academic years 1963–64 and 1964–65, 9,100 professors left one college to accept employment at another. An additional 4,200 left college teaching altogether. Thus, simply to maintain their faculties, colleges and universities had to hire 13,300. Still another 15,200 new professors were recruited to

5 |

Flow in the Academic Labor Market, 1963–64 to 1964–65[a]

Factors Involved		Number of Faculty
Professors in 1963–64[b]		160,000
Minus: Professors *lost* between 1963–64 and 1964–65:		
Death, retirement, graduate school	3,700	
Administration in higher education	650	
Business, government, industry (hired by)	850	
Primary and secondary education (hired by)	(c)	
Higher education (hired by another college)	9,100	
Total lost		−14,300
Professors *continued* between 1963–64 and 1964–65		145,700
Plus: Professors *gained* between 1963–64 and 1964–65:		
Graduate students	13,100	
School teachers (primary and secondary)	2,900	
Nonacademics (business and government)	3,000	
Administrators (returning to teaching)	400	
Professors (hired from another college)	9,100	
Total gained		+28,500
Professors in 1964–65		174,200

[a] These figures are obtained by multiplying the percentage distribution of "balanced sample" by 28,500. For example, 10.2 percent of my sample were school teachers during the previous academic year; thus .102 times 28,500 equals 2,900. The figure 28,500 is my estimate of the total of those newly hired in 1964–65. In response to my request, college presidents representing 93.7 percent of all students enrolled in two-year and four-year colleges and universities listed 31,181 new appointees. The 31,181 figure was multiplied by 100/93.7 to get 33,300 which is an estimate of the names that would have been received if 100 percent of the college presidents had responded. The 33,300 was reduced to 28,500 by eliminating new appointees to two-year institutions.

[b] All data include only full-time professors in four-year colleges and universities. Lawyers, M.D.'s and theologians are excluded. Minor exclusions are also made of professors at special and technical institutes.

[c] Number is unknown but very small.

meet expansion needs. In all, the number of newly hired professors was 28,500. This means that each year between 15 and 20 percent of a typical institution's faculty is new. College faculties change rapidly. College professors expect to switch schools several times, at least, during their careers.

A general indication of the rate of mobility is given by the accession rate—"the number of newly hired faculty" divided by "the total faculty in the preceding year."[1] For the 1964–65 academic year, the average college and university accession rate was 17.9 percent (for every five faculty members in 1963–64 the typical college had to recruit and hire one new faculty member to start the following fall) and is amazingly comparable to the 18 percent Hardin Craig observed in 1927–28.[2]

Accession rates varied between zero percent and 80 percent with nearly one-fourth of all schools hiring at least one new for every four old faculty members and, at the other end of the spectrum, one-sixth of all schools hiring less than one new for every ten old (see table 6).

6 |

Accession Rates

ACCESSION RATE[a]	PERCENTAGE OF ALL COLLEGES AND UNIVERSITIES[b]
.00–.09	15.5
.10–.14	21.9
.15–.19	20.8
.20–.24	17.1
.25 and over	24.6

[a] Computed as number of newly hired faculty divided by the total faculty in the preceding year.
[b] Based on data from 939 four-year colleges and universities, for the 1963–64 and 1964–65 academic years.

Source: survey data.

[1] This statistic is typically larger than the more traditional "turnover rate," for it includes not only the new hiring necessitated by replacement of personnel who leave the market and those who shift to other academic institutions, but also the hiring for newly created positions resulting from expansion. Since it is the number of jobs taken, not the number of quits and layoffs, that most directly concerns both demanders and suppliers in academic labor markets, the more inclusive measure is most relevant for this study.

[2] "Method of Appointment and Promotion in American Colleges and Universities," *AAUP Bulletin*, XV (March 1929), 175–217.

In 1942 Logan Wilson observed that "on the whole, the more mediocre the university, the higher the annual turnover of staff."[3] The same is true today. In markets where knowledge is imperfect, mismoves are frequent. Personnel migrate to both good and poor institutions without a full understanding of what to expect. The dichotomy arises not at the point of attraction but of retention. A few months on a job gives an individual an opportunity to assess its value. Those persons at poor jobs seek others. The institutions with better jobs, therefore, have relatively low turnover rates because they avoid the annual ritual of attracting new and unsuspecting candidates to replace the discontended.[4]

As shown in table 7, the highest rated schools experience only 14.7 percent accession, compared to 19.9 percent for the poorest schools.[5]

7

Accession Rates, by Quality of School

QUALITY OF SCHOOL	AVERAGE ACCESSION RATE[a]
	%
Top 20 percent	14.7
20 to 40 percent	17.5
40 to 60 percent	17.1
60 to 80 percent	19.0
Bottom 20 percent	19.9

[a] For method of computation, see table 6, p. 26.
Source: survey data.

To cite additional data not included in the table, very high accession rates are common for the poorer schools, where a majority of the

[3] *The Academic Man: A Study in the Sociology of a Profession* (New York: Oxford University Press, 1942), p. 59.

[4] Identifying the institutions which offer better jobs is not an easy task. Because individuals will give different relative weights to the various factors involved when offered identical jobs and because two individuals are unlikely to be offered identical jobs even by the same institution, it is unlikely that two individuals will give the same score to any one institution. Here I assume that the better institutions offer identical men better jobs and that the Prestige Index used in this study identifies the better institutions.

[5] In interpreting these data, the exclusion of persons teaching at the same institution where they are studying toward a degree must be kept in mind.

rates exceeds 20 percent. Accession rates in excess of 20 percent are experienced by only one-fifth of the best schools. Academic employers apparently do have the real option of offering attractive jobs and thereby reducing their quit rates and, on the other hand, combining poor jobs with great hiring effort.

Reasons for Vacancies

Since accession rates reflect not only turnover but also expansion, it is desirable to break down the crude rate into several components: temporary demand, shift demand, replacement demand, and expansion demand. As shown in table 8, the largest number of vacancies (43 percent) are newly created positions that represent a net expansion in the numbers of college faculty. Twenty-three percent of the movers are called to their current appointments because their predecessors have accepted employment at another institution of higher education. Another 18 percent are filling positions left vacant by individuals who left the teaching force due to death, retirement, or a more attractive offer outside academia. And seven percent are keeping shop while the permanent occupant of the position is taking his

8 |

Reasons for Vacancies[a]

TYPE OF DEMAND	PERCENTAGE TOTAL DEMAND
Expansion demand (newly created job)	
Replacement Demand	
Death	1.5
Retirement	5.1
Move to administration	2.2
Return to studies	6.3
Move to business	1.8
Move to government	1.0
Total	18
Shift demand (predecessor switched colleges)	23
Temporary demand (predecessor on leave)	7
Unknown	9

[a] Summary of the answers of new appointees to the question, "What is your predecessor doing this year?"
Source: survey data.

sabbatical, visiting at another institution, serving the government temporarily, or acting in some other short-term capacity with the expectation of returning to his position one year hence.

The predominance of expansion demand and the insignificance of death-caused vacancies reflect special market conditions unique to extended periods of expansion and excess demand. In many institutions, a majority of the faculty were not yet trained as college teachers as recently as the end of the Korean War. As a result, for the nation as a whole over two-thirds of all faculty are under 50 years old. This, combined with longer life expectancies, means that death-caused vacancies are few. In 1936–37, when William J. Haggerty and George A. Works conducted their study of North Central colleges, the demographic picture was quite different: though death-caused vacancies were fewer in number, they represented a considerably higher proportion of all vacancies—seven percent. Most of the vacancies, 58 percent, resulted from resignations (replacement plus shift plus temporary demand as categorized here).[6]

The academic labor market of today differs considerably from that of the pre-World War II era. Today all types of institutions are expanding, at an average rate of 8.5 percent as shown by table 9. The expansion is not, however, evenly concentrated throughout the system. Reluctant to endanger the quality of program by losing the distinction of a close-knit community of learning and pressured less by public demands for universal access to higher education, the high quality, small, private colleges are the least expansive. In contrast, as shown in table 9, already large, state-supported institutions of mediocre stature are increasing enrollments the most rapidly.

Staffing problems differ. Whereas the small private colleges are hiring to keep even with a high turnover, the large public universities, which typically enjoy lower turnover rates, are hiring to expand. Each year almost five percent of the faculty at the poorest schools leave college teaching—to return to graduate school, to enter a nonacademic profession, to retire, or by death. Another 4.6 percent of these same faculties switch to other college teaching positions. Still another 1.3 percent go on leave and must be replaced by a temporary appointment. In all, the poorest schools must rehire 10.7 per-

[6] "Faculties of Colleges and Universities Accredited by the North Central Association of Colleges and Secondary Schools during 1936–37," *North Central Association Quarterly*, XIII (January 1939), 309–407.

9

Hiring Rates, by Selected Institutional Characteristics[a,b]

Characteristics of Schools	Percentage Expansion Rate[a]	Percentage Replacement Rate[b]	Percentage Shift Rate[c]	Percentage Temporary Rate[d]	Percentage Accession Rate[e]
All 4-year institutions	8.5	3.4	4.4	1.4	17.7
Size					
Under 1,000 students	6.8	4.7	5.9	1.7	19.1
1,000–5,000 students	9.1	4.3	4.9	1.6	19.9
Over 5,000 students	9.2	2.4	2.4	1.1	15.1
Control					
Public	11.2	4.2	5.1	1.5	22.0
Private	7.3	3.8	4.7	1.6	17.4
Quality[f]					
Top 20%	7.6	1.9	4.0	1.2	14.7
Middle 60%	8.6	3.4	4.5	1.4	17.9
Bottom 20%	9.2	4.8	4.6	1.3	19.9

[a] *Expansion rate* = the number of faculty hired into newly created positions for fall 1964 divided by the total number of faculty in spring 1964.

[b] *Replacement rate* = the number of faculty hired to replace persons who were teaching in the spring of 1964, but had left college teaching altogether as of the fall of 1964 divided by the same denominator.

[c] *Shift rate* = the number of faculty hired to replace persons who switched from one faculty to another between the 1963–64 and 1964–65 academic years divided by the same denominator.

[d] *Temporary rate* = the number of faculty hired in the fall of 1964 as temporary, one-year, replacements for persons on leave and so forth divided by the same denominator.

[e] The *accession rate* is the sum of columns one through four. It may be computed independently by dividing the total number of newly appointed faculty members as of fall 1964 by the total number of faculty members as of spring 1964.

[f] Rated according to the Prestige Index.

Note: Here the nine percent of vacancies listed in table 8 as unknown were distributed proportionately over the four reasons cited.

Source: survey data.

cent of their faculty each academic year, a figure more than 50 percent higher than that of the better schools (table 10). Though a man joining a high prestige school has typically made more moves before getting there,[7] once in place he has a greater tendency to remain.[8]

Because vacancies by resignations are less predictable, the schools with large shift and replacement demands tend to enter the market

[7] Both the Lazarsfeld-Thielens and Stecklein-Eckert studies reveal that the faculty accepting positions at the better schools have, on the average, held a greater number of different jobs. Paul F. Lazarsfeld and Wagner Thielens, Jr., *The Academic Mind* (Glencoe, Ill.: The Free Press, 1958), p. 9. John E. Stecklein and Ruth E. Eckert, *An Exploratory Study of Factors Influencing Choice of College Teaching as a Career* (Washington: U.S. Office of Education, Government Printing Office, 1961), p. 18.

[8] Confirming evidence is presented in table 9.

10 |

Importance of Expansion and Replacement Demands,
Compared by Institutional Size, Level, Control, and Quality

CHARACTERISTIC OF INSTITUTION	PERCENTAGE OF ALL VACANCIES CREATED BY EXPANSION DEMAND
*Size**	
Over 5,000 students	61
Under 1,000 students	36
*Level**	
University	52
College	44
*Control**	
Public	51
Private	42
Quality	
Top 20%	52
Bottom 20%	46

* Means that by a chi-square test at the .05 level, the difference in matched pairs is significant.

Sources: survey data and table 9.

later, and with a greater sense of immediate need, than the schools filling expansion demands.[9] Whereas 26 percent of the newly created positions are not filled before March 31, 43 percent of the vacancies created by faculty shift are still to be filled.[10] Whereas the large public universities tend to dominate the market prior to March 31 as they hire into newly created positions, the main activity in late spring and summer is that of the smaller, private colleges scrambling to cover needs not known until late in the season.

Regardless of cause, turnover is disruptive to an institution. Faculty offices must be changed or built; orientation to administrative procedures must be pursued; often courses must be added and deleted; research facilities may need to be altered and expanded; students must adjust to different advisors, different course offerings, and

[9] For a more complete discussion of the different implications of expansion and replacement demand, see Brown, *The Market for College Teachers: An Economic Analysis of Career Patterns among Southeastern Social Scientists* (Chapel Hill, N.C.: University of North Carolina Press, 1965), pp. 49–51.

[10] The differences between expansion demand and each of the other demands are significant at the .05 level, by chi-square.

different instructors. Especially faculty departures, but also additions, involve costs both to the institution and the individuals concerned.

But there are also benefits. To the institution, new faculty members mean new ideas, new orientations, new courses, new vitality. The replacement of old staff with new allows for a fresh perspective and exposes students to several different professors. The new professor brings a different background, a different set of experiences, and often a different bias to his classroom—thus affording varied exposure. The turnover of faculty almost certainly prevents the development of mutual admiration societies of like-minded scholars who may have lost touch with the realities of their discipline. Since the academic tradition is hiring at the bottom and promoting from within, the turnover evidenced in this study means that, even at the top, there is some room for new people.

Some mobility is good, and it should not be implied otherwise: in a dynamic economy where some sectors shrink and others grow, labor must follow the newer demands to the needed areas. When consumers' tastes change to increase the desires for college education, resources must flow to the collegiate industry if marginal social costs and marginal social benefits are to be moved toward equality.[11] *Mobility should occur.*

It seems reasonable to question if, however, the extent of mobility that many of the poorer institutions are experiencing is good for them. The schools in the bottom 20 percent by prestige are faced with the necessity of locating and hiring one-fifth of their last year's faculty, a task that requires much time. Very high turnover rates must endanger the continuity of both instruction and administration. In a market that is expanding as rapidly as the academic labor market is at this time, the large rates of replacement- and shift-caused turnover are probably more detrimental than beneficial to the institutions. The vitality and the fresh view offered by new faculty could be lent by eight percent per year faculty expansion. Though the lack of the possibility of movement for veteran faculty would certainly be detrimental to all institutions—indeed to the entire academic com-

[11] One of the more concise treatments of the theory behind this statement is provided by Harry S. Mills and Royal E. Montgomery, *Labor's Progress and Some Basic Labor Problems* (New York: McGraw-Hill Book Co., Inc., 1938), p. 119.

munity—most of the colleges and universities, and especially those institutions with high replacement and shift demands, would stand to benefit from a lessening of movement within the market.

Sources of Candidates

Filling these many vacancies are several distinct groups of new professors. Emerging graduate students fill 40 percent of the jobs. Experienced professors switching colleges account for another 32 percent; together these two groups constitute almost three-quarters of all movers. The other new professors are hired away from business, government, secondary schools, and other noncollegiate employers. (These data are summarized in table 11, and analyzed below.)

11

Activity Last Year of All Movers[a]

Activity Last Year	Number of Movers[b]	Percentage of All Movers[b]
Teacher in higher education	9,100	32.0
Student	11,300	39.6
Teacher in primary or secondary education	2,800	9.7
Business, government, or foundation	2,900	10.2
Other	1,300	4.6
Unknown (nonresponse)	1,000	3.4
Total	28,400	100.0

[a] Data are for four-year colleges only, except that a person who taught in either a two-year or a four-year college last year is counted as a "teacher in higher education."
[b] The absolute figures are computed on the basis of the percentages and rounded to the nearest 100. For this reason the total does not equal the 28,500 figure cited earlier in this chapter.

Source: survey data.

PROFESSORS: AN OCCUPATIONAL PROFILE

In 1962–63, 1,177 four-year colleges and universities[12] employed nearly 200,000 full-time faculty members:[13] 82 percent male, one-third over 50 years old, one-half Ph.D. holders, and 55 percent associ-

[12] As listed in Allan M. Cartter, ed., *American Universities and Colleges,* 9th Edition (Washington: American Council on Education, 1964), p. 27.

[13] U.S. Office of Education, *Digest of Educational Statistics* ("OE-10024–63, Bulletin 1963, No. 43"; Washington: Government Printing Office, 1963), p. 66.

ate or full professors.[14] Universities with graduate schools, though the number is fairly small, are the primary employer of faculty, employing nearly half of them.[15] The still expanding public sector employs 57 percent of all faculty. Concentrated in a few large disciplines such as mathematics, physical education, music, and history, and otherwise spread among many smaller disciplinary specialties, approximately 27 percent of all professors are scientists, 30 percent social scientists, 26 percent in the humanities, and 17 percent are associated with professional schools such as law and medicine. Geographically faculty locate more in the North Atlantic (29 percent) and Middle West (29 percent) than in the Southeast (19 percent) and the West-Southwest (22 percent).

As indicated by the diversity of social origins, the professiorial labor force is a culturally heterogeneous group. The American Association of University Professors reported in 1938 that a sample of 4,667 members revealed the following social origins of professors, according to the occupational status of their fathers: businessmen, 26.6 percent; farmers, 24.7 percent; manual workers, 12.1 percent; clergymen, 10.6 percent; teachers, 5.1 percent; physicians, 5.1 percent; lawyers, 4.1 percent; professors, 3.9 percent; chemists and engineers, 3.0 percent; public officials, 1.9 percent; editors and writers, 1.2 percent; artists and musicians, 1.0 percent.[16] Historically academicians have been more of an intellectual than a social elite.[17]

[14] U.S. Office of Education, *Teaching Faculty in Universities and Four-Year Colleges,* by Ralph E. Dunham, Patricia S. Wright, and Marjorie O. Chandler ("OE–53022–63"; Washington: Government Printing Office, 1966). This study is subsequently referred to as COLFACS.

[15] This number excludes junior college faculty.

[16] B. W. Kunkel, "A Survey of College Faculties," *AAUP Bulletin,* XXIV (March 1938), 262. For a more recent commentary see Richard H. Shyrock, "United States" in *The Status of University Teachers* (Paris: UNESCO, 1961), pp. 179–94.

[17] It is good to remember that the stock of college teachers is not the sole source of supply to the academic labor markets. Traditionally in economic theory, the employed represent only a portion of supply. Even after adjusting for the fact that many potential suppliers of teaching services are currently employed outside academia, total supply is something more than all persons employed. The employed are a "quantity hired" which at best includes all persons who offer their services under unique employment terms. Total "quantity supplied" includes others who might have worked under similar conditions if jobs were vacant. And total supply must, in one instance, include still others

The extent of mobility. In any one year not all professors are actively looking for a new job; yet few consider their present job permanent. Among those serving on new jobs 15 percent expect to leave at the end of the academic year, another 38 percent expect to stay less than four years. Only 17 percent consider their new jobs as permanent. Interviews with southeastern social scientists revealed that 22 percent of the faculty who had been on their jobs for less than three years had reentered the market and were actively seeking another job, and that virtually all (98 percent) of the interviewed professors wanted to be kept posted on employment opportunities for which they might qualify.[18] Marshall found that 22 percent of the economists that he studied were actively seeking new jobs and that by the time a man reaches the full-professor stage of his career, he has typically changed institutions at least three times.[19]

Considering the character of their jobs and the nature of their training, the high mobility of professors is not at all surprising. Escape from provincialism, exposure to a variety of intellectual settings and critical examination of one's ideas by different audiences undoubtedly strengthens a man's preparedness to teach and for research. At the same time, skills developed in one university are almost certain to be directly relevant in another. The basic similarity in institutional structure, and in instructional and research procedures, means that only the employers differ significantly, not the demands of jobs.[20] Moreover the very training that qualifies a man to

---

who would have taught if the terms were more favorable and, in another, exclude those who would not have taught if the conditions were less favorable. Total supply also includes the flow of new teachers into the market who have not yet landed jobs. Thus, although the above description of labor supply includes the major portion of labor supply and therefore represents a reasonably accurate description of the stock of labor services, it is not a total picture.

[18] See Brown, *The Market for College Teachers,* p. 67.

[19] Marshall, *The Mobility of College Faculties* (New York: Pageant Press, Inc., 1964), pp. 49–51. See also Venkatraman Anantaraman, *Mobility of Professional Economists in the United States: A Report on the Survey of Patterns and Factors in Their Mobility* (Madison: Industrial Relations Research Center, University of Wisconsin, 1961), p. 5. (Mimeographed.)

[20] This is not to suggest that there are no costs of moving. Time is lost in the actual process of moving, of job hunting, and of getting to know the new institutional procedures. However one can contend that the time involved here is relatively small when compared with that required of other persons switching occupations and industries.

become a college teacher conditions him to adjust to mobility. The conditioning of the college teacher, a history of geographic dislocations, starts with his movement from home to college and continues as he moves from school to school in search of advanced degrees. Anti-inbreeding traditions require, even at the end of the training period, still another geographic move. By the time he becomes "fully certified," the typical college professor has had ample opportunity to know and appreciate varied living experiences.

Rewards of mobility. Job-changing pays. Because his new employer has to make the terms sufficiently attractive to overcome the costs of movement, the typical mover almost always advances in salary and often in rank and in the quality of the school. The data are cited in table 12. Sixty-nine percent of the moves result in increased annual income. Twenty-eight percent advance in rank and 30 percent move to a better-rated institution. One-sixth of the movers increase both rank and quality. Those persons who accept lower ranks (27 percent) or less prestigious institutions (49 percent) usually trade off one factor for another: for example, a lower rank for a better school.

12

Change in Rank, Income, and Institution Prestige between Old Job and New[a]

FACTORS CHANGED	PERCENTAGE EXPERIENCING		
	Increase	Decrease	No Change
Income[b]	69	16	15
Rank	28	27	45
Prestige of institution	30	49	21

[a] These figures include only persons who switched from one institution to another.
[b] Incomes compared are current versus the income that would have been made if the man had remained at his old job.
Source: survey data.

The largest gainers of all are those who have many publication credits and men over women. "Publishers" have between a 25 percent and 30 percent greater chance of increasing in each of the factors (rank, quality, salary) than nonpublishers;[21] men move to higher

[21] Publishers are defined as persons who have published more than ten articles or the equivalent; nonpublishers as persons who have published nothing.

prestige schools twice as frequently as women (30 percent versus 15 percent). But all groups move ahead. Even those told to leave their previous jobs gain in rank (34 percent) and income (95 percent), though their chances of gaining in prestige (20 percent) are not as great as voluntary movers (35 percent).

THE MOBILE PROFESSORS

To the candidate-seeking employer, the knowledge that many current teachers will change jobs is of little help. He needs to know where and who the most mobile are.

Unlike most blue collar worker markets, active supply is not obvious.[22] Only rarely do professors resign their current positions *before* seeking another. The flexibility of most teaching jobs allows a man to job hunt inconspicuously "during working hours." Thus it is difficult to identify job hunters.

Moreover, after identifying those who act as if they are seeking a new job, it is necessary to differentiate true prospects from "lookers." Because of the absence of commonly accepted and widely known market intermediaries, the traditions of secrecy that abound in academic labor markets, the heterogeneity of individual professors, and a variety of special motives (some of them relating to the process of higgling with present employers), a significant number of professors make it known that they are available to be moved, when in fact they are not.[23]

To determine what sectors of the total stock of current college teachers are most movable, it is helpful to identify those who are likely to gain the most and lose the least by moving. The likelihood that an individual professor can be moved should be predictable relative to his family financial situation, department and university peer group, institutional commitment, research and other job obligations, status, and the relative positions of his current and prospective institutions in the hierarchy.

The high benefit group. For the young professor the gains from mobility are greater than of an older man, because the young enjoys the greater attractiveness of the new opportunity for a longer period

[22] Lloyd G. Reynolds, *The Structure of Labor Markets: Wages and Labor Mobility in Theory and Practice* (New York: Harper & Bros., 1951), p. 211.

[23] These are the spectators, confidence seekers, telegram wavers, and heaven hunters as described in Brown, *The Market for College Teachers*, pp. 63–5.

of time.[24] That job-changing activity actually does decrease with age is shown in table 13: for example, the probability that Professor X will switch collegiate employers in any given year is 19.5 percent if X is under 30 years old, but only 1.2 percent if X is over 60. Although professors under 40 are only two-fifths of the teaching force, they are slightly over three-fifths of the movers.

13 | Age and Mobility

Age	Percentage Faculty Moving from One Faculty to Another[a]	Percentage of All College Faculty	Probability of Moving[b]
Under 30	25	7	.195
30 to 39	37	33	.061
40 to 49	17	30	.031
50 to 59	9	20	.024
60 and over	2	10	.012

[a] These data exclude all newly hired professors who were not also full-time faculty members in the previous year.

[b] Probabilities are computed by dividing the number of movers in each age group by the number of faculty members in that group.

Sources: survey data and Ralph E. Dunham, Patricia S. Wright, and Marjorie Chandler, *Teaching Faculty in Universities and Four-Year Colleges: Spring, 1963* ("OE-53022-63"; Washington, D.C.: Goverment Printing Office, 1966), p. 5. The latter study is subsequently cited as COLFACS.

Another hypothesis, almost too obvious to mention, is that professors who are dissatisfied at their current jobs can profit greatly by switching jobs.[25] The trick is identifying those who are dissatisfied. A priori three groups stand out:

1. professors in poor jobs—for example, instructors at poor institutions and at low salaries;

[24] The inverse relationship between mobility-propensity and age has been noted by students in a wide range of markets. Cf. Reynolds, *The Structure of Labor Markets,* p. 21; Anantaraman, *Mobility of Professional Economists,* p. 5; U.S. Department of Labor, Bureau of Labor Statistics, *The Mobility of Electronic Technicians, 1940–1952: The Work Experience, Training, and Personal Characteristics in a New Skilled Occupation* ("Bulletin 1150"; Washington: Government Printing Office, 1954), p. 9; and Industrial Relations Center, University of Minnesota, *Minnesota Manpower Mobilities, Bulletin 10* (October 1950), pp. 12–3.

[25] Data confirm the obvious. The probability that Professor X will switch collegiate employers in any given year is 14.1 percent if X is dissatisfied, but only 4.3 percent if X is not.

2. professors who have recently outgrown what was once a satisfactory job—for example, assistant professors with blockage problems, professors with an increasingly impressive list of publications, instructors who have just completed their Ph.D. while teaching at a mediocre institution, and scholars at the salary ceiling in a low salary institution, or at the teaching load minimum in a high-load institution;

3. professors whose jobs have changed in an undesirable way since they first accepted them—for example, the flight of a superstar from the department, discontinuation of a special curriculum or research project, threatened loss of accreditation, addition of an obnoxious colleague to the departmental faculty, and change of administrators.

The small amount of quantitative data that I have been able to assemble suggests that these groups are in fact more prone to switch jobs. The probability that Professor X will switch jobs in a given year is 13.7 percent if X is an instructor but only 1.2 percent if X is a full professor (table 14). It is 6.4 percent if X is at a bottom quintile school but only 5.2 percent if X holds an appointment at a school in the top quintile (table 15). Finally, support of the hypothesis that persons who receive their Ph.D. while out teaching are prone to move is lent by the observation that 13 percent of all the professors who switched between collegiate teaching jobs had received their terminal degree within the last year.

14

Rank and Mobility

Rank before Move	Percentage Faculty Moving from One Faculty to Another[a]	Percentage of All College Faculty	Probability of Moving[b]
Instructor	40	16	.137
Assistant professor	42	25	.079
Associate professor	10	24	.021
Full professor[c]	7	28	.012

[a] These data exclude all newly hired professors who were not also full-time faculty members in the previous year.

[b] For example, .137 means that in any given year it is 13.7 percent likely that a full-time faculty member who holds the rank of instructor will leave to accept an appointment on another faculty. Persons who leave to pursue a noncollege teaching job are not considered.

[c] The final figures in columns one and two do not total 100 percent because some professors are not assigned an academic rank.

Source: survey data and COLFACS data.

15

Prestige of Previous Job and Mobility

Prestige of School Before Move	Percentage Moving from One Faculty to Another[a]	Percentage of All College Faculty	Probability of Moving Voluntarily[b]
Top 20 percent	19	20	.052
Bottom 20 percent	23	20	.064

[a] These data exclude: (1) all newly hired professors who were not also full-time faculty members in the previous year, and (2) the 17 percent of all professors who moved involuntarily.

[b] Calculated as number of voluntary moves divided by total faculty.

Sources: survey data and Prestige Index.

The low cost group. Job switch is costly, especially if the place of residence must be changed. Beyond the actual expenses of moving homes and families between campuses, in many cases houses must be sold, investments in local real estate must be terminated, valuable contacts which enable outside income must be left behind, and new and even unknown opportunities for advancement at the same job or in other jobs offered must be sacrificed. And, in addition to the direct economic costs, job-switching often requires drawing children out of a familiar school situation and placing them in an unfamiliar one, leaving behind close personal friends and professional colleagues and facing the necessity of making new ones, abandoning a laboratory facility or a library collection that years of hard work have built and gaining the prospects of repeating the task, leaving behind second- and third-year graduate students without a mentor and substituting the need to establish rapport with a new set of students, and making irrelevant the storehouse of personal knowledge both of students and of administrative procedures. Virtually no job switch can be made that does not involve one or more of these costs.

Where costs are high, resistance to mobility is great. It therefore behooves the collegiate recruiter to identify those sectors of the teaching labor force for which the costs of movement are likely to be relatively low: for example, those professors who have small families and are spared the complications of moving voluminous home furnishings and children, those who have moved so recently that they have not had the time to develop strong ties to their community, those who have little "job capital" that cannot be moved easily (specifically social scientists and humanists as contrasted to physical scientists with their expensive laboratory equipment that they have convinced their employer to buy over the years), or those who have not developed sources of outside income.

This hypothesis helps to explain why married professors are less mobile than unmarried ones, even after adjustments are made for differences in age and rank.[26] It explains why, even though they are less visible, associate professors move no less frequently than full professors.[27] It accounts for the observation of Anantaraman that economists make 64 percent of their career shifts in the first ten years of professional experience.[28] It partly explains why the probability of Professor X moving in any given year is 10.3 percent if he is a social scientist but only 4.0 percent if he is a physical scientist; additionally, if his field is humanities, his probability of moving is 7.9 percent, whereas if his field is engineering it is 1.5 percent (see table 16). And it helps to explain why the probability of moving is significantly lower in those disciplines where outside income earning is greater (6.9 percent versus 7.9 percent).

The involuntarily mobile. The entire discussion of low costs and high benefits assumes that it is the professor, not the employer, that initiates mobility. It assumes that the candidate has the choice to remain. Although this assumption is generally valid, a minority of the

[26] Because statistics on the entire population of college professors are not available, it is impossible to know if the hypothesis that homeowners and heads of large families are less mobile is true. My guess is that the hypothesis is valid. Of the newly hired professors between ages 30 and 50, 21 percent are unmarried, another 28 percent are married but have no children, and another 31 percent are married with fewer than three children. Only 15 percent have three or more children, and 5 percent are separated or divorced. Of the newly hired professors who were also professors in the previous year, only 32 percent owned homes at their previous jobs. Furthermore, according to a study by Fred J. Kelly ("How Do Faculty Members Like Their Jobs?" *Higher Education,* V [May 1, 1949], 196), when asked about their intentions of remaining at their current institution, a much higher percentage of instructors indicated lack of attachment than full professors. Only 29.3 percent of the instructors indicated "Yes, I'm almost certain I will stay," whereas the comparable percentage for full professors was 65.9 percent.

[27] The data do not confirm the hypothesis that the less visible associate professors are less mobile than full professors, an hypothesis advanced by, among others, Theodore Caplow and Reece J. McGee, *The Academic Marketplace* (New York: Basic Books, Inc., 1958), p. 42.

[28] Anantaraman, *Mobility of Professional Economists,* pp. 5, 29.

16

Subject Matter Specialty and Mobility

SUBJECT MATTER SPECIALTY	NUMBER MOVING FROM ONE FACULTY TO ANOTHER[a]	ALL COLLEGE FACULTY	PROBABILITY OF MOVING*
Sciences[b]	1,190	29,600	.040
Engineering	150	9,500	.015
Humanities[c]	3,050	38,500	.079
Social Sciences	1,750	17,000	.103

[a] These data exclude all college professors who did not hold a full-time faculty position during the previous year.

[b] Sciences = agriculture and related fields, biological sciences, physical sciences, psychology in the COLFACS study.

[c] Humanities = English and journalism, fine arts, foreign languages and literature, law, philosophy, religion and theology in the COLFACS study.

* Means that differences are significant by a chi-square test at the .05 level.

Sources: survey data and COLFACS data.

mobility is employer-initiated. Seventeen percent of the professors switching colleges are responding to the unavailability of their original job.[29]

In the areas and institutions that can carry it off, there are definite signs of "up or out" promotion policies. At the better schools the nontenured positions are testing grounds; only the very best performers are invited to join the ranks of the tenured. The residual, the men forced out, have often neither published nor completed their degree (table 17). They are concentrated in areas where replacements are relatively easy to find—in the surplus disciplines, at the lower academic ranks, and at the schools of greatest stature. "The man who stays at the same college for a long time may often do so be-

[29] One-eighth of the registrants at the American Economic Association's convention placement service who left jobs during the last three years were *asked* to do so by their employers. Edwin Gooding, "The Seven-Year Lag . . . The Market for Economists," *Business Review* (Federal Reserve Bank of Boston, December 1964), p. 10.

The 17 percent statistic undoubtedly understates the percentage of all terminations which are involuntary in that professors hired by nonacademic institutions after being fired are not included. Also excluded are those who enter the market involuntarily from nonacademic jobs. There are still other professors who are pressured to leave their old positions, who are likewise not recorded in this statistic; they are men who had tenure, but received the old Army treatment of "you don't have to leave, but we'll make it very unpleasant if you don't." In many of these cases, the school acts so diplomatically that the individual himself is not aware that he is being pushed out. His only impression is that the school was especially helpful in finding him other job offers.

cause he has not received enough professional attention to bring an attractive invitation from another institution."[30] When all mobility is voluntary, the self-selecting process keeps the poorest candidates off the market—but not so in the case of involuntary mobility.

17 | Involuntary Mobility

Characterisic of Individual or Institution	Percentage of Involuntary Mobility of All Terminations[a]
Highest Degree*	
Ph.D.	15
Less than Ph.D.	22
Rank at Job Left*	
Instructor	27
Assistant professor	12
Associate professor	8
Full professor	6
Extent of Publications*	
No publications	24
Up to 10 journal articles	16
Publications exceed 10 journal articles	8
Discipline	
8 surplus disciplines	17
8 shortage disciplines	15
Quality of School Left*	
Top 20 percent	23
Middle 60 percent	17
Bottom 20 percent	13

[a] Percentages cited probably represent a slight understatement of involuntary mobility insofar as persons who are involuntarily terminated are more likely to accept a nonteaching job rather than another college teaching position.
* Grouped percentages are significantly different by a chi-square test at the .05 level.
Sources: survey data and Prestige Index.

THE NEW PROFESSORS

Although many vacancies are filled by "raiding" faculties at other colleges, even more are filled by recruiting emerging students. For most graduate students the market-entry decision follows naturally from the anticipated completion of a degree. They rarely have the easy option of remaining in place. Benefits from market entry are high.

And costs are low: since a change of residence is anticipated when studies are completed, and since most of the students' peers are also

[30] Lazarsfeld and Thielens, *The Academic Mind,* pp. 9–10.

moving, the community ties developed by permanent faculty are not relevant to graduate students. Moreover emerging students are often single or married without school-age children. Many students reside in housing available only to students and become ineligible to remain in place upon completion of their studies. This means that a change of residence must take place whether or not a new job is taken, so that the marginal moving costs involved in accepting a new job are often quite low. Both because benefits are high and because costs are low, most emerging graduate students enter the market.

From the employers' viewpoint, emerging graduate students may be a preferred source of supply: the concentration of graduate students in a small number of schools makes them quite visible.

Although graduate students are inexperienced and unknown in the classroom situation, difficult to evaluate regarding future prestige value and research interests, and prone to move on to another school after only a few years service, they are also willing to work for less pay, to accept a position at the bottom of the departmental hierarchy, and to receive constructive criticism. Graduate students are recently trained and knowledgeable about the latest developments in their fields. Because graduate students have recently been in close contact with some of the better-known men in the field, the hiring department is usually able to locate a trusted and respected recommender.[31]

Some selected characteristics of emerging students are statistically summarized in table 18.

18 |

Selected Characteristics of Emerging Students versus Job-Switching Professors

Characteristics	Percentage among Emerging Students	Percentage among Switchers from One Faculty to Another
Under 30 years old*	64	26
No publications*	67	41
Single marital status*	30	21
Highest degree less than doctorate*	65	37
Male sex	83	85
No professional association memberships*	16	6
1-year appointment*	19	12

* Difference between two groups of movers is statistically significant by a chi-square test at the .05 level.
Source: survey data.

[31] See Brown, *The Market for College Teachers,* p. 58.

"Of the 180 universities that conferred doctorates in the period 1936–1956, over half averaged five or fewer a year," and "of the 175 institutions that conferred one or more doctorates in 1957–58," a third gave fewer than ten.[32] Three-fourths of all doctorates granted between 1936–56 were from 30 institutions.[33] Even in 1959–60, after many new institutions had expanded into the doctoral field, the ten top-producing universities granted 35.8 percent of the doctorates and only 30 universities granted more than 100.[34]

The active sources of new recipients of master's degrees are far more numerous, but still considerably fewer than the different loci of the same men after they have accepted their first jobs. In 1959–60, 195 different institutions granted more than one hundred master's degrees with one, Columbia University, granting 2,744. Many of these institutions, however, grant almost all of their advanced degrees in the field of education[35] to students headed toward a teaching career in primary and secondary education and are, therefore, not substantial suppliers of prospective teachers for four-year colleges and universities.[36] Thus at both the M.A. and Ph.D. levels, graduate students are concentrated at a relatively small number of institutions.

For the recruiter who has decided to go after a graduate student, the problem is determining when the student will leave school to accept his first full-time job. Practices in different disciplines vary widely. As a rule, the incentives to obtain the Ph.D. before leaving school are greatest in the sciences: here financial aid is most generous;[37] mentors place the least value on a full-time teaching experience as a part of graduate training; the Ph.D. is typically earned in the fewest years,[38] with assurance of a strong sellers' market candi-

[32] Bernard Berelson, *Graduate Education in the United States* (New York: McGraw-Hill Book Co., Inc., 1960), p. 104.

[33] M. H. Trytten, *Doctorate Production in United States Universities 1936–56: With Baccalaureate Origins of Doctorates in the Sciences, Arts, and Humanities* ("Publication 582"; Washington: National Academy of Sciences/National Research Council, 1958), p. 17.

[34] U.S. Office of Education, *Earned Degrees Conferred, 1959–1960.*

[35] Berelson, *Graduate Education in the United States*, p. 94.

[36] U.S. Office of Education, *Earned Degrees Conferred, 1959–1960.*

[37] National Science Foundation, "Highlights of a Survey of Graduate Enrollments, Fellowships, and Assistantships, 1954," *Scientific Manpower Bulletin,* July 29, 1955

[38] Berelson, *Graduate Education in the United States*, p. 158.

dates are least reluctant to pass by a good job offer in the fear that such a good offer will not be forthcoming in future years; and the income differential between doctoral degree holders and master's is the largest.[39]

As shown in table 19, the opportunity costs of not getting the Ph.D. are highest in the sciences. Whereas the student emerging

19

Worth of Ph.D. to Emerging Students, by Discipline

Subject Matter Specialty	Percentage Holding Ph.D.[a]	Salary Advantage	Rank Advantage[b]	Fewer Hours Teaching Load Advantage
All fields (weighted average)	36	$1,300	.60	2.3
Eight shortage disciplines	(c)	1,600	.62	4.6
Eight surplus disciplines	(c)	1,000	.56	1.4
Sciences (weighted average)	55	1,400	.58	3.1
Biochemistry	78	2,000	.56	3.2
Civil engineering	74	1,100	.83	3.0
Electrical engineering	69	1,100	.61	1.7
Chemistry	62	2,500	.98	4.7
Mechanical engineering	62	900	.62	1.4
Physics	49	1,100	.61	1.7
Earth sciences	43	1,200	.50	2.6
Clinical psychology	42	800	.55	2.1
General zoology	40	1,600	.56	3.6
General biology	14	1,100	.33	2.8
Humanities (weighted average)	16	1,000	.58	1.6
English and literature	19	800	.64	1.5
Music	18	1,300	.61	2.4
Art	11	1,700	.42	1.7
French	9	900	.50	1.6
Social Sciences (weighted average)	32	1,000	.63	1.8
Political science	46	1,200	.61	2.6
History	36	800	.43	1.2
Economics	26	800	.64	1.6
Sociology	24	1,100	.85	1.7
Other Fields				
Educational services	69	−200	.50	−3.0
Counseling and guidance	56	1,900	.72	1.8
Mathematics	38	1,800	.65	6.9
Secondary education	36	1,600	.81	−1.5
Physical education	2	1,500	1.48	1.2

[a] Based upon all new professors who were students in the previous year.
[b] The rank average was derived on a scale which assigns a weight of 1 to instructors, 2 to assistant professors, 3 to associate professors, and 4 to full professors.
[c] Data are not available.

Source: survey data.

[39] These arguments are elaborated in Brown, *The Market for College Teachers*, pp. 58–60.

with his humanities or social science Ph.D. receives only $1,000 more starting pay than the same student without the Ph.D., the Ph.D. is worth $1,400 more in the sciences. It also means a teaching load in the sciences 3.1 hours lower than for the non-Ph.D., compared to less than a two-hour difference in the humanities and social sciences.

Why those specialists in greatest demand are the least likely to leave graduate school without the Ph.D. is explained by a similar contrast between *shortage* and *surplus* disciplines. The degree buys a salary that is $1,600 more and a teaching load that is 4.6 hours less in shortage disciplines, compared to only $1,000 more and 1.4 fewer hours for those in *surplus* disciplines. Because the pull of excess demand is less important than the adhesion of opportunity costs, it is easier to draw a student in the humanities out of graduate school before he completes his degree than it is to attract personnel from a data discipline.

The Loosely Connected Group as Supply

The supply of professors available to American higher education is not, even in a given year, fixed and rigid. The data indicate considerable flexibility in total supply. Recruitment of faculty does more than redistribute individuals already committed to teaching: it actually increases the total number of available professors. In a limited sense, demand brings forth supply. One-third of all newly hired faculty (over 10,000 individuals) would not be teaching in higher education if an active recruiter had not interested them with a specific offer. Among these individuals (the loosely connected group) are former employees of nonacademic institutions who needed a concrete offer to persuade them to teach, former high school teachers who had not considered seriously their opportunities at the college level, and former graduate students who originally intended to continue their studies without interruption.

The best schools rely heavily upon the loosely connected. Because they are more likely to want experienced professors, more likely to have professional schools, and more able to manage extensive recruitment and to compete successfully with salaries outside the academic community, 57 percent of the new professors at the better schools are members of the loosely connected group. The lowest quintile schools hired only one-fourth of their newly appointed from this source. When compared with the other new faculty hired, the

loosely connected, strongly reflecting the characteristics of the schools which hired most of them, tends to be research-oriented (14 percent versus 7 percent), publication-minded (17 percent versus 10 percent), and highly trained (54 percent with Ph.D.'s versus 42 percent with Ph.D.'s). It signs contracts earlier (38 percent before March versus 30 percent before March for other newly hired), and at higher rank.

Sources of Immobility

The multifarious sources of demand and of supply have both been identified. Now let us return to the market. When two parties, one a supplier and the other a demander come together and agree upon mutually satisfactory terms of employment, turnover results. Mobility occurs. But two parties do not always come together. And even when they do, mutually satisfactory terms are not always defined. In many instances, mobility would occur *if* the two parties found one another or *if* special noneconomic constraints were not placed upon negotiations. *But it does not.*

Since economic theory posits that the best allocation of scarce resources (college professors, for example) depends upon suppliers moving toward the demanders that offer the best jobs, it is important to understand any forces that prevent such movement, to know what constrains professors from following the best job opportunities, and to know why the market for professors is not perfect. Classical wage theory tells us that in an ideal market, where resources are allocated with perfect economic efficiency, five conditions must exist: (1) entry into and exit from the market is unrestricted; (2) complete knowledge exists among all participants in the market; (3) movement of resources is instantaneous and costless; (4) all decisions are economically rational, made in accordance with the principles of profit maximization; and (5) decisions are made by a large number of demanders and suppliers acting independently of each other. By contrasting these conditions to the reality of academic labor markets, some measure of economic efficiency can be gained.

1. MARKET ENTRY: RESTRICTED OR UNRESTRICTED

The assumption concerning free entry into and exit from the academic labor market applies both to universities and colleges as the demanding firms, and to teachers as the suppliers of resources. This study focuses upon suppliers, upon the practices that restrict the

movement of teachers. Issues relating to the entry and exit of demanders (e.g., why are colleges established and are they allowed to fail)
though important, are not treated because the collection of the appropriate information would be a quite different study. The firm is
studied only insofar as it influences some characteristics of the
resources it employs.

The ethics of the market. Ethics of the profession restrict the tim-
ing and the frequency of job change. An individual professor is not
free to change jobs whenever he pleases. He cannot move in the middle of an academic term because the disruption in course continuity
would receive general condemnation. Moreover, he will not give notice of resignation after May 15 for the following September, for this
deadline is set by the American Association of University Professors
(AAUP) in cooperation with the Association of American Colleges
(AAC) and adhered to by most members of the profession.

Similarly, employers are constrained. The AAUP-AAC code of ethics states that each professor should understand his status for September by March 15, so that he can seek another appointment if necessary. Faculty raiding after May 1 is condemned.

Thus the calendar restricts the freedom of both professors and
their employers. Decisions not to rehire reached after March 15 may
not be implemented until seventeen months later. Just as resignations after May 15 may not become effective until a year beyond the
following September.

Whereas codes of ethics are more easily defined than enforced, evidence suggests that deadlines are generally honored. Before the end
of May, 80 percent of the professors switching colleges sign a binding
contract with their new employer. It is reasonable to expect that
most of the remaining 20 percent have informed their employers of
their intention to leave and are deciding among several alternative
offers.

A second immobilizing ethic is the antipirating pact, or gentle-
man's agreement between institutions against the wooing away of
faculty from a sister institution. Job-switching costs both employees
and their employers. In most cases the costs are somewhat commen-
surate. Occasionally, however, the costs of movement for individuals
are substantially less than those for their employers and it behooves
employers artificially to restrict movement. Two schools located in
the same city are a case in point. For the individual to switch em-

ployers does not involve the usual cost of uprooting community ties and moving furniture. But the school is left with a vacancy and must undergo the same costs of recruitment, orientation, and general disruption as if its departed faculty member had moved a thousand miles. Since the institution which hired the new faculty member is likely to be on the losing end of a similar transfer at a future date, both schools will probably gain by a collusive agreement not to hire one another's faculty. Here the individual faculty member loses, but the institutions gain. Institutional gains from antipirating agreements normally extend beyond the particular situation to relate to preservation of harmonious relations.[40] Pacts maintain equilibrium between closely related universities but place the professionals at the schools in an immobile position even if a special opportunity exists.

A third immobilizing ethic is folklore condemning too much mobility. The professors themselves still feel that too much mobility is bad per se, that the relatively stable teacher is the more marketable. Potential movers remain in place to avoid getting a reputation as too mobile. Thus benefits that might be obtained from a move may be passed up in fear of the sanctions resulting from too much mobility.

Promotion from within. One practice impeding interinstitutional mobility is the promotion of lower ranked faculty within the college or university (table 20). Eighty-eight percent of all hiring is heavily concentrated in the two lowest ranks. But a majority of all college teachers are associate and full professors. A shift in the distribution of this magnitude indicates that most senior faculty appointments are reached from within. Hiring at the upper ranks is the exception.

20 |

Academic Rank of Newly Hired Professors*

ACADEMIC RANK	PERCENTAGE OF NEWLY HIRED FACULTY	PERCENTAGE OF ALL COLLEGE FACULTY[a]
Instructor	40	16
Assistant professor	44	29
Associate professor	10	24
Full professor	6	27

[a] Totals 96% because some faculty not assigned rank.
* Means that distributions are significantly different by chi-square at least at the .05 level.
Sources: survey data and COLFACS data.

[40] For further discussion see Brown, *The Market for College Teachers*, pp. 78–9.

The result of the hire-low-and-promote policy is a narrowing of the size and degree of competition in the markets for senior professors. The markets become less perfect as one progresses in rank. An individual's mobility is concentrated in the lower ranks and more limited in respect to senior positions.[41]

Inbreeding and outbreeding. Caplow and McGee have coined the phrases, "inbreeding" and "outbreeding," to cover practices of hiring one's own graduates and of requiring graduates to complete an internship at some other acceptable institution before returning to their alma mater.[42] Although the extent of inbreeding appears to be declining,[43] it is still a force that limits the supply considered by college administrators. My study of schools in the Southeast suggests an increasing taboo against hiring one's own graduates, especially directly from graduate school.[44] The feeling is that both the school and the individual benefit from requiring graduates to get experience in at least one other institution. This may be a stimulus to mobility in the short run, but it does not necessarily extend to the long run.

The practice of outbreeding indicates that the factors which originally work against teaching at the same school where the highest degree is received dissipate over time. At some point advantages of bringing a man back begin to outweigh the disadvantages. Since the candidate is known to the department, he can be rated accurately and is probably "safer" than an unknown candidate. He is familiar with the institution and already knows what is expected of him. Finally, the expense and effort of recruiting him is relatively small.[45]

Tenure. A common interpretation of the tenure principle[46] is that, after a probationary period (maximum duration seven years), college professors are assured permanent and continuous employment until

[41] For discussion of promotion from within, see Brown, *The Market for College Teachers*, p. 37; also see pp. 36–41.

[42] Caplow and McGee, *The Academic Marketplace*, pp. 49–50.

[43] In 1943, J. B. Roberts suggested that inbreeding between 1931 and 1941 had been on the wane: *Inbreeding Practiced in Appointing College and University Teachers and Administrators* (Nashville: George Peabody College for Teachers, 1943).

[44] See Brown, *The Market for College Teachers*, p. 77.

[45] Wilson, *The Academic Man*, p. 53. See also J. S. Cleland, "Inbreeding in College and University Faculties," *School and Society*, March 18, 1944, pp. 193–5.

[46] "Academic Freedom and Tenure: 1940 Statement of Principles," *AAUP Bulletin*, XLVIII, No. 1 (Spring 1962), 51.

retirement. The first thing to say is that *tenure is essential to preserve the freedom of academic inquiry. Without denying the truth that tenure is essential, an interesting question is "What is the effect of tenure upon the market?"* The effect may be considerable, for tenure policies may freeze professors in place by decreasing competition. Tenure may isolate senior professors from the market pressures that would otherwise goad them to greater productivity. On the other hand, the assurance of continued employment may free scholarly minds from mundane concerns and generate a productivity-increasing loyalty to employer.[47] And, the prospect of tenure may attract talent to careers in college teaching. The mobility of tenured professors is lower than that of the nontenured, even after a correction is made for age differences. Assuming that all associate and full professors are tenured and that no assistant professors or instructors have tenure, table 21 shows that the persons with tenure are a smaller portion of movers than of the total population of professors.[48] For both the group of professors under 40 and the group over 40, the senior professors are less likely to move than the junior ones.[49]

21 |
Tenure and Mobility

AGE GROUP	PERCENTAGE AT SENIOR RANK	
	Of Movers	Of All Professors
Under 40 years old*	19[a]	22
40 and over*	69	73

[a] Nineteen percent of all movers under 40 are currently employed as associate or full professors.

* Means that the difference between 19 percent and 22 percent and between 69 percent and 73 percent is significant by a chi-square test at the .05 level.

Sources: survey data and COLFACS data.

[47] Edwin O. Stene, "Bases of Academic Tenure," *AAUP Bulletin,* XLI (Autumn 1955), 587

[48] The rank of professor used in table 21 is the rank assumed at the new job. Since more movers advanced in rank than accepted lower rank positions in moving, if the rank at the previous job were used the percentages in column one of the table would have been smaller. Correspondingly, the contrast between the two columns would have been more striking, even if slightly deceiving.

[49] Even this conclusion must be guarded. Age is not the only factor multicollinear with academic rank. It may be that senior professors are less mobile because they have attained their career goals, *not because they have tenure.*

Yet, tenure is not always immobilizing. Over one-fourth of the professors switching colleges leave tenured appointments, and within this group 21 percent move to nontenured jobs. In some instances tenure may increase mobility. First, the AAUP ruling that tenure must be granted after seven years or the man must be dismissed undoubtedly gives rise to involuntary movement among some professors who would have remained at the same institution indefinitely if that employer had not been forced to a decision. Also some professors will move from a job that offers little prospect for immediate tenure in order to obtain the security of a tenured position at another school. And finally, it may be that for the man contemplating a move between two senior positions the guarantee of tenure at the new position reduces the uncertainty of the new situation so that the move is made when, without tenure, the man would have remained in place.

Over all, the influence of tenure upon turnover rates does not appear to be high. In markets of excess demand, such as those existing today in most academic disciplines, tenure (and security) is not a major element in decisions to move and not to move.

Fringe benefits. A third practice often linked to immobility is the payment of income in the form of nonwage benefits. For the entire American labor force fringe benefits have become increasingly important in the past two decades, so much so that

> It is said that seniority systems, health and welfare plans, and negotiated pensions have chained the worker to his job; that the adaptability and flexibility of the labor force are being "sacrificed" and that a new industrial feudalism is being built. The crux of the problem, it is held, is that the worker can no longer afford to quit his job.[50]

In spite of these fears, several recent studies of blue collar labor markets have shown that, except for special subgroups, fringe benefits do not significantly reduce worker mobility.[51] Apparently the same conclusion also applies to academic institutions. Melvin Lurie's recent study of the higher education industry divides all academic institutions according to the type of pension plan offered to

[50] Arthur M. Ross, "Do We Have a New Industrial Feudalism?" *American Economic Review,* XLVIII (December 1958), 903.

[51] *Ibid.,* 918. Also H. S. Parnes, "Workers' Attitudes toward Job Changing: The Effect of Private Pension Plans," in Gladys L. Palmer, *et al., The Reluctant Job Changer* (Philadelphia: University of Pennsylvania Press, 1962), pp. 45–80.

the faculty.[52] One group of institutions has fully vested plans: their faculty may take their pension rights with them when they move. A second group offers plans that are nonvested in the sense that their faculty lose all rights to a pension if they leave. If pensions are a substantial consideration in decisions to move and not to move, we would expect that turnover in the nonvested group of schools would be considerably lower than in the vested group. But this is not the case. Lurie concludes that the turnover rates are essentially the same.[53]

This study reaffirms the Lurie finding. *When academic institutions are dichotomized according to those which contribute more than five percent of salary to pensions and those that do not, the accession rates[54] for the two groups are virtually identical.* The institutions paying high pensions must do about the same amount of hiring as those offering less attractive plans.[55] Hypothesizing that not pensions, but tuition plans for faculty children and sabbatical leaves, are the mobility-reducing fringe benefits, similar dichotomizations were drawn on these variables. Though the differences in average accession rates are not significant, the schools with sabbatical leave plans (accession rate: 19.6 percent) evidence slightly higher turnover than those without (18.1 percent), and the institutions with a tuition plan for faculty children have a somewhat higher average accession rate (18.4 percent) than those with no such plan (17.7 percent). Taking all three types of fringe benefits together, when the 33 institutions that offer all three types of fringe benefits are compared with the 49 institutions that offer none of them, the accession rates are 16.7 percent and 16.5 percent, respectively. In no instance is the accession rate significantly higher among institutions that fail to offer

---

[52] "The Effect of Non-vested Pensions on Mobility: A Study of the Higher Education Industry," *Industrial and Labor Relations Review,* XVIII (January 1965), 224–337.

[53] Lurie's general conclusion does not, however, apply to certain submarkets. He notes, for example, that vesting does affect mobility in expected ways when only universities are considered, and when only certain regions are studied.

[54] The accession rate is "total full-time faculty newly hired for 1964–65" divided by "total full-time faculty 1963–64" and is calculated for each institution according to the method explained earlier in the chapter. The rates are 17.4 percent for low pension schools; 18.8 percent for high.

[55] Not only the average accession rates but also the distributions of accession rates are not significantly different for the two groups: of all schools in the high retirement group 29 percent have turnover rates over 20 percent, compared to 39 percent for the group of schools offering less than 5 percent of salary in retirement benefits.

large fringe benefits. Unless there is some generally prevalent third factor that causes the institutions with unusually high fringe benefits to have a higher accession rate than institutions with lower fringe benefits, it would seem that high fringe benefits are not a strong restraining influence upon mobility.[56]

2. Perfect Knowledge Versus Ignorance

Another constraint upon mobility is the lack of communication. Candidates are often ignorant of the very vacancy that would interest them most. And employers, not knowing about the availability of the best candidate, often hire the second or third best. In this regard, academic labor markets are similar to others, where the sellers of labor services are unable to identify all potential customers, and the buyers do not know about all the sellers. In the academic labor market the ignorance is the product of both the unjustifiably high costs of pursuing a complete market search and the "culture of the market" which condemns overt advertising of availabilities.[57]

Although it is not possible to determine what the volume and character of mobility would be if perfect market knowledge did exist or whether the increase in information would in fact improve the functioning of the academic labor market, an indication of the extent of ignorance can be gained by noting the knowledge that professors have of the market when they do move. It is evident that professors' market knowledge, even those who actually switch jobs, is most incomplete. The typical professor (median) investigates fewer than two jobs (not counting the job he is leaving). Although he has a vague impression that many jobs are available, he actually knows of less than five openings.

[56] It is appropriate to issue several caveats about the data on which this conclusion is founded. First, accession rates were used when it would have been most desirable to have a measure of voluntary outward mobility. That is, I studied "hires" when I should have studied "quits." Although there is certainly a strong connection between the amount of hiring and the amount of outward mobility, differences in expansion rates, rates of retirement, and involuntary mobility may also affect accession rates. Secondly, though it seems improbable, it may be that high turnover causes an institution to adopt an extensive fringe benefit program and that the program reduces the turnover rate to an average level. The fact that the turnover rate is no higher in the schools with fringe benefits does not necessarily mean that the fringe benefits have had no effect.

[57] A more complete discussion of the role of ignorance in the labor market is given in Brown, *The Market for College Teachers*, pp. 87–90, 146–50, 166–8, and 173–6.

If the southeastern social scientists interviewed in my previous study are typical, professors often lack vital information not only about the job offers they consider and reject but also the one they actually accept: over one-fourth of the more than one hundred professors interviewed confessed that they did not know about matters such as library facilities, office facilities, fringe benefits, the quality of students, promotion possibilities, and committee responsibilities at the time they signed their contracts.[58]

The frustration that job-changing professors experience in learning about alternative jobs available received expression when, in the present study, 35 percent of newly hired professors rated opportunities for finding jobs in their field as either "poor" or "very poor."

Employers, too, faced with cost constraints and the acceptance deadlines of competitive recruiters, must limit their market searches and, as a result, have only an incomplete knowledge of the candidates available. For most positions no more than four or five candidates are considered seriously and, except for the beginning positions, employers rarely recognize more than ten potential suppliers.

No doubt ignorance on both sides of the market changes the character of mobility and perhaps its extent. Ignorance generates false moves that would not be made with perfect knowledge. It cannot be determined, however, whether the benefits that would be received from the consequent reduction of ignorance and false moves are sufficient to compensate for the expenditures involved in any concerted campaign to increase the flow of market information. It may be that the false movement resulting from market ignorance is economically justifiable, or it may not.

3. MOVING RESOURCES: COSTLY OR COSTLESS

Because almost all job changes require geographic relocation, moves are expensive. In answer to the question "How many days of productive time did you lose moving between jobs?" the mean response was 10.7 days (table 22). As expected, individuals with the greatest personal involvement at their previous location experience the greater costs: e.g., married more than single (12 days versus 8 days, couples with children more than those without (19 versus 9), last year's faculty more than students (13 versus 7), and researchers with nontransferable job capital more than teachers (17 versus 12).

[58] *Ibid.*, p. 175.

22

Days of Productive Time Lost in Moving

NUMBER OF DAYS	PERCENTAGE OF ALL MOVERS
1 or less	28
2–7	37
8–14	17
15–30	11
Over 30	7
Total	100

Source: survey data.

Since most candidates pay their own expenses (table 23), the monetary expense of moving must also be weighed against the gains from the new job. Add to these time and money charges the "strain" of leaving behind good friends and familiar surroundings in exchange for the uncertainty of new work in a little known setting, and the result is less movement, although precisely how much less movement is uncertain.

23

Payment of Moving Expenses

PAYER OF MOVING EXPENSES	PERCENTAGE OF ALL MOVERS
Candidate	65
Employer	12
Candidate and employer	6
Third party	2
No move of residence	15
Total	100

Source: survey data.

4. ECONOMIC RATIONALITY: FACT OR MYTH

From a solely economic viewpoint, the optimal use of scarce resources requires that these resources flow to the producers who need them most, and it is assumed that need is expressed in the market by the willingness and ability to bid these resources away from other employers. Thus in academic labor markets optimal allocation of faculty members requires that prospective professors accept those positions that offer the greatest "net advantage." To the extent that professors have uneconomic regional preferences, loyalties to particular schools and environments, the production of teaching and research services is less than it might be.

Why professors choose jobs is discussed extensively in chapter 6. It is noted that the reasons for job choice are not solely economic. To a considerable extent, professors fail to accept the offers from the institutions that would pay them the highest salary and place them at the highest rank. It is sufficient at this point to say that many of the laborers in the groves of academe are not economic men and this gives rise to a market imperfection.

5. INDEPENDENCE OF ACTION

One of the problems in academic labor markets is generating a volume sufficient to make a market. Scholars are highly specialized. They are differentiated by factors such as the quality and extent of training, regional preferences, and attitudes toward the importance of research versus teaching. As a result, the academic labor market has become divided and redivided into units too small to generate effective competition. Instead of many suppliers anonymously meeting the forces of many demanders, the markets are characterized by individual higgling where bargaining tactics and persuasiveness complement, in an economically undesirable way, the action of economic forces in setting market rates. *The smallness of markets contributes far more to imperfection than collusion among buyers or sellers.*

Professors have no strong unions. If there is a general labor organization for professors it is the American Association of University Professors, which is a voluntary, nationwide organization open to all college teachers, both full time and part time. Slightly over 100,000 members, about one-fourth of those eligible, pay ten dollars annual dues to the organization which is pledged to promote the interests of higher education and to advance the standards and ideals of the profession.[59] If an academic institution acts against the academic freedom of a college faculty member, AAUP mobilizes its legal and diplomatic corps to reverse the decision. If unsuccessful in gaining a reversal, delegates to a national convention, aided by the recom-

---

[59] "Systematic Examination of the Current Structure and Functioning of the Association," *AAUP Bulletin,* LI, No. 2 (May 1965), 110.

mendations of a specially appointed investigating committee, decide whether the institution's action should be sanctioned. If sanction is chosen, the AAUP publicizes the violation of academic freedom and the name of the violator. In another regard, the AAUP is an active lobbyist for bills advancing higher education.

But the AAUP differs from other craft unions in many substantial ways. It is not exclusive unionism: initiation fees are nonexistent. The only requirement to join is the payment of annual dues and a signed statement that the prospective member is, in fact, a college teacher. Initial membership is contingent upon being a college teacher, but the reverse is not true. It is not necessary to belong to the AAUP to teach. The AAUP is not a collective bargainer, for academicians are proud of the higgling tradition and are offended by any intimation that they are unable to bargain for themselves. More a lobbyist than a trade unionist, the AAUP is not a major force in the market.

If the AAUP has any effect upon mobility, it is to increase it. By providing information on the salaries offered by nearly six hundred institutions of higher learning in its annual survey,[60] by urging the institutions to adopt fringe benefit programs transferable without lapse or loss from one employer to another, and by making available pages of the *AAUP Bulletin* for "jobs wanted" and "candidates available" advertisements, the AAUP increases awareness in the academic community of market conditions and attempts to reduce one of the major costs of moving (possible loss of fringe benefits).

Although the AAUP is the largest, solely academic, professional association, it is only one among hundreds. In each major discipline there is a primary association to which economists, or historians, or physicists belong. Each of the major disciplines is then divided regionally into a northeast association, a southern association, a western association, and so forth. The major disciplines are also subdivided into subspecialty associations such as the Econometrics Society, the Industrial Relations Research Association, the Regional Science Association, and so forth. The academic profession does not lack membership associations: only a partial list compiled by Carlton Bowyer includes approximately five hundred such organizations.[61]

[60] See "The Economic Status of the Academic Profession: Taking Stock," *AAUP Bulletin,* LI, No. 3 (Summer 1965), 248–301.

[61] Carlton H. Bowyer, *The Directory of Educational Associations* (Emporia, Kan.: Kansas State Teachers' College Press, 1962).

In spite of their numbers, disciplinary professional associations are not usually a major factor in academic markets, at least not consciously so. Professional associations exist primarily to provide a forum for the exchange of ideas and opinions among men of similar training or similar research interests. Their two major tasks are to publish a journal containing papers on subjects of common interest and to organize a meeting where members may convene for intellectual and social exchange. The professional association is a medium for transmitting technical information which is of little interest to a mass audience and of special interest to a selected one.

These same associations often are media providing information about employment opportunities for the persons of specialized interest and training who belong to them. Not all talk at an annual physics convention is about physics: much is said in the corridors about employment opportunities. Whenever specialists are brought together, some type of market information is likely to be exchanged, and annual conventions are notorious for their job talk.[62] Even if the professional association makes no attempt to provide any type of convention placement service, the very act of bringing specialists together undoubtedly increases the flow of market information.

At these same conventions, many professional associations provide a formal communications center where job-seeking candidates are put in touch with candidate-seeking employers. Illustrative of this service is the convention placement service provided by the American Chemical Society where fifty staff members are hired to run it.

In much the same manner between conventions, through the pages of their journals and special publications (for example, "Vacancies Available" published by the American Chemical Society) and in their association headquarters offices, these same professional associations continue to provide liaison services. In each instance the associations are increasing the flow of information and thereby improving mobility.

Whatever the strength of academic unions may be, they do not effect immobility in the same manner that trade unions do. Because of the national character and the high prestige associated with the teaching profession, the academic unions do not make a professor immobile. The unions are able to increase mobility through their in-

[62] See Brown, *Placement Services for College Teachers,* A Report to the Office of Manpower, Automation and Training, U.S. Department of Labor, 1965.

formation facilities. A professor can improve his job search techniques if he is a member of one of the large, active, professional unions and thereby decrease his immobility. Thus immobility will be decreased as the union distributes job information which helps to widen the horizon for the less informed professors.[63]

Summary

The forces preventing the academic labor market from being perfectly competitive are many. Although artificial constraints such as employee unionization and employer collusion common in other markets are unimportant in academia, a number of other factors operate to decrease the extent and effectiveness of mobility.

When viewed against classical wage theories concerning mobility in an economic utopia, the academic labor market appears to be a maverick. Entry into and exit from the market are not unrestricted. Because of such practices as inbreeding, promotion from within, antipirating pacts, tenure, and fringe benefits, along with adherence to the code of ethics, movement within the market is not free. Nor is movement costless; it involves both monetary and emotional costs. Decisions to relocate are seldom made within the confines of economic rationality or profit maximization. Also, academicians have specialized talents and skills making individual higgling necessary.

Part of the problem is the sheer market size. Since colleges are so numerous and scattered, and many elements of a good teaching job are necessarily subjective and therefore difficult to determine without lengthy on-site investigation, perfect knowledge cannot be expected. Similarly, employers cannot realistically hope to tap all of the potential sources of college teachers and meticulously evaluate candidates.

What can be hoped for is the development of intermediaries that facilitate market flows and reduce sources of immobility. To this objective, several policy recommendations are posed in the final chapter.

[63] There are at least two exceptions to this general statement. First, the tenure policy of AAUP which states that a man automatically should be given tenure at least by the end of seven years service probably reduces the amount of employer-initiated mobility (involuntary movement). The importance of this constraint, though small in the excess demand markets of 1964–65, might increase in less favorable times. Second, the division of college teachers into disciplines such as history, economics, and political science reduces the visibility of the generalist (the social scientist), for he has no disciplinary home.

4

Divided Markets

The concept of *the* academic market place is strictly a theoretical fetish. The realistic iconoclast that replaces it is a series of submarkets partially isolated from each other by geography, subject matter, research interest, demographic characteristics, purpose, and stature. All employers do not come into contact with all candidates, nor do all candidates contact all colleges. Horizons are confined to the feasible and relevant.

Dividing the markets are at least three forces. First, professors are heterogeneous. Not fully substitutable, the musicologist cannot conduct the physics lab, the female faculty cannot teach men's physical education, and the inexperienced teaching specialist cannot provide the same services as the experienced publisher. Different assignments require different skills, and different skills are marketed separately.

Second, both demander and suppliers choose to limit their participation. Because he can afford neither the time nor the money to search exhaustively for all possible vacancies, the candidate must confine his search to a feasible area, to a limited number of people and places. Based upon his personal preferences and a realistic evaluation of his chances of being offered good jobs, the job-changing professor may arbitrarily choose not to search for jobs on the West Coast, in disciplines outside his specialty, at very large universities, and so forth. Similarly, employers choose to confine their search and choice to a subsector of the entire market such as Ph.D.'s, publishers, and disciplinary specialists. The result is a divided market.

Third, institutional traditions such as promotion from within, avoidance of hiring too many faculty with graduate training, anti-inbreeding, antipirating pacts, and specialized lines of communication between established ex-students and their former mentors also create submarkets.[1]

In this chapter, the products of these divisive forces are considered. The more important to be discussed are divisions by subject matter specialty, sex, religion, race, and academic rank of the individuals and by region, stature, size, type, and sponsorship of the academic institution.

A Babel of Specialists

The knowledge explosion[2] has left us the choice of dilettantism or specialization. The possibility of a universal man has long past. Today the choice is half-trained, half-current teachers who are conversant in several disciplines or scholars fully trained and up-to-date in a narrow subspecialty. Although a few colleges consciously hire the dilettante in order to effect their education of the "whole man," the vast majority of colleges and universities are organized by departments according to specialized subject matter. Following the logic of the economic law of comparative advantage, most academic institutions, especially universities, hire specialists. Today's professors are rarely specialists in "science," sometimes in "physics," but usually in "thermodynamics" or some other subspecialty. Not "chemists," they are experts in "inorganic catalysts." Though specialization is vital and advantageous, it divides markets and places strains upon the administrators of institutions of higher learning, particularly those at impoverished schools who must cope with the changing demands and staff courses in each field. Insubstitutability makes it increasingly difficult to maintain the community atmosphere often desired at small colleges. Specialists are frequently in closer contact with col-

---

[1] For a more complete discussion of balkanization, particularly the institutional variety, see Clark Kerr, "The Balkanization of Labor Markets," in E. Wright Bakke, ed., *Labor Mobility and Economic Opportunity* (New York: John Wiley and Sons, Inc., 1954).

[2] A residual estimate is that increases in knowledge were responsible for 20 percent of the growth of Gross National Product from 1929 to 1957. Considering that the GNP more than doubled in this period, the growth of knowledge must have been considerable. Edward F. Denison, *The Sources of Economic Growth in the United States and the Alternatives Before Us*, p. 266 and chapter 21.

leagues at other institutions who specialize in the same field, than they are with colleagues in other departments at their own schools.

SUBSTITUTABILITY OF SPECIALISTS

To gain an indication of the extent of specialization in present-day academia, individuals were asked, "Are you teaching in the same field as the one in which you received your highest degree?" and "Is your principal teaching assignment in the same field as your primary research interest?" The answers, summarized in table 24, indicate that, although markets are balkanized, a substantial degree of substitutability does exist. Before a man becomes superspecialized he is usually required to obtain a general background in related disciplines. The American system of higher education is not producing narrow specialists who know only nuclear physics and know nothing about mathematics and chemistry. Most narrow specialists have a broadly based training that allows them to teach in several areas when there are not sufficient demands to justify the allocation of all their teaching hours to courses in a narrow subspecialty. As seen in table 24, when subject matter areas are subdivided into 73 speciali-

24

Extent of Specialization

SUBJECT MATTER AREA	PERCENTAGE TEACHING IN TWO OR MORE AREAS	PERCENTAGE TEACHING IN AREA DIFFERENT THAN HIGHEST DEGREE
Narrowly defined areas (73 disciplines)	21	21
Broadly defined areas[a] (13 subject matter areas)	5	4

[a] Broad subject matter areas are groupings of the 73 individual disciplines into 13 categories: biological sciences, business and commerce, education, engineering, English and journalism, fine arts, foreign languages and literature, health fields, physical sciences, psychology, religion and philosophy, social sciences, and all others.

Source: survey data.

ties (bacteriology, biochemistry, religion and theology, economics, history, etc.), 21 percent of all newly employed faculty teach in more than one field and 21 percent have primary teaching responsibilities in a field other than that of their highest degree. Many physicists also teach a course in mathematics. French professors teach some Spanish. Clinical psychologists often offer a course in experimental psychology.

Substitutability is definitely limited, however. There is almost no substitution across broad subject matter areas (table 24, line 2). Persons trained in a social science discipline will often teach another social science subject, but rarely will they be involved with a course in the natural sciences or the fine arts. Virtually all substitution is within broad subject matter areas.

The few substitutions that do occur between broad subject matter areas are typically the result of the incorrect compartmentalization of knowledge and interests. Some scholar-specialists concentrate upon a given genera of *problems,* drawing techniques from all disciplines as necessary. Thus, there are specialists in ancient history who may be found teaching in the departments of both classics and history, specialists in the problems of home and family who may be centered in the home economics department but teaching a course in the sociology of family life, specialists in the teaching of English at the primary and secondary school levels who may have responsibility for both English and education courses, and so forth. A detailed analysis of the few persons who are teaching in several broad subject matter areas reveals that they are not generalists, as it at first appears, but that they are problem-oriented specialists. *Virtually all college faculty are specialists, substitutable only within broad subject matter areas. Markets are deeply balkanized by discipline.*

The only indication that the extent of specialization is dependent upon market conditions is the greater splintering of the responsibilities of those hired in the *shortage* areas. *Within* the categories of engineering, biological sciences, and physical sciences—which include many *shortage* disciplines—a man is more likely to be teaching in several of the 73 disciplines (for example, mechanical and civil engineering), than if he were teaching within the categories of humanities or social sciences.[3] This may simply reflect differences in the structure of disciplines: for example, that there are fewer courses to offer in physics than in English. But there is at least a suggestion that some academic institutions may be reducing the number of course offerings in the scarcity areas so that one professor may cover all the related courses in several disciplines. Knowing that both physicists

[3] A special case is education where it is traditional to be trained in a specific subject matter such as English as well as in the methodology of teaching.

and mathematicians are in short supply, the data suggest that some schools are hiring one man to cover both fields and keeping the course offerings to a level where this is possible. Economy-minded employers are not, however, hiring linguists to teach physics.

DIFFERENCES IN MARKET BEHAVIOR

Although there is a modest degree of substitutability *within* broadly defined subject matter areas and *between* narrowly defined ones, the barriers between even the narrowly defined disciplines are strong enough to give rise to substantially different market conditions. For each of the 32 disciplines represented in this study, these differences are summarized in table 25. Since many of the differences have been highlighted at other points in this report, it will suffice to cite only a few illustrations. To the average new Ph.D. without teaching experience, $9,800 is paid electrical engineers whereas historians receive only $7,200. Economists draw $8,350; French Ph.D.'s only $7,350. Eighty-four percent of the new Ph.D. chemists and sociologists are appointed at an academic rank above instructor while only 66 percent of the new Ph.D.'s in history, French, and English are. The average teaching load for newly hired professors (not just emerging Ph.D.'s) is less than nine hours in chemistry, biochemistry, civil and electrical engineering, and agriculture whereas it is more than eleven hours in elementary education, accounting, art, music, French, and classical literature.

Less than one-twelfth of the appointments in secondary education, electrical and mechanical engineering, and physical education are for "one year only," compared to over one-fifth in educational administration, French, and classical literature. Involuntary mobility exceeds 30 percent in both political science and civil engineering but is only six percent in secondary education.[4]

In the disciplines that draw heavily from secondary schools (e.g., general biology and secondary education) the incidence of "reluctant

---

[4] Repeated attempts to explain the differentials in market behavior by dividing the disciplines into shortage and surplus have not produced any conclusive evidence of the expected relationships. Shortage specialists are slightly younger when they attain full professor (39 years versus 41.4 years), move involuntarily or "at the will of the employer" slightly less often (21 percent versus 24 percent), and receive slightly more job offers (2.3 versus 2.1)—but the differences are not statistically significant. One weak explanation of the similarities is that all disciplines are confronted with excess demand. Rather than excess supply disciplines, there are only disciplines with relative excess demand.

maidens," persons who do nothing to seek a job, is considerably higher than in engineering and most other fields. This probably indicates that employers who can use secondary school teachers must actively recruit them, since the teachers do not think they have the opportunity to teach in a college.

One of the greatest contrasts among markets is the importance of research and researching competence. Here there is a sharp dichotomization between the "data" disciplines, which emphasize research, and the "word" disciplines, where research is less important. The attitudes of individuals within the disciplines are illustrative. When asked "During a typical week do you spend more time 'teaching and counseling' or more time 'researching and writing,' or equal time at both?," more than one out of every eight chemists, physicists, biochemists, sociologists, and economists indicated "research and writing." This contrasts with those trained in English, music, physical and elementary education, and general biology and zoology where less than one-sixteenth were primarily "researching and writing."

In answer to another question, "Which of 17 factors were 'very important' in your job choice decision?," the research emphasis of the data disciplines is confirmed. In *all* of the physical and engineering sciences and in all of the biological sciences except the very general disciplines of general biology and general zoology, "research facilities" was mentioned more often than any other factor, whereas "research facilities" never ranked first among persons trained in the humanities and social sciences. Still another indication[5] of the greater

[5] The publication habits of movers differ little from their more stable colleagues, when a comparison is made across disciplines. The COLFACS data, where the discipline groups are identical to ours, are illustrative:

Subject Matter Area	Percentage with Any Published Article
Biological sciences	85
Physical sciences	77
Psychology	74
Health fields	69
Engineering	61
Social sciences	61
Education and related fields	58
Religion and philosophy	52
Business and commerce	50
English and journalism	46
Foreign language and literature	46
Mathematics	43
Fine arts	36
Physical education	32

Source: Kenneth G. Nelson, "Professional Publications of Teaching Faculty in Higher Education," a paper presented at the American Association for the Advancement of Science, December 27, 1964.

25

Characteristics of Newly Hired Faculty, by Discipline

VARIABLE	SOCIAL SCIENCES				
	Economics	History	Political Science	Anthropology	Sociology
a. Ph.D.'s	41%	55%	53%	65%	45%
b. Emerging students with Ph.D.	26%	26%	45%	52%	24%
c. *Last Year's Activity*					
Student	46%	44%	43%	28%	42%
College faculty	34%	43%	41%	46%	43%
Secondary/primary teacher	1%	7%	2%	1%	2%
Other	17%	6%	13%	25%	13%
d. *Mean Salary*					
Student Ph.D.'s	$8,400	$7,200	$7,600	$7,700	$7,800
Student non-Ph.D.'s	$7,300	$6,400	$6,800	$6,800	$6,700
All faculty	$8,400	$7,700	$7,800	.8,200	$7,900
e. Mean hrs. teaching load	10.3	10.9	10.7	9.1	10.6
f. Mean number conventions attended	0.8	1.1	1.1	1.1	1.1
g. *Publications*					
No publications	60%	60%	55%	29%	45%
Big publishers[a]	11%	12%	16%	17%	14%
h. Remaining only one year	19%	16%	18%	21%	16%
i. Did nothing to find job	10%	11%	8%	21%	17%
j. *Orientation*[b]					
Research	14%	11%	11%	17%	13%
Teaching	68%	71%	71%	58%	73%
k. Involuntary movers	21%	22%	32%	20%	10%
l. Teaching and researching in same field	96%	92%	96%	93%	98%
m. *Appointed Instructors*					
All students	38%	64%	50%	46%	57%
Student Ph.D.'s	3%	35%	22%	13%	15%
n. Shortage Index[c,d]	+		0	n.a.	0
o. Mean number job options	2.7	1.9	2.2	1.9	2.3
p. Mean age emerging students[e]	29.6	29.7	29.4	31.0[f]	29.8
q. Job choice criterion[g]	COURS	COURS	COURS	COURS	COURS
Respondents in discipline	357	318	316	121	345

[a] At least one book or ten journal articles, art objects included.
[b] Based on the answer to the question. "During a typical week do you spend more time 'teaching and counseling' or more time 'researching and writing'?"
[c] (+) means one of eight shortage disciplines; (—) means one of eight surplus disciplines; (0) means one of seven in-between disciplines.
[d] *n.a.* Means "not available" or "not applicable" or "sample too small to be statistically meaningful."
[e] Indicates *median* age used rather than *mode.*
[f] Data for emerging students are not available. Age given is for "all newly hired" faculty.

	PSYCHOLOGY			HUMANITIES AND LANGUAGE			
	Clinical	Experimental	Counseling and Guidance	English and Literature	French	Art	Music
	72%	76%	59%	29%	35%	14%	28%
	42%	54%	56%	19%	9%	11%	18%
	24%	41%	33%	52%	43%	42%	27%
	29%	35%	37%	31%	41%	32%	42%
	0%	0%	2%	7%	10%	11%	19%
	47%	25%	28%	10%	6%	15%	12%
	$7,900	$7,800	$8,300	$7,500	$7,300	$8,000	$7,600
	$6,800	$6,900	$6,700	$6,700	$6,400	$6,700	$6,000
	$8,600	$8,300	$8,100	$7,100	$7,900	$7,100	$7,400
	9.6	9.1	n.a.	11.3	11.4	n.a.	13.6
	1.4	1.6	1.4	0.7	0.7	0.7	1.0
	37%	20%	47%	70%	70%	11%	64%
	20%	16%	12%	11%	18%	49%	11%
	11%	12%	20%	16%	23%	18%	12%
	18%	12%	11%	11%	14%	11%	21%
	7%	15%	0%	5%	12%	16%	6%
	79%	64%	96%	83%	75%	62%	84%
	14%	19%	18%	29%	10%	25%	12%
	68%	85%	59%	95%	96%	88%	93%
	26%	29%	33%	81%	82%	67%	72%
	12%	17%	0%	36%	40%	33%	33%
	0	n.a.	0	—	—	0	—
	2.2	2.0	n.a.	2.6	2.1	1.8	1.3
	29.0	30.1[f]	33.0	28.0	28.0	29.7	28.4
	RES	RES	n.a.	COURS	COURS	COURS	COURS
	102	171	54	345	143	72	148

[g] That one factor receiving the most "very important" votes in answer to the question, "Which of 17 factors were 'very important' in your final job choice decision?"

"RES" means research facilities
"LOAD" means teaching load
"FUTUR" means future salary prospects
"COURS" means courses taught.

Source: survey data.

25

Characteristics of Newly Hired Faculty, by Discipline (continued)

VARIABLE	BUSINESS	EDUCATION		
	Accounting	Elementary	Secondary	Services: Administration and Supervision
a. Ph.D.'s	n.a.	n.a.	40%	54%
b. Emerging students with Ph.D.	n.a.	n.a.	36%	69%
c. *Last Year's Activity*				
Student	n.a.	n.a.	19%	24%
College faculty	n.a.	n.a.	31%	30%
Secondary/primary teacher	n.a.	n.a.	42%	28%
Other	n.a.	n.a.	8%	18%
d. *Mean Salary*				
Student Ph.D.'s	n.a.	n.a.	$8,000	$9,200
Student non-Ph.D.'s	n.a.	n.a.	$8,200	$7,300
All faculty	$8,200	$8,200	$8,000	$8,800
e. Mean hrs. teaching load	n.a.	11.9	n.a.	n.a.
f. Mean number conventions attended	0.9	2.0	2.0	n.a.
g. *Publications*				
No publications	n.a.	n.a.	60%	n.a.
Big publishers[a]	n.a.	n.a.	5%	n.a.
h. Remaining only one year	n.a.	n.a.	5%	21%
i. Did nothing to find job	26%	22%	24%	18%
j. *Orientation*[b]				
Research	n.a.	3%	n.a.	n.a.
Teaching	n.a.	90%	n.a.	n.a.
k. Involuntary movers	16%	6%	6%	n.a.
l. Teaching and researching in same field	73%	86%	52%	n.a.
m. *Appointed Instructors*				
All students	n.a.	n.a.	25%	23%
Student Ph.D.'s	n.a.	n.a.	0%	11%
n. Shortage Index[c,d]	n.a.	n.a.	n.a.	n.a.
o. Mean number job options	2.2	2.4	2.2	n.a.
p. Mean age emerging students[e]	n.a.	n.a.	32.5	35.2
q. Job choice criterion[g]	FUTUR	FUTUR	COURS	n.a.
Respondents in discipline	62	112	63	71

[a] At least one book or ten journal articles, art objects included.
[b] Based on the answer to the question, "During a typical week do you spend more time 'teaching and counseling' or more time 'researching and writing'?"
[c] (+) means one of eight shortage disciplines; (−) means one of eight surplus disciplines; (0) means one of seven in-between disciplines.
[d] *n.a.* Means "not available" or "not applicable" or "sample too small to be statistically meaningful."
[e] Indicates *median* age used rather than *mode*.
[f] Data for emerging students are not available. Age given is for "all newly hired" faculty.

	BIOLOGICAL SCIENCES					
General Biology	General Botany	General Zoology	Bacteriology	Biochemistry	Microbiology	Physiology
17%	55%	52%	n.a.	84%	73%	69%
14%	43%	40%	n.a.	78%	67%	63%
33%	48%	41%	n.a.	30%	35%	41%
16%	36%	43%	n.a.	25%	31%	26%
44%	5%	4%	n.a.	0%	2%	7%
7%	12%	12%	n.a.	45%	32%	26%
$7,600	n.a.	$7,500	n.a.	$7,900	$7,900	$7,800
$5,700	n.a.	$6,400	n.a.	$5,800	$6,500	$6,400
$6,200	$7,700	$7,600	$8,500	$8,800	$8,100	$7,900
11.5	10.6	10.0	9.3	7.1	9.1	9.4
1.7	1.2	1.1	1.3	1.0	1.7	1.3
71%	41%	42%	n.a.	14%	23%	29%
10%	5%	10%	n.a.	13%	14%	11%
12%	22%	n.a.	n.a.	14%	17%	12%
19%	12%	12%	12%	13%	13%	14%
5%	7%	5%	n.a.	21%	18%	14%
91%	83%	86%	n.a.	49%	72%	69%
11%	21%	17%	11%	22%	20%	10%
74%	73%	63%	43%	45%	53%	53%
71%	59%	48%	n.a.	7%	33%	36%
0%	33%	12%	n.a.	0%	30%	14%
0	n.a.	—	n.a.	—	n.a.	n.a.
1.6	1.6	1.9	1.9	1.8	1.8	2.5
28.6	29.7ᶠ	28.9	n.a.	29.3	31.9ᶠ	30.7ᶠ
LOAD	RES	LOAD	RES	RES	RES	RES
43	60	121	25	63	52	116

[g] That one factor receiving the most "very important" votes in answer to the question, "Which of 17 factors were 'very important' in your final job choice decision?"

"RES" means research facilities
"LOAD" means teaching load
"FUTUR" means future salary prospects
"COURS" means courses taught.

Source: survey data.

25

Characteristics of Newly Hired Faculty, by Discipline (continued)

VARIABLE	ENGINEERING			
	Chemical	Civil	Electrical	Mechanical
a. Ph.D.'s	83%	60%	62%	57%
b. Emerging students with Ph.D.	78%	74%	69%	62%
c. *Last Year's Activity*				
Student	38%	57%	38%	41%
College faculty	28%	19%	26%	22%
Secondary/primary teacher	0%	0%	0%	1%
Other	34%	24%	36%	36%
d. *Mean Salary*				
Student Ph.D.'s	$8,500	$8,800	$9,800	$8,900
Student non-Ph.D.'s	$7,800	$7,700	$7,300	$7,900
All faculty	$9,900	$8,800	$9,500	$9,000
e. Mean hrs. teaching load	6.8	8.8	8.5	9.0
f. Mean number conventions attended	1.1	0.9	1.0	0.8
g. *Publications*				
No publications	22%	43%	29%	36%
Big publishers[a]	15%	1%	16%	8%
h. Remaining only one year	11%	13%	7%	7%
i. Did nothing to find job	8%	7%	10%	9%
j. *Orientation*[b]				
Research	15%	2%	11%	9%
Teaching	63%	86%	71%	72%
k. Involuntary movers	0%	31%	14%	15%
l. Teaching and researching in same field	83%	98%	93%	93%
m. *Appointed Instructors*				
All students	44%	12%	22%	22%
Student Ph.D.'s	8%	6%	0%	5%
n. Shortage Index[c,d]	n.a.	+	+	+
o. Mean number job options	3.3	2.2	2.3	2.2
p. Mean age emerging students[e]	29.7[f]	31.0	29.5	28.8
q. Job choice criterion[g]	RES	RES	RES	RES
Respondents in discipline	48	88	138	96

   [a] At least one book or ten journal articles, art objects included.
   [b] Based on the answer to the question, "During a typical week do you spend more time 'teaching and counseling' or more time 'researching and writing'?"
   [c] (+) means one of eight shortage disciplines; (−) means one of eight surplus disciplines; (0) means one of seven in-between disciplines.
   [d] *n.a.* Means "not available" or "not applicable" or "sample too small to be statistically meaningful."
   [e] Indicates *median* age used rather than *mode*.
   [f] Data for emerging students are not available. Age given is for "all newly hired" faculty.

MATHEMATICS AND PHYSICAL SCIENCES				
Mathematics	Chemistry	Earth Science and Geology	Physics	Physical and Health Education
41%	74%	57%	61%	15%
38%	62%	43%	49%	2%
53%	34%	39%	42%	31%
25%	22%	26%	25%	35%
9%	4%	2%	3%	26%
14%	40%	33%	30%	8%
$8,300	$7,800	$7,600	$8,300	$8,000
$6,500	$6,500	$6,800	$6,700	$6,400
$8,000	$8,200	$8,400	$8,900	$6,900
10.9	8.8	9.4	8.6	10.8
0.8	1.1	1.5	1.5	1.9
66%	24%	31%	29%	71%
6%	9%	20%	16%	8%
16%	14%	17%	14%	6%
13%	11%	21%	16%	17%
12%	14%	12%	17%	0%
71%	69%	74%	61%	89%
22%	24%	24%	20%	11%
97%	96%	90%	93%	99%
55%	34%	55%	45%	77%
24%	16%	24%	22%	n.a.
+	−	+	0	+
2.3	2.2	1.7	2.3	1.8
27.7	27.9	30.3	28.0	26.0
COURS	RES	RES	RES	FUTUR
761	447	145	447	156

[g] That one factor receiving the most "very important" votes in answer to the question, "Which of 17 factors were 'very important' in your final job choice decision?"

"RES"	means research facilities
"LOAD"	means teaching load
"FUTUR"	means future salary prospects
"COURS"	means courses taught.

Source: survey data.

emphasis upon research in the data disciplines, as shown in table 26, is that only 40 percent of those in data disciplines have not published, compared to 59 percent in the word disciplines.

In the data disciplines, where research training and experience are more directly relevant to the learning process, the Ph.D. degree is expected. Over three-fifths of all movers in the markets for biochemists, electrical engineers, civil engineers, chemists, physicists, and clinical psychologists have their Ph.D.'s. In these same disciplines, a majority of the graduate students entering teaching have the Ph.D. degree in hand before leaving school. The contrast between these data disciplines and English, art, music, and physical education, where less than 30 percent of all movers and less than 20 percent of last year's students have Ph.D.'s, emphasizes the very different compositions of supply which exist.

26

Emphasis upon Research in Data versus Word Disciplines

VARIABLE	PERCENTAGE IN DATA FIELDS[a]	PERCENTAGE IN WORD FIELDS[b]
Spend more time researching and writing*	13	6
Published something*	60	41
Research facilities are "very important" factor in job choice more than any other factor	All fields	No fields
Average teaching load*	9.5 hrs.	11.2 hrs.
Teaching and researching in *same* fields*	93	83
Holding Ph.D.'s*	50	17
Last year's occupation outside academia*	29	8

[a] Data fields =civil, mechanical, electrical engineering; mathematics; physics; chemistry; earth science and geology; biochemistry.
[b] Word fields =art; secondary, physical education; music; English; French; educational services.
* Means that difference is statistically significant by a chi-square test at the .05 level.
Source: survey data.

What at first seems surprising is that the very markets in which employers are most adamant about maintaining quality by hiring only Ph.D.'s are the ones where the pressures to compromise standards are the greatest, where the faculty shortages are the most severe. Cause and effect are curiously intermingled. The explanation is that research ability is regarded as more essential in the data disciplines. Compromising Ph.D.-type experience in these research-oriented disciplines will result in a sharp decrease in the quality of output. Scarcity in the data disciplines is created by the low substitutability of non-Ph.D.'s for Ph.D.'s. At the same time, individuals, contemplating careers in several academic disciplines, are not responding to the higher remunerations offered in the data disciplines because the barriers to entry into the market (receipt of a Ph.D.) are greater. Thus another cause of excess demand in the data disciplines is the high training costs involved in entering.

The case is clear and conclusive. Each of these differences is in itself evidence that the academic market place is divided. For if divisions did not exist, the excess supply in one subsector would move to meet the demand in another and the flow would continue until the two market rates became equal. Though there is some substitutability of professional manpower within broad subject matter areas (for example, natural sciences), the low coefficients of substitutability limit flows of manpower among markets and give rise to the continuation of significant differences in levels of remuneration.

Inequality in the Market Place

The academic market place is also divided by personal characteristics such as sex and religion. There are submarkets in which women predominate, submarkets for Catholics and for Methodists, submarkets for nonwhites and for whites. Women tend to be concentrated at women's colleges where they teach more hours than men and are paid less. Agnostics are concentrated at public and nondenominational schools, Catholics are at Catholic schools, and Protestants are at Protestant schools. Disproportionately large segments of the staff at Negro colleges are nonwhite.

The differing compositions of the teaching staffs at various types of schools are so pronounced that there is no doubt that submarkets do in fact exist. Are the submarkets created by the actions of suppliers, preferring one type of institution to another (e.g., women making themselves available to women's colleges at a lower price than to coeducational and all-male institutions), or by the actions of the demanders, hiring only supply with certain personal characteristics? *Why* is there a special submarket for women? For Catholics? For Negroes?

In the course of answering these questions data will be presented that will illustrate division of sex and religion in the market place.

TWO TYPES OF INEQUALITIES

The word "discrimination" in popular usage connotes a conscious policy, stemming from malice or prejudice, to treat equals unequally, irrationally to impose disfavor upon a selected group, to exploit unfairly, to violate fundamental rights as a consequence of following a course of action contrary to the course deemed most rational by objective standards.

There is another specie of inequality that is sometimes confused with discrimination. It is often not immoral, but rather amoral. Call it "differentiation." Differentiation may involve treating two persons who are equal "in the eyes of God" as unequals—because they are not equally productive. It is allowing the best player, regardless of religion or race, to represent the U.S. in Davis Cup competition. When carpentry must be done, it is hiring the trained carpenter instead of the store clerk. It is paying more to the better qualified and more productive professor. It is justifiable inequality.

DISCRIMATION AGAINST WOMEN

Women *are* treated unequally. They are paid lower salaries (at least to start) and given lower academic rank but are assigned heavier teaching loads. They fill disproportionately high percentages of the positions at the least prestigious schools and are underrepresented in the most prestigious ones. As a rule they have fewer alternative job options from which to choose. These data are summarized in table 27.

Inequalities exist. The question is "Why?" Is it discrimination or differentiation? There are at least three arguments for differentiation.

1. Women are less qualified and less committed to an academic career. This is perhaps the strongest argument. One of the major reasons that women are paid less is that they produce less: their productivity is lower. Male faculty, on the average, increase educational output more.

Much of the evidence in support of the argument is summarized in table 28. By all indices of quality, women appear to offer less productivity than men. Only one-half as many have earned their Ph.D.'s. Women have considerably less interest in research, the type of activity demanded by the top quality schools; the portion of big publishers

27

Remuneration: Newly Hired Men versus Women

Variable	Men	Women
	%	%
Academic Rank[a]		
Instructor	66	34
Assistant professor	87	13
Associate professor	87	13
Full professor	91	9
Average income (only persons who received their last degree in the decade following World War II)[b]*	$11,650	$11,100
Average income (only last year's students emerging from top quintile institutions)[b]	$8,100	$7,300
Average teaching load*	10.4 hrs.	12.0 hrs.
*Quality of Hiring Institutions**		
Top 10 percent	91	9
10 to 20 percent	88	12
20 to 40 percent	86	14
40 to 60 percent	84	16
60 to 80 percent	80	20
Bottom 20 percent	79	21
Average number of job offers*	2.2 offers	1.7 offers

[a] The distribution by sex and academic rank for all faculty, not just newly hired ones, are in accord with these data (*source:* COLFACS):

Rank	Men	Women
	%	%
Instructor	71	29
Assistant professor	79	21
Associate professor	85	15
Full professor	92	18

These narrowly defined groups are used in an attempt to keep constant quality and experience.
* Difference between men and women is significant by a chi-square test at the .05 level.

Source: survey data.

28

Quality of Supply: Men versus Women

Index of Quality of Supply	Percentage of Men	Percentage of Women
Holders of doctorate degrees*	50	25
*Orientation**		
Spend more time teaching	73	88
Spend more time researching	11	2
*Publications**		
None	50	77
More than 10 articles	14	4
*Quality of Graduate School**		
Top 20 percent	45	37
Bottom 40 percent	12	18
Experience		
Faculty last year	33	28

* The difference between men and women is significant by a chi-square test at the .05 level.

Source: survey data.

among men is over three times that of women and the portion of
women who have published nothing is 27 percent greater than that
of men. Moreover, women are less experienced and are more often
educated at the lesser schools.

Furthermore, it may be argued that the large differentials in
starting salaries are not discrimination, but instead represent the rational recognition by the institutions that they are taking a bigger
gamble on whether or not the newly hired teacher is professionally
committed. The employers realize that one-fourth of all women
Ph.D.'s leave the labor force, a percentage that is much lower for
men.[6] Even when women are equally qualified the nature of the
products they produce are not as prestige-giving to their employer:
". . . women tend to be discriminated against in the academic profession, not because they have low prestige but because they are outside
the prestige system entirely . . ."[7] This suggests that women are not
only quantitatively less productive but also qualitatively so, as the
quality is judged by the community of scholars.

Extending the argument further, it may be that women, with their
emphasis upon teaching, are of more economic value to the poorer
schools. The types of products that they would be asked to produce
at the top-rated schools are not ones they desire, whereas the lower
echelon schools which emphasize teaching are willing to pay more
for their services.

All of these arguments simply show that women should earn less
because they are less productive. They do not indicate how much less.
It may be that, even after the differential abilities of women are accounted for, women are hired less than they should be by the better
schools.

To measure the extent of discrimination, let us assume that a professor's publication record is his most critical characteristic. All academic institutions want to hire publishing scholars.

Every institution has three pools of supply that it may draw upon:
big publishers (10 or more articles), small publishers (less than 10 articles), and nonpublishers. The top decile schools draw 29.1 percent
big publishers, 40.1 percent small publishers, and 30.8 percent nonpublishers. If the top decile schools were not discriminating, they

[6] Jessie Bernard, *Academic Women* (University Park, Pa.: The Pennsylvania
State University Press, 1964), p. 66.
[7] Caplow and McGee, *The Academic Marketplace*, pp. 111, 226.

would be indifferent whether they drew *a man or a woman* from any one of the pools. They would reach into the big publishers pool and draw out 29.1 percent of their supply, 1.6 percent women and 27.5 percent men, since 5.6 percent of the big publishers are women. Similarly, they would reach into the small publishers pool and draw out 40.1 percent, 4.1 percent women and 36 percent men. And they would draw out 30.8 percent nonpublishers, 7 percent women and 23.8 percent men. Adding the percentages of women together (1.6 + 4.1 + 7.0) we find that if the top decile had not discriminated they would have hired 12.7 percent women. This figure appears in column 2 of table 29. Column 1 of the same table shows that in fact, of the persons hired by the best schools, only 8.8 percent are women. Discrimination exists. The top decile should have hired more women.

29

Actual Hirings versus Nondiscriminatory Hirings, by Prestige of Institution

Prestige of Hiring Institution	Actual Percentage of Women Hired	Percentage of Women That Should Have Been Hired If Employment Policy Were Not Discriminatory[a]
Top 10 percent	8.8	12.7
Top 20 percent	12.4	14.4
20 to 40 percent	14.0	16.2
40 to 60 percent	15.9	16.3
60 to 80 percent	19.9	17.8
Bottom 20 percent	21.1	19.2

[a] Method of calculation is explained in the text.
Sources: survey data and Prestige Index.

Similar figures are calculated for all echelons. They indicate that the top 60 percent of all institutions of higher learning do discriminate against women by hiring too few of them, even after accounting for their differential research productivity. Though some of the discrimination against women pursued by the top-rated schools is due to the fact that women are less productive, not all of it is.

2. **Women express a preference for the schools that pay the least and are the least prestigious.** Though women could go to the more prestigious and better paying schools, they choose not to do so. Thus

discrimination exists but it is the women who discriminate against the more prestigious and better paying employers, not vice versa.

In the first place, women place constraints upon the types of jobs that they will accept, constraints that are not as common among men. For example, the married woman is often unwilling to consider any job that is not within commuting distance of her spouse's employment.

Even within the geographic area, the type of job desired by a woman may be quite different than that desired by a man. Wishing to assume the dual role of college teacher and homemaker, many women may feel that the workload requirements of a major university are not compatible with their dual role. Late nights in the laboratory, midnight "runs" on the computer, frequent travel to conventions to deliver papers, long hours in the library perusing professional journals and other publications are not always compatible with the homemaker role. As indicated by our finding that 88 percent of the women spend more time teaching than researching, women want to teach. Women are not subject to the same prestige motivations as men, Jessie Bernard argues, and frequently do not aspire to the best schools.[8] Women actually prefer to accept jobs in institutions that emphasize teaching and do not expect research.

It is difficult to explain the fact that 41 percent of the staff at women's colleges is female, compared to only three percent at men's schools and four percent at coeducational institutions.[9] One plausible explanation of the overhiring of females by women's colleges is that the hiring institutions feel that teaching effectiveness is increased when teacher and student are of the same sex and, in order to get the relatively few women in the market, the women's colleges pay them more than they could earn at other institutions. Though plausible, the statistics do not bear out the hypothesis. Women's colleges, on the average, pay men $1,200 more than women. Not only do the women's colleges pay less to females than males but, of the four groups of schools considered in table 30, women's colleges are the second worst discriminators, paying men 16.8 percent more than women. Furthermore, after adjusting for differences in ability to pay (by drawing a sample of coeducational schools matched in ability to

---

[8] Bernard, *Academic Women*, p. 151.

[9] These percentages are for only selected groupings of predominantly male, predominantly female, and coed institutions; the sample is not a balanced one.

30

Salaries Paid to Men and Women
by Selected Men's, Women's, and Coed Institutions

Type of Hiring[a]	Men	Women	Percentage Men Higher
Women's schools*	$8,350	$7,150	16.8
Men's schools*	9,350	7,200	29.9
Coed schools I*	8,300	7,250	11.4
Coed schools II*	9,700	8,450	11.5

[a] Data are based on the new faculty at ten schools in each category. The schools in the category, "women's colleges," and those in "coed schools I" are matched pairs, matched according to prestige level. The same is true for "men's schools" and "coed schools II."

* Means that differences in male and female salaries are significant by a chi-square test at the .05 level.

Source: survey data.

pay with the schools in the women's-college category), females are paid less by women's schools ($7,250 versus $7,150) and are (proportionally) discriminated against more. Evidently, women prefer to work in women's colleges, even at some sacrifice in salary.

Since women's colleges tend to emphasize teaching, to pay low salaries, to schedule large teaching loads, and to be rated relatively low in the prestige hierarchy, it is not surprising that when women are compared with men they appear to be discriminated against by employers. The fact is that only part of the discrimination is employer-initiated. Just as the woman's preference for women's colleges means that she will receive less remuneration, so also does her preference for emphasis upon teaching. Much of the apparent discrimination against women appears to be self-imposed.

3. Technical explanations. There are two "technical" considerations that help explain why women are remunerated at lower rates than men. They need only be mentioned. First, women tend to be concentrated in the low paying disciplines. Disproportionately few women are in the high paying, *shortage,* scientific disciplines. Secondly, partly because of the concentration of women's schools, disproportionately high numbers of women are concentrated in the lowest paying region, the North Atlantic.

Implications. Each of the three points presented above indicates that not all of the discrimination against women evolves from discrimination by employers. Part of the difference in rates of remuneration can be explained by the lesser productivity of women, part by the preference of women to teach at colleges with low abilities to pay, and part by technical considerations. Women are not always located in the poorer schools because they could not have the opportunity to be elsewhere.

In defense of women, their lower productivity, lesser training, and preference for appointments that emphasize teaching may manifest a discrimination by society. Though employers may be only differentiating, society may impose prior discrimination. For example, opportunities may not be equal for women to attend graduate school, publish in the scholarly journals, and gain financial assistance.

Regardless of the cause of the inequality, it is interesting to reflect upon the implications. The situation as it exists, the concentration of women at the poorer schools, may be an optimum allocation of resources. In a qualitative study conducted at the Pennsylvania State University, it was found that:

> Women tended to be relatively more successful with less able students, as measured by college aptitude tests, than with the abler ones. They were relatively better than the men with the students of average aptitude, but not as good with the superior students.[10]

Since the poorer students tend to be located at the poorer schools, it may be desirable that women are there also.

INEQUALITIES ACCORDING TO RELIGION[11]

Like women, teachers of the Catholic faith are remunerated at lower rates than others. Though Protestants earn more than Catholics, they earn less than teachers of "other"[12] faiths. These differences are significant for all aspects of compensation: salary, teaching load, academic rank, and prestige level of appointment. For example, the average salary earned by Catholics is $7,700, by Protestants $9,000, and by "others" $9,300. Again, it is appropriate to ask "Are the inequalities discrimination or differentiation?" "Are the inequalities initiated by demanders or by suppliers?" As with inequalities by

---

[10] Bernard, *Academic Women,* pp. 253–5.

[11] These data are based upon a selected sample of schools which are probably slightly better than all schools in the population. The absolute salaries are probably, therefore, slightly overstated—but the differentials, which is what is important here, should not be affected.

[12] Other includes non-Christians and agnostics. This group is 36 percent of the sample.

sex, the answers to both of these questions are somewhat ambiguous.

Inequalities among employers. Part of the inequality is employer-initiated and is differentiation. Employers tend to hire persons of the same faith as the college. The tendency is strongest in the Catholic schools but evident in all. Developing an index similar to that used in table 29, the estimates of staff that would be of the same religious faith as the school if hiring were egalitarian are presented in column 2 of table 31. When comparing the percentage that "should be hired" with the percentages "actually hired," the evidence shows that Catholic schools are overhiring Catholics, Protestant schools are overhiring Protestants, and public and nondenominational schools are hiring more than their share of agnostics and non-Christians.

31

Actual Hirings versus Nondiscriminatory Hirings, by Religion[a]

CONTROL OF HIRING INSTITUTION	ACTUAL PERCENTAGE OF ALL HIRES	PERCENTAGE OF SAME FAITH THAT SHOULD HAVE BEEN HIRED IF EMPLOYMENT POLICY WERE NOT DISCRIMINATORY
Catholic schools hire Catholics*	67	15
Protestant schools hire Protestants*	75	54
Public and nondenominational hire agnostics and non-Christians	37	33

[a] All data exclude faculty paid directly as a member of a religious order.

* Means that matched pairs (e.g., 67 percent versus 15 percent) differ significantly from a random distribution by a chi-square test at the .05 level.

Source: survey data.

Also evident is a tendency for academic institutions to overhire (proportionally) college teachers with previous experience at schools under the same control. As shown in table 32, 45 percent of the new professors at Catholic institutions hold their first degree from Catholic schools, a percentage significantly greater than the five percent of all movers with Catholic baccalaureates. In table 33, although five percent of all switching from one faculty to another come from jobs at Catholic schools, 42 percent of experienced faculty hired by Catholic colleges and universities come from another school of similar control. Obviously, Catholic institutions are attracting disproportionate numbers of those with prior experiences in Catholic institutions.

32

Actual Hirings versus Nondiscriminatory Hirings, by Undergraduate Degree of Those Hired

CONTROL OF HIRING INSTITUTION	ACTUAL PERCENTAGE OF ALL HIRES	PERCENTAGE THAT SHOULD HAVE BEEN HIRED IF EMPLOYMENT POLICY WERE NONDISCRIMINATORY[a]
Catholic schools hire persons with baccalaureate from a Catholic school*	45	5
Protestant schools hire persons with a baccalaureate from a Protestant school[b]*	46 (29)	19 (4)
Nondenominational schools hire persons with baccalaureate from a nondenominational school*	38	76

[a] Column two totals 100 percent. Five percent of all job-changers held baccalaureates from Catholic schools, 19 percent from Protestant schools, and 76 percent from all others.

[b] The figures in parentheses refer to specific denominations (e.g., Methodist baccalaureates hired by Methodist schools, Presbyterians hired by Presbyterian schools) whereas 46 percent and 19 percent refer to all Protestants grouped together (e.g., Methodist baccalaureates hired by Presbyterian schools as well as by Methodist schools).

* Means that matched pairs (e.g., 45 percent versus 5 percent) differ significantly from a random distribution by a chi-square test at the .05 level.

Source: survey data.

33

Actual Hirings versus Nondiscriminatory Hirings, by Control of Previous School

CONTROL OF HIRING INSTITUTION	ACTUAL PERCENTAGE OF ALL HIRES	PERCENTAGE THAT SHOULD HAVE BEEN HIRED IF EMPLOYMENT POLICY WERE NONDISCRIMINATORY[a]
Catholic schools hire person away from faculty of another Catholic school*	42	5
Protestant schools hire person away from faculty of another Protestant school[b]*	33 (16)	13 (4)
Nondenominational or public schools hire faculty away from nondenominational or public school*	91	81

[a] Column two does not total 100 percent because of rounding. Five percent of all job-changers who were hired away from another teaching position came from Catholic schools, 13 percent from Protestant schools, and 81 percent from schools without a specific religious relationship.

[b] The figures in parentheses refer to specific denominations (e.g., Methodist schools hiring away from other Methodist schools) whereas the 33 percent and 13 percent refer to all Protestant schools grouped together (e.g., Methodist schools hiring away from Presbyterian schools as well as other Methodist schools).

* Means that matched pairs (e.g., 42 percent versus 5 percent) differ significantly from a random distribution by a chi-square test at the .05 level.

Source: survey data.

What is true of the Catholic institutions is also true—to a lesser extent—of Protestant institutions and of public and nondenominational schools.

To the extent that professors of similar faith or similar experience are more productive, the preference of institutions of higher education in hiring represents differentiation rather than discrimination. To the extent that this is not the case, employers are discriminating. Professors with religious beliefs fully consistent with the objectives of the college may well be more productive, especially if the college stresses the teaching of faith as well as fact. Similarly, professors with experience in similar colleges are more likely to understand what their responsibilities will be. Moreover, they have proven their ability to work within the value structure of the sponsoring faith. To separate discrimination from differentiation is not possible until the effects upon productivity of the factors mentioned above are quantified.

Inequalities by candidates. To what extent is the discrimination that exists due to the preference of supply? As a rule individuals tend to seek schools of their own faith even at a sacrifice in salary (table 34).

34 |

Acceptances: Individual Religion versus Institutional Control

Religion of Candidate	Percentage Teaching at Institutions Affiliated with Their Church	Jobs Sponsored by Church as a Percentage of All Jobs
Catholic*	29	6
Protestant Iᵃ*	21 (11)	15 (3)
No religious preference	89ᵇ	79

ᵃ Similar to table 33.
ᵇ A "no religious preference school" is defined as a private nondenominational or public school.
* Means that matched pairs differ significantly by a chi-square test at the .05 level.
Source: survey data.

Twenty-nine percent of the Catholics take jobs at Catholic schools, though such jobs represent only six percent of total vacancies. A Protestant (e.g., Methodist) is 11 percent likely to locate in a Protestant (e.g., Methodist) school, though each of the four largest Protestant denominations generates only three percent of the vacancies.

The average Protestant earns $500 less at a Protestant school than at one that is not sponsored by a Protestant denomination, and the average Catholic earns $200 less at a Catholic school. This fact, more than any other, suggests that supply is discriminating against colleges sponsored by religious groups other than their own. It suggests that at least a portion of the difference in remuneration of Catholics versus Protestants versus agnostics and non-Christians results from the preference of supply.

Differences in ability. Professors at church-related institutions conform to the stereotype of teachers: they are not researchers. With interest more student-oriented than profession-centered, they neglect publication and place less emphasis upon receiving their Ph.D. (see table 35).

35 |

Characteristics of Newly Hired, by Control of Institution

CONTROL OF INSTITUTION	PERCENTAGE OF NON-PH.D.'s*	PERCENTAGE TEACHING-ORIENTED[a]	PERCENTAGE WITH NO PUBLICATIONS*	PERCENTAGE STUDENTS LAST YEAR	PERCENTAGE AT BOTTOM 20 PERCENT INSTITUTIONS*
Public	54	77	54	40	30
Nondenominational	43	63	44	39	15
Catholic	65	78	64	41	40
Baptist	77	86	79	47	40
Presbyterian	54	86	69	43	25
Methodist	49	91	51	38	26
Lutheran	76	86	71	49	58

[a] Spend more time teaching than researching.
* Means that differences among four groups (public, nondenominational, Catholic, and all Protestant institutions) are statistically significant by a chi-square test at the .05 level.
Sources: survey data and Prestige Index.

Perhaps because research accomplishments are more easily identified and judged or because research skills are naturally more rare, the man who stresses publications in a profession-centered career is more highly valued in the market place. An institution that hires staff primarily to teach, without an expectation for research, is employing a skill that has a lower market value. Since church-related institutions do in fact stress teaching, in a nondiscriminating world their salary levels should be slightly lower. To the extent that institutions of higher education hire different types of ability, abilities that are valued differently, the inequalities in compensation are differentiation.

Summary. Inequalities among religious groups are partly discrimination, partly differentiation. They are based upon lesser qualifications overall, greater productivity of individuals working within familiar situations and situations that are consistent with their own beliefs, different orientations of deeply religious professors, and preferences of some professors to teach at schools sponsored by the church of which they are a member.

DISCRIMINATION BY RACE

I suspect that the inequalities by race result from a complex interaction of many forces. Negro faculty is concentrated in the lower paying Negro schools. The concentration reflects the idea that Negroes teaching Negroes are more effective than whites teaching Negroes (an idea that is probably mistaken), the fact that Negroes have received less training at less prestigious schools and have published less, the attitude among Negroes that they would prefer to teach in a familiar environment and the practices among employers that discriminate against Negroes. The sample represented in this survey has not resulted in any significant data for Negroes. Rather than present misleadingly sparse data, the racial empiricism will be left for future research.[13]

Nationwide Markets

Numerous studies indicate that for blue collar workers geography is the most divisive element in the labor market. Faced with labor shortage, employers will pay to train new workers before they will recruit in other regions. However, when costs of training will exceed costs of transporting, it is to the employer's advantage to recruit already trained men even though they must be transported great distances.

When workers are homogeneous and unskilled, essentially the same skills may be recruited within the employer's home region as in

[13] For some information, see Patricia S. Wright and Earl E. Huych, "Faculty in White and Negro Colleges," *Health, Education, and Welfare Indicators,* February 1965, pp. 16–30.

others. There is little incentive to recruit nationally for unskilled and semi-skilled workers. When workers are highly trained and heterogeneous, the likelihood of finding a substantially superior worker in another region is high. That the gain in value productivity resulting from finding that better worker in that other region will exceed the costs of searching and recruiting is likely.

What is true for employers is also true for employees. Unskilled workers will rarely find substantially better jobs in foreign regions, whereas workers who own special skills relevant to a limited number of jobs within the region may benefit greatly by extending their search: for example, the demand for a specific type of professor may be limited so that within an entire region only one or two vacancies are pertinent. To extend the market to include a sufficient number of alternatives requires a nationwide perspective.

Because training costs are high and markets are specialized, geography is not an important divider of academic labor markets. To serve at their new jobs 26 percent of all professors move over 1,000 miles.[14] A total of 46 percent move over 500 miles. Fourteen percent remain in place. Over two-thirds consider a concrete offer in another region. Because veteran faculty have contacts more widely dispersed throughout the country and have less reason to remain close to their graduate school, they are more prone to switch regions (50 percent) than emerging students (41 percent).

REGIONAL PREFERENCES

The small amount of regionalism that does exist is primarily the product of the personal preference of professors. The influence of background is obvious in movement. Fifty-seven percent of the movers accept jobs in the region where they attended high school. Fifty-six percent choose the region of their baccalaureate school, and 56 percent return to the region of their graduate school. There is a constant tendency for supply to return to regions known best. All regions show a drawing power greater than 50 percent for all categories. The power is strongest in the Southeast where, for all categories, over 63 percent return.

[14] Of those who move over 1,000 miles, 40 percent of the movement is to the Far West. Even high moving expenses do not substantially discourage the professorial tendency to view markets nationally. Of those who move 1,000 miles, 69 percent pay the major portion of their moving expenses without subsidization by the new employers.

The lure of home is evident in dreams as well as actions. When asked to identify their "El Dorado" (the institution of higher learning where they would most like to teach), a majority picked their home region (refer to table 36). As in actions, midwesterners are least loyal in their dreams. The loyalty of southeasterners is more apparent than real: 13 percent who do return home would prefer (if the opportunity were available) an appointment outside the region. Partly because of the concentration of most prestigious institutions in these regions the professors from the West and North Atlantic retain the greatest loyalty to their home regions.

36 |

Region of El Dorado Compared to Region
of Selected Background Influences

REGION OF EL DORADO JOB AND BACKGROUND INFLUENCE	PERCENTAGE OF EL DORADOS IN SAME REGION AS			
	High School	Baccalaureate School	Graduate School	Average for All Schools[a]*
North Atlantic	63	66	64	64
Great Lakes and Plains	42	45	41	43
Southeast	51	56	54	54
Far West and Southwest	66	68	68	67
All regions[b]	55	58	56	56

[a] Column four is an unweighted average of columns one through three.

[b] This is a weighted average. Weights are the number of current jobs in each region. Since there were more vacancies in the Midwest than the Southeast, 43 percent was weighted more heavily than 54 percent.

* Means that this distribution differs significantly from the distribution of vacancies by a chi-square test at the .05 level.

Note: For example, for "North Atlantic" the data show that 63 percent of those who went to high school in the North Atlantic want to return. Similarly, 66 percent of those who attended undergraduate school in the North Atlantic want to return, and 64 percent of those who attended graduate school in the North Atlantic want to return to that region.

Source: survey data.

What is important to note from both the recent movements and the ideal locations are the policy implications. If regions can be viewed as trading countries, it is to their advantage to educate their own faculty, for there is a definite tendency for faculty to desire to remain in that region, with the possible exception of the Midwest. The reward to institutions in initiating graduate programs and in giving hiring preferences to men educated in the same region will be reduced turnover rates.

THE REGIONS THEMSELVES

Arbitrage has failed to eliminate small differentials among regions. Consider variations in average annual income. Comparing new Ph.D.'s emerging from graduate school, the two regions with the strongest loyalties offer the lowest salaries, whereas the Southeast, generally regarded as the region to avoid, is forced to pay slightly higher salaries in order to attract needed manpower (table 37). As time passes, how-

37

Mean Annual Income for Ph.D.'s, by Region[a]

REGION OF CURRENT JOB	BEGINNING PH.D.'S	VETERAN PH.D.'S[b]
North Atlantic	$7,700	$9,900
Great Lakes and Plains	8,200	9,600
Southeast	8,100	9,200
Far West and Southwest	7,900	9,400

[a] The figures are rounded to the nearest 100.
[b] Includes only persons holding Ph.D.'s and who switched from one faculty to another in 1964–65.
Source: survey data.

ever, the wealth of schools in the regions becomes more apparent and the salary advantages of the Midwest and Southeast recede and vanish: e.g., newly hired, experienced Ph.D.'s earn, on the average, from $200 to $700 less in the Southeast than in any other region. In the more experienced group, the North Atlantic is the leader.

What is true of salary is also true of rank, as shown by table 38. To

38

Academic Rank of Appointments of Student Ph.D.'s, by Region

REGION OF CURRENT JOB	PERCENTAGE APPOINTED AS INSTRUCTORS	PERCENTAGE APPOINTED AS ASSOCIATE OR FULL PROFESSORS
North Atlantic	33	3
Great Lakes and Plains	13	9
Southeast	11	17
Far West and Southwest	12	8

Source: survey data.

attract beginning Ph.D.'s, the least preferred regions hold out the highest ranks. The biggest contrast in hiring traditions is between the North Atlantic and Southeast. Institutions in the North Atlantic region are able to offer the lowest rank of instructor to one-third of the emerging Ph.D.'s that they hire. Beginning professors are able to demand a senior rank in only three percent of the hirings. In the Southeast, only 11 percent of the newly appointed Ph.D. holders will settle for less than an assistant professorship and 17 percent demand a senior rank.

In spite of its ungenerous policies on starting rank and salary, the North Atlantic hires more than its "share" of Ph.D.'s. The prospect of substantial increases in salary and rank is part of the explanation, but not all. Another factor is the high prestige of the institutions in the region: the North Atlantic houses the highest percentage of the top 20 percent institutions and the lowest percentage of the poorest quintile. The high quality institution usually means better facilities, brighter students, and more illustrious and more competent colleagues, all of which will enhance productivity. Still another advantage is that the North Atlantic has the largest portion of graduate students in the country (36 percent) and, consequently, the greatest number of the coveted positions involving graduate-level teaching.

When competing for similarly qualified faculty at the beginning levels, the regional differentials appear to conform closely to the theory of compensating differentials. The regions that have the least to offer in terms of prestige and graduate-level teaching are the very regions that offer the highest salaries and ranks.[15]

[15] Inducements can overcome preferences. For the right job, professors can be lured between regions. The campaign of the disadvantaged regions to offer higher salaries and higher ranks does bear fruit, though it is sometimes frustrated by the higher prestige offered by an institution in one of the preferred regions.

To attract individuals from outside their home regions, most institutions do find it necessary to offer special inducements. Of the persons drawn from outside their regions, 30 percent had to be offered promotions in rank, compared to only 28 percent for those drawn from within their regions.

When an employer goes out of his region, he must then draw from a slightly lower quality pool. Thirty-eight percent of the professors who move between regions are drawn from schools of lesser quality (than the job that they are drawn to), whereas only 28 percent of the supply drawn from within the region are located at lesser quality schools. Also, higher salaries have to be offered to 31 percent of the persons attracted from other regions, compared to only 25 percent of the intraregion movers.

VARIATION: IN PROVINCIALISM

The crucial factor determining the geographic breadth of submarkets is *size*—specifically, the number of employment alternatives acceptable to an individual job seeker within the confines of a single geographic region. The individual qualified for an assistant professorship will usually find a plentitude of vacancies within his home region, probably some quite good ones. Because his home region offers a large sample of available vacancies, even though the sample is not random, the assistant professor will find little advantage in extending his horizons to different geographic areas. In contrast, to obtain an adequate sample (if this can ever be achieved), the individual seeking a chairmanship in a highly specialized field must extend his search to several regions: because his home region sample is so small, the probability of finding a better job in another region is quite high.

To generalize from this example, individuals with a small number of acceptable vacancies within their own regions will broaden horizons to other regions, and individuals with relatively numerous opportunities in all regions will tend to confine the search. For example, since the number of universities within a single region is less than the number of colleges, persons seeking *university*-level appointments move interregionally more often. For the same reasons, professors seeking positions at large schools and at the highest quality schools move between regions more often than their opposites. Similarly, professors in small disciplines move farther than specialists in the larger disciplines such as English and history. Since they move in smaller markets, publishing professors and Ph.D. holders are less provincial. They are more likely to require an appointment at a high stature university, the type that are few and far between.[16]

Because of the hire-at-the-bottom-and-promote tradition within colleges and universities, more vacancies occur at the lower ranks. Correspondingly, we would expect more interregional mobility at the higher ranks. In this case, however, the data cited in table 39 neither

[16] The size of market theory of interregional mobility breaks down when movers are dichotomized by sex and by age (see table 39). The greater interregional mobility of men, and of younger professors, reflects the larger net benefits (high benefit minus low cost) of these groups discussed earlier, the differences in net benefits being so large that they override size of market considerations.

deny nor confirm the hypothesis. Evidently the fact that the individuals eligible for junior ranks are younger and have not yet developed strong regional attachments offsets the "size of market" effect.

39

Size of Market and Interregional Mobility, for Selected Groups of Veteran Faculty

Characteristics of Individual's Current Job or the Individual	Percentage Who Switch Regions	
	Small Market	Large Market
University vs. college*	56	43
Large institutions vs. small*	56	42
Top 20% institutions vs. bottom 20%	57	41
Senior faculty vs. junior	49	52
Small disciplines vs. large	60	53
Big publishers vs. nonpublishers*	59	47
Ph.D.'s vs. non-Ph.D.'s*	51	41
Old faculty vs. young*	45	54
Female faculty vs. male*	42	51

* Means that the difference is significant by a chi-square test at the .05 level.

Note: The figures for discipline include *all* newly appointed college teachers. All other data refer to only those who move from one faculty to another. The twelve disciplines with the largest absolute number of full-time professors, according to COLFACS data, are mathematics, English, physical education, music, history, chemistry, physics, art, economics, political science, elementary education, and sociology. The twelve smallest disciplines included in our study are bacteriology, journalism, chemical engineering, social work, anthropology, clinical psychology, other engineering, microbiology, classical languages and literature, general botany, physiology, and experimental psychology.

Sources: survey data, COLFACS data, and Prestige Index.

SUMMARY

Academic labor markets are national. Movement across regional boundaries is typical. Few job changes are made without geographic relocations. There are variations in the geographic breadth of submarkets according to factors such as the absolute number of vacancies of the type sought, demographic characteristics of supply, characteristics of the hiring institutions, and preferences of supply. And there are some differences in the types of opportunities offered by various regions. But the continuance of these differential opportunities appears to be the result of differentials in the necessity and ability of the regions to make competitive offers, not the unwillingness of supply to cross regional boundaries.

Charmed Circles and Scholars' Siberia

Behind the walls of academia, an individual's reputation, his prestige and stature are, to a large extent, enabled and determined by the stature and renown of his employing institution. Because of this link, the stature of competing colleges and universities is believed to be a significant determinant in job choice. Willingly sacrificing the immediate possibility of both rank and salary, professors aspire to appointments at highly prestigious schools in order to gain both immediate prestige and the research facilities and teaching loads that expedite career advancement and maximum future earnings.

But the charmed circle of highly prestigious schools is quite exclusive. Only a very talented few who are not already within the circle are allowed entry, and many who once attain entry are soon to be cast off to the schools of lesser prestige. In academic labor markets, the majority of movement is believed to be downward, from high stature schools to schools of lesser stature.[17] Any upward movement is rare. The academic hierarchy, it is argued, carefully separates good institutions and bad so that rigid divisions arise within the academic market place. In each of these beliefs there are both truthful and mythical elements, as we shall see in this section.

Throughout this section, as in others, institutions are rated according to a "Prestige Index." The index is a composite rating based upon eight factors believed to be concomitants of "prestige in the eyes of scholars": (1) percentage of faculty with Ph.D.'s, (2) mean faculty compensation, (3) percentage of undergraduate students continuing to graduate school, (4) percentage of enrollment that is graduate, (5) ratio of faculty to students, (6) total size of the faculty, (7) number of volumes in the library per full-time student, and (8) total income per student. The methodology used to construct the index is detailed in appendix B.

THE EDIBILITY OF PRESTIGE

Appointments at the highly prestigious schools should be cherished, for these schools offer all the advancement-facilitating resources—greater specialization,[18] better libraries and larger labora-

---

[17] Caplow and McGee, *The Academic Marketplace*, pp. 147–54.

[18] Eighty-seven percent of new professors at top quintile schools are teaching in only one field, compared to 75 percent of the bottom quintile professors.

tories, more diversified research programs, fewer hours of classroom teaching,[19] more outlets for publication through captive journals and monograph series, greater stimulation from more active and better-known colleagues,[20] better students, greater assurances of academic freedom, and environments more conducive to productivity.

But the potential monopsonists, the highly prestigious schools, do not take full advantage of the bargaining power afforded by their greater nonmonetary attractions, at least not by the conventional method of paying lower compensations. To the emerging Ph.D. top schools offer salaries that are virtually identical to the institutions of lesser prestige, except for the bottom 20 percent of schools where the salaries are lower instead of higher. The new Ph.D. does not need to trade off salary to locate at the more prestigious schools[21] (table 40).

40

Average Starting Salaries for Ph.D.'s,[a] by Institutional Prestige

Prestige of the Institutions	Moved from One Faculty to Another	Moved from Student to Faculty
Top 10 percent	$10,800	$8,100
Top 20 percent[b]	10,500	7,900
20 to 40 percent	9,900	8,100
40 to 60 percent	9,300	8,200
60 to 80 percent	9,200	8,000
Bottom 20 percent	8,800	7,600

[a] Only Ph.D.'s are used so as to promote homogeneity of supply. If non-Ph.D.'s are used the salary structure declines from top to bottom.
[b] The top 20 percent includes the top 10 percent.

Sources: survey data and Prestige Index.

What is true for *new* Ph.D.'s is even more true for experienced faculty holding Ph.D.'s. Not only is it unnecessary for persons desiring to locate at top schools to sacrifice salary, the lower the school is

[19] Whereas the average new professor at a bottom 20 percent school spends more than 12 hours in the classroom, the top 20 percent spends less than eight.

[20] Twenty-six percent of the big publishers (10 articles or a book) are located at the top 10 percent schools, compared to eight percent at the bottom 40 percent schools.

[21] More significant than the necessity to give up salary for *prestige* is the salary sacrifice required of those who wish to locate in the North Atlantic. The salaries for any quality grouping in the North Atlantic are below the salaries for the same quality groups in all other regions.

in the prestige hierarchy, the lower the salary it is likely to pay. Whereas the top 10 percent schools are paying an average of $10,800, the bottom 20 percent are paying only $8,800.

From the individual's perspective there seems to be little reason not to go to the higher prestige schools if the opportunity affords itself.[22] Prestige need be only slightly edible, even in the short run.[23]

Although the low quality schools do pay the market wage for emerging Ph.D.'s, the inability of the poorer schools to attract and retain experienced, highly qualified faculty is not only a product of lower prestige but also of lower salary.

To some undetermined extent, the poorer schools are paying a higher salary than they are getting credit for. The similiarity of salaries may be more apparent than real: the top schools are getting better men (the stars) for the same wage. If the lower echelon schools could have these stars for the same salaries they are paying their current faculty, they would prefer them. Extending the argument, it may be that the lower echelon schools would be willing to pay to these stars more than they are paying the men they are currently hiring if only the stars would come. When viewed this way, the top schools are not neglecting their favored market position. Their monopsonistic power is being used not to hire the same quality supply at a lower rate, but to make more refined judgments about the quality of supply.[24] The top schools are able, for instance, to hire more persons with superior graduate training with their terminal degree, and with substantial records of publication (table 41).

THE PORTS OF ENTRY

With all of the advantages offered by the top schools, there is no doubt that they can be selective in their hirings. At the same time

[22] The top schools offer better fringe benefits and greater opportunities for "outside" incomes. Whereas the average professor moving to an institution in the top 20 percent group expects to earn outside income of almost $1,200, the comparable figure for professors at the bottom 20 percent schools is only $250.

[23] Academic rank has such different meanings at various schools that it is not included in the above discussion. If the improbable assumption that rank means the same thing at different schools is made, then nine percent of those persons moving between two faculty appointments sacrifice rank in order to gain prestige. Or, in a slightly different vein, 15 percent sacrifice quality to increase rank.

[24] For a theoretical discussion of such use of monopsonistic power, see Martin Bronfenbrenner, "Potential Monopsony in Labor Markets," *Industrial and Labor Relations Review*, IX, No. 4 (July 1956), 577–88.

the *competition* for the openings will be greater. Despite the individuality of each professor, there is *apparent* homogeneity. A large segment of supply is very likely to be of apparently equal ability, a segment larger than can be hired by the top schools. Selection will, therefore, often depend upon other criteria.

The receipt of the doctorate is apparently one such criterion, as was seen in table 41. But even the doctorate is not sufficient to place a man in competition for a top position.

41 | Characteristics of Newly Hired Faculty, by Institutional Prestige

Prestige of the Current Institution	Percentage with Doctorate*	Percentage of Big Publishers*	Percentage with Last Degree from Top 20 Percent*
Top 10 percent	74	67	80
10 to 20 percent	67	52	64
20 to 40 percent	54	47	49
40 to 60 percent	52	24	34
60 to 80 percent	39	31	43
Bottom 20 percent	32	28	28

* Means that the differences among groups are significant by a chi-square test at the .05 level.
Sources: survey data, Prestige Index, and Productivity Index.

The stature of the doctorate-granting institution is tremendously important, especially for emerging students. The top schools are reluctant to recruit outside the charmed circle. Of last year's students hired by schools in the top 10 percent group, 69 percent were drawn from the graduate departments of other top-rated schools. A student from a top-rated school[25] has a 16 percent chance of accepting employ-

[25] There are other advantages of attending top-rated graduate schools. More offers are received: 25 percent of the students from top schools receive two or more offers, compared to only 13 percent from the bottom group of schools (bottom 20 percent). After adjustments are made for differences in the prestige of the appointing institution and the degree attainment of the appointed individual, students from the better schools are hired in at higher academic ranks and higher salaries. Students from the better schools are also able to bargain for lower teaching loads: average teaching loads of eight hours for the students from the top 20 percent of schools compared to 13 hours for those from the bottom 20 percent. Almost 90 percent of the students from the top 10 percent of schools move to positions requiring nine or fewer hours of teaching, compared to 20 percent of the students from bottom echelon institutions.

ment in another top-rated school, whereas a student from a school outside the top decile has only a two percent chance.

In his extensive survey of graduate education Bernard Berelson concludes: "Where one ends up, by these institutional classifications, depends a great deal on where one starts with his doctorate." Studying all faculty by analyzing degrees listed in catalogues, Berelson notes that 83 percent of the present faculty in the top twelve universities hold their highest degree from one of these same schools.[26]

If career options are determined by the prestige level of one's graduate school, it is important to know how to become a student at a high quality graduate school. Some indication is offered by the current survey. Of those respondents who had attended a top quintile graduate school, 36 percent received baccalaureates from a top-rated undergraduate school whereas only 12 percent had entered from a bottom quintile undergraduate school. To cite Berelson's findings again, 32 percent of those receiving doctorates from his select group of the top twelve universities had completed baccalaureates at these same schools.[27] Although Trytten's ambitious study of the baccalaureate origins of Ph.D.'s shows that there are many exceptions,[28] the general rule is that the students who attend the best undergraduate schools are most likely to attend the best graduate schools and, ultimately, to be placed in the best faculty positions.

EXTENT OF DIVISION

Primarily because the institutions require different skills, movement of faculty between institutions of high and low prestige is limited. Market divisions by prestige do exist, but they are vaguely defined. Not to be characterized as a rigid hierarchy of self-contained clusters where equally prestigious institutions trade faculty within the group and never allow outsiders participation, the academic ladder is more appropriately seen as a spectrum of circles with broadly overlapping membership. Movement among quality levels is common, even at the extremes.

If the academic labor market is divided into fifths according to

[26] Berelson, *Graduate Education in the United States*. pp. 112–5.

[27] *Ibid.*, p. 112.

[28] M. H. Trytten, *Doctorate Production in United States Universities 1936–56: With Baccalaureate Origins of Doctorates in the Sciences, Arts and Humanities* ("Publication 582"; Washington: National Academy of Sciences/National Research Council, 1958).

prestige so that we think of the one-fifth of all faculty appointments that are most prestigious, the one-fifth that are second most prestigious, and so forth—a quite broad definition of "tight cluster"—we find that no one of these clusters draws even a majority of its veteran faculty from within itself (refer to table 42). Of the faculty leaving

42 |
Intragroup Hirings, by Prestige of Institution

Prestige of the Previous Institution	Percentage Moving between Faculties of Schools in the Same Prestige Group[a]
Top 20 percent[b]	36
20 to 40 percent	18
40 to 60 percent	26
60 to 80 percent	31
Bottom 20 percent	44
Weighted average	28

[a] For example, 36 percent of the last year's college teachers who moved from the top 20 percent of schools went to a top 20 percent school.
[b] The percentage for the top 10 percent only is 27.

Sources: survey data and Prestige Index.

the top (20 percent) schools, only 36 percent return to another top school. At the other extreme, intragroup movement is only 44 percent which is still less than half. In the middle groups, where faculty are neither the leading specialists in the field nor the least qualified, intragroup movement of veteran faculty is less than one-third.[29] Thus, throughout the entire spectrum of quality, and especially in the middle, market divisions by quality are extremely imperfect.

The Academic Ladder

The existence of between-group mobility does not necessarily imply, however, that movement is free. Between-group movement may be one-way downward. Once outside the charmed circle of the

[29] What is true of veteran faculty is also true of emerging students. Because the better schools educate disproportionately large numbers of graduate students, at first it appears that within-group hiring is very high at the good schools and very low at the poor ones. After accounting for the differences in graduate student populations, however, again it is found that the extent of intragroup movement is not large for any group and that it is smallest for the middle groups.

top 20 percent schools return may not be possible. The road to "Siberia" may be one-way.

The physical necessity of downward mobility is obvious. As one
leaves graduate school, professorial manpower is concentrated at the
top of the academic ladder—for it is these institutions that have graduate programs. For 1964–65, the top 20 percent schools supplied
5,000 emerging students to the market but employed only 1,300. At
least 3,700 had to move downward. In fact, for all quintiles of graduate schools, a majority of the emerging students accept first jobs in
institutions of lesser prestige. As shown by table 43, 64 percent of all
emerging students move downward.

43 |

Direction of Interprestige Movements of Last Year's Students

Prestige of Graduate Institution	Percentage Prestige of Present Institution*		
	Higher	Same	Lower
Top 10 percent		16	84
10 to 20 percent	4	8	88
20 to 40 percent	7	23	70
40 to 60 percent	18	28	54
Bottom 20 percent	28	72	
Weighted average	10	26	64

* Means that the distributions for the various "prestige groups" differ significantly by a chi-
square test at the .05 level.

Sources: survey data and Prestige Index.

The necessity of descent does not, however, preclude the possibility of ascent. Upward mobility is a definite possibility, as proven by
the 10 percent of emerging students and 32 percent of veteran faculty who do it (table 44).

As would be the case in an undivided market, whether a mover
switches up or down is primarily dependent upon his original position in the prestige hierarchy. If his original placement is such that
there are many more institutions below than above, his move is likely to be downward. But if he starts low, most likely he will move up:
for example, 73 percent of the veteran faculty starting at the top
move down, whereas 56 percent starting at the bottom move up.

44

Direction of Interprestige Movements of Last Year's Faculty

PRESTIGE OF PREVIOUS INSTITUTION	PRESTIGE OF PRESENT INSTITUTIONS*		
	Percentage Higher	Percentage Same	Percentage Lower
Top 10 percent		27	73
10 to 20 percent	14	11	75
20 to 40 percent	24	18	58
40 to 60 percent	31	26	43
60 to 80 percent	40	31	29
Bottom 20 percent	56	44	
Weighted average	32	28	40

* Means that the distributions for the various "prestige groups" differ significantly by a chi-square test at the .05 level.

Sources: survey data and Prestige Index.

Avoidance of downward movement is increased by publication (table 45). Among professors leaving second quintile schools, upward movement is far more common for big publishers (33 percent) than for others (20 percent). And probability of moving to a bottom 60 percent school is over twice as low for the big publishers (30 percent versus 62 percent).[30] Though it is certainly easier to start at the top and resist the downward push, the professor publishing his way out of Siberia into the Charmed Circle is not entirely legendary.

45

Direction of Interprestige Movements and Extent of Publication

PRESTIGE OF PREVIOUS INSTITUTION	PROBABILITY OF MOVING UP		PROBABILITY OF MOVING DOWN	
	Big Publishers[a]	Others	Big Publishers[a]	Others
Top 20 percent*			67	79
20 to 40 percent*	33	20	30	62
40 to 60 percent*	46	25	41	41
60 to 80 percent*	42	38	12	30
Bottom 20 percent*	72	53		

[a] Big publishers are defined as persons who have published ten or more journal articles or at least one book.

* Means that for each "prestige group," big publishers and others are significantly different by a chi-square test at the .05 level.

Sources: survey data and Prestige Index.

[30] Similarly, the probability of moving up is higher for Ph.D.'s (one-third) than for non-Ph.D.'s (one-fifth).

Being in the right field also enhances an individual's chances for moving up. In the more rapidly expanding disciplines, such as mathematics, physics, and mechanical engineering, where the creation of many new positions creates a series of leapfrogging job chances that extends throughout the entire quality spectrum of institutions, upward mobility is greatest (see table 46).[31]

46

Direction of Interprestige Movements by Disciplines Selected According to Rates of Expansion[a]

DISCIPLINE	PREVIOUS TOTAL	PERCENTAGES OF PREVIOUS PRESTIGE AND PRESENT PRESTIGE COMPARED[*]		
		Present Higher	Same	Present Lower
Rapidly expanding disciplines	100	49	22	29
Slowly expanding disciplines	100	43	21	36

[a] The figures in the table represent all last year's college teachers except those located in the top 20 percent and bottom 20 percent of institutions. These individuals are excluded because they do not have the possibility of moving both up and down. For example, it is impossible for an individual who is already teaching at a top 20 percent school to move up because there is no higher category.

[*] Means that differences are significant by a chi-square test at the .05 level.

Note: For 24 disciplines an expansion rate was computed as "the number of positions filled in 1964–65 for which there was no predecessor" divided by "the number of positions filled in 1964–65." The eight disciplines with the highest rates are included in the "rapidly expanding" group: mathematics, mechanical engineering, electrical engineering, physics, biochemistry, clinical psychology, chemistry, and educational services. The eight disciplines with the lowest rates, the slowly expanding group, are sociology, English and literature, physical education, history, general zoology, French, music and general biology.

Source: survey data.

THE QUALITY NEUROSIS

Apparently there is no barrier to interquality movement except a lack of ability or desire. If there is a neurotic group, it is the professors at the bottom institutions. Of those who accept a job in a top school, eight percent reject higher salary offers from schools of lower quality. This probably reflects the fact that expected long-run productivity is greater at the top schools than are the short-run gains to be had at the lower quality schools. More irrational are the five per-

[31] For a similar description of the leapfrogging effect, see Reder, "Theory of Occupational Wage Differentials," *American Economic Review*, XLV, 833–52.

cent of those who accept their current jobs in the 60 to 80 percent level school[32] and reject concrete offers of higher salaries at better schools. Not only is upward mobility possible for these people, destroying a commonly held myth, but the neurosis is reversed entirely.

Deficient upward movement, if any, stems from the personal preference of the lower groups, and not discrimination on the part of the upper groups. These high quality schools have become "established firms" by operating according to some maximization principle, and will continue to hire the best qualified individuals *wherever* they are.

Small Colleges Versus Large Universities

Professors prosper in different environments. For some, their comparative advantage rests in teaching freshmen women, others are most productive in the graduate classroom, and still others find that research is their forte. Some professors prefer the environment of a small campus, where student-faculty relationships can be closer, while others demand the elaborate research facilities provided only on a university campus. Correspondingly, colleges and universities prefer to hire the types of professors who promise to be the most productive in their environment: for example, most small colleges place a lower premium on interest and ability in research-publication.

Since neither professors nor institutions change ability and emphasis very rapidly, we would expect that, except for occasional false moves, a professor who once chose a small college as "the type of institution that best matches his ability" would tend to remain in a small college. Though he might switch jobs, the switch would be between similar type schools. As a result, markets would become divided. There would be a small college market, and a large college market. There would be a market for university professors, and one for college professors. Such is the case.

Division by Size of Institution

Researchers are concentrated in the large universities where teaching loads are lower, opportunities for specialization are greater, research facilities are more adequate, and an environment conducive to research prevails (see table 47). Large institutions wishing to uti-

[32] This group is used not to distort the results, but only because the data on the 80 to 100 percent group were not significant.

47 |

Terms of Employment, by Size of Institution

TERMS APPLIED TO NEWLY HIRED FACULTY	SIZE OF INSTITUTION	
	Less Than 1,000 Students	More Than 5,000 Students
Percentage teaching in only 1 field*	71	86
Percentage teaching and researching in the same field*	80	88
Average teaching load*	12 hrs.	9 hrs.
Mean salary (last year's students)*	$6,550	$7,350
Mean salary (last year's faculty)*	$8,050	$9,550

* Means that the difference is significant by a chi-square test at the .05 level.
Source: survey data.

lize their resources for research, want researchers as much as researchers want them, even though competition with other large schools forces a premium salary. As a result, 60 percent of the researchers are located at schools enrolling over 5,000 students, compared to only eight percent at small schools. Sixteen percent of the staff newly hired by large colleges and universities are research-oriented, compared to less than one-half of this percentage by the middle-sized institutions.

Large and small schools have different types of demand for faculty and they operate in separate markets that are partially independent. Overall, 46 percent of all job-switching faculty move between schools of the same size. Even though small colleges account for only 17 percent of all vacancies, 27 percent of last year's faculty leaving small colleges moved to other small colleges. In contrast, only 15 percent of those leaving middle-sized institutions and 11 percent of those leaving large ones locate in small colleges. At the opposite end of the size spectrum, 52 percent of the experienced faculty coming from large schools move to other large schools compared to only 20 percent of those coming from small schools (table 48).

There is a clear preference to remain in the "same size league." Whether the cause of the market division is primarily due to the preferences of supply, desiring to remain in a similar setting, or the preferences of demand, desiring to hire manpower experienced in working in a similar production function, cannot be determined.

48

Faculty Mobility, by Size of Institution[a]

Size of New Institution	Percentage of Those Newly Hired by Group	Size of Former Institution (percentage at)[*]		
		Small	Medium	Large
Small	17	27	15	11
Medium	46	53	49	37
Large	37	20	37	52
Total	100	100	101	100

[a] "Small" means under 1,000, "medium" means 1,000 to 5,000, "large" means over 5,000 students.
[*] Means that differences are significant by a chi-square test at the .05 level.
Source: survey data.

DIVISION BY TYPE OF INSTITUTION

The multicollinearity between size and type of institution is so great that independent discussion of the factors promises to be redundant. With few exceptions the larger institutions are universities; the smaller, colleges.

The college and university markets are somewhat different. Sixty-two percent of faculty moving between two academic institutions move from college to college or from university to university; only 38 percent move from one type of institution to the other (table 49).

49

Faculty Mobility, by Type of Institution

Type of New Institution	Type of Institution Left (percentage at)[*]	
	College	University
College	57	43
University	34	66

[*] Means that differences are significant by a chi-square test at the .05 level.
Source: survey data.

Most definitely isolated are junior colleges. Universities hire only two percent of their experienced faculty from them; colleges, only 8.5 percent. Only six percent of the supply that accept an appointment to the faculty at a four-year institution have even one offer from a two-year academic institution.[33]

By paying more ($9,350 versus $8,200 for veteran faculty) for teaching fewer hours (12 hours versus 9 hours) with greater specialization (85 percent versus 75 percent), universities attract 78 percent of the research-oriented and the best emerging students. Whereas only nine percent of the students hired by universities come from the bottom 40 percent of institutions, 67 percent of the students hired by colleges come from the same source.

Outside the Halls of Academia

Academic and nonacademic positions offer different opportunities to an individual, so different that one might expect very little movement from one type of position to another. In teaching positions there is an unusual amount of independence, absence of direction from superiors, latitude in both the quantity and distribution of work hours, escape from the pressure of tight deadlines, and the opportunity to imbibe the cultural and intellectual prerogatives that go along with living in an academic community. There are the rewards of enlightened students, notoriety through publications, and the satisfaction of revealing a previously unknown truth, even an obscure one. In nonacademic jobs both tasks and compensations differ. Output must have more immediate use; deadlines are more necessary; work is often more timely. Self-discipline is less necessary; progress is more obvious; rewards are more tangible and conventional.

According to a recent study of salaries paid to Ph.D. economists hired through a convention placement service, the government pays $9,800, business pays $10,400, and academic institutions pay only $8,400. The differentials are larger for non-Ph.D. economists.[34] A 1964 report of the United States Department of Labor shows government biochemists earn $9,025, compared to $6,800 in academia.[35] A

[33] That junior college staffing problems are more similar to those in secondary schools than colleges is documented extensively in David G. Brown, *The Instructor Exchange: Staffing Junior Colleges* (A report of the Center for Research, Development, and Training in Occupational Education at North Carolina State University for the U.S. Department of Health, Education, and Welfare under the administration of the Division of Adult and Vocational Research, 1966).

[34] Edwin C. Gooding in Brown, *Placement Services for College Teachers*, p. 159.

[35] *Occupational Outlook Quarterly*, February 1964, p. 15.

more general study of salaries in science for the same year reports that scientists are paid $11,000 by the federal government, $12,000 by industry-business and nonprofit organizations, and only $9,600 by academic institutions.[36]

The existence of work-load differentials and salary differentials is strong evidence that the academic and nonacademic markets are divided. Further evidence is the type of offers received by persons entering academic positions. Newly hired professors were asked to list all of the offers they considered seriously. Analysis of these lists indicates that only eight percent are for nonteaching positions. Seven out of eight new college professors never consider *any* nonacademic offer. Only five percent consider high school teaching and 11 percent consider other types of nonacademic employment. Most college teachers obviously do not envision themselves as candidates for jobs outside college teaching.

Several students of academic labor markets have indicated that the division between the academic and the nonacademic is largely imposed by the community of scholars. To quote Caplow and McGee:

> Although non-academic positions . . . may pay much more than what their incumbents could ever earn in an academic post, the acceptance of such employment is always interpreted by a man's colleagues as moving down in or out of the profession . . . men who take this path . . . are rarely able to return to academic employment, and when they do, any minimally respectable academic position is regarded as an opportunity for them. For the men of the major league, the route out of the academic profession is generally a one-way street.[37]

In the same vein, Everett G. Hughes states:

> The general disposition of the faculties . . . is never to let anybody come back to the academic world if he has been out and has had a taste of some other kind of life. He is a traitor.[38]

Two Very Different Flows

The separation of markets is not, by any means, complete: in 1964–65, 8,600 newly hired professors came from outside academia (table 50). There are two distinct types of individuals who are drawn

[36] National Science Foundation, "Salaries and Professional Characteristics of U.S. Scientists, 1964." *Reviews of Data on Resources,* I, No. 2 (December 1964), 6.

[37] Caplow and McGee. *The Academic Marketplace,* p. 150.

[38] *Review of Economics and Statistics,* August 1960, p. 121.

50 |

New Faculty from Outside College Teaching

Last Year's Activity	Number Hired by Four-Year Institutions
Primary and secondary school teachers and administrators	2,800
Government (excluding military)	950
Business	1,800
Administration in higher education	300
Military service	250
Foundation employees	150
Others (including postdoctoral fellowships, housewives)	2,400
Total	8,650

Source: survey data and COLFACS data.

back into the academic community after having once left it for employment elsewhere.

First, there is the "sought-after" group, comprised mainly of publishing scholars who have broad experience in nonacademic work that is closely related to their specialty (a teacher of architecture with experience in an architectural firm, for example) or who have been loaned temporarily to the nonacademic community as a long-term consultant (e.g., a member of the Council of Economic Advisers).

The second group, the "supply of last resort," is comprised mainly of high school teachers who are drafted into college teaching as a desperate solution to the staffing problem of some little-known college. Between these two groups there is probably a third, the "qualified activists," comprised of those who are disenchanted with the nonacademic life and desire to return to the contemplative atmosphere of academia. They are no doubt qualified, but they must be active participants in the labor market if they are to find jobs.

As shown in table 51, most of the hiring of the supply of last resort is concentrated in institutions other than the top 20 percent. This is not surprising, in light of the poor qualifications of the average person drawn from this source of supply: only 20 percent have earned Ph.D.'s and only five percent have published ten or more articles. In sharp contrast, the ex-foundation employees who come back to academia with strong records of publication are sought after and hired by the top schools.

51 |

Characteristics of Those Hired and Hirers, by Sources of Supply

Last Year's Activity	Percentage with Ph.D.'s	Percentage of Big Publishers[a]	Percentage Hired by Top Quintile Institutions[b]
College faculty	63	20	15
Primary and secondary school teacher	20	5	3
Business	44	13	10
Government	58	21	13
Foundation	79	23	48
Other[c]	58	20	17

[a] Ten articles or one book.
[b] This means that three percent of the primary and secondary school teachers who moved to a four-year institution moved to a top 20 percent school.
[c] Includes college administrators, military personnel, housewives, unemployed, post-doctoral fellows, and others not easily identified.
Source: survey data.

DISCIPLINARY INFLOW

The heaviest traffic between worlds is in the sciences and the field of education. These are the disciplines which have the greatest contact with nonacademic circles when first emerging from graduate school and, consequently, if only by mere numerical strength they should dominate the return to academia. They are also the disciplines which often do not lose the professional status gained in graduate school. Engineers and scientists are constantly using their professional "tools," and can thus be easily reacademized. In contrast, theoreticians in the word disciplines often have little place outside academia. Their professional skills often lead to pragmatic enterprises. Whatever research orientation a linguist may have acquired in graduate school, it becomes rusty in most nonacademic pursuits. Whereas nonacademicians fill one-third of the vacancies in data disciplines and one-half in secondary education, they fill less than one-sixth the vacancies in word disciplines (except education).

Implications of Divided Markets

SUMMARY OF THE DIVISIONS

"The" academic labor market is in fact a set of overlapping submarkets divided by employer demands, candidate preferences, and community traditions. Vaguely separate markets exist for chemists and engineers, men and women, Catholics and Protestants, assistant professors and full professors, publishers and nonpublishers. Arbitrage does not completely eliminate the differentials among institutions for higher learning of various regions, sizes, types, and controls. For any single vacancy or candidate only a small portion of the total academic labor market is relevant.

IMPLICATIONS FOR EMPLOYERS

Whatever the reasons may be for limited participation, the resultant market divisions provide benefits and costs to the participants.

If he has sufficient flexibility, the alert administrator may take advantage of divided markets. For example, if sex is not a factor that influences productivity, he may substitute a female English teacher for a male one and, as a result, pay less. Or, if it doesn't matter to his institution, he may hire disproportionately large numbers of musicologists at relatively low salaries, salaries that have not been pushed upward by the shortage of physicists. Divided markets imply differential rates of pay. To the extent that an employer may shift his demands from the market of premium pay (e.g., physics) to the markets of surplus, he can save money.

Divided markets also save time and effort. There are fewer contacts to make, fewer applications to process (as a result of many professors' recognition that they are unqualified or in some other way ineligible for the positions), and fewer campus interviews to finance. This work reduction results in turn in decreased costs of hiring and increased knowledge of a particular market.

IMPLICATIONS FOR PROFESSORS

Separation of markets involves benefits and costs for professors as well. Divided markets favor specialists who are most scarce and the candidates who are least qualified at the expense of their opposites.

When markets are undivided, the best candidate will get the best job—for employers are free to examine the entire field and to choose from a wide range of supply. When markets are divided, however, the employer is not exposed to some segments of supply. He may not be exposed to the best candidates and, as a result, the candidacy of the second best may be enhanced and he may get the best job. The best candidate may get the second- or third-best job.[39]

[39] A qualified but inferior professor may thus gain a position more easily at a more prestigious institution because he is one of only a few known candidates. A denominational school may hire an inferior professor if he is of that religion and his only substitute is of another faith.

For the physicists (and others in short supply) balkanization means higher pay. If employers are unable to substitute low paid musicologists (or others in excess supply), they are forced to bid up the wage in order to attract one of the scarce physicists. Employers are unable to dissipate their excess demand, except by moving to higher price-quantity relationships. By the same token, the musicologists are worse off because they are unable to benefit from a "spill-over" of the demand for physicists.

IMPLICATIONS FOR SOCIETY

There are basically two types of market divisions, the implications of which differ. *Intra*market divisions occur when two professors who are *equally productive* do not receive the same consideration. For example, a man and woman may be equally qualified but an employer may choose the man. Another example: two candidates may be equally productive but the employer on the West Coast may never find the one candidate who is currently teaching at a small northeastern college. *Inter*market divisions occur when two professors have substantially different abilities: for example, physicists and musicologists. Here there are two markets, not one market divided. Only *intra*market divisions are conclusively costly to society. *Inter*market divisions give rise to costs but also to benefits.

*Intra*market divisions prevent professors from contributing as much as they could to the social product. In an ideal world, the college that is able to offer the top job to Professor X needs him most. It is at this school that Professor X can make the greatest contribution to the social product. To the extent that market divisions prevent Professor X from learning about that best offer or inhibit him from accepting it, the nation's teaching force is misallocated. Another professor, less appropriate for the job than X, will be paid too much; and X will be paid by another employer at a rate lower than he deserves. Both exploitation and unnecessary economic rent will be furthered. If the less qualified but better paid professor and X could switch positions, the social product could be increased.

It is not correct, however, to reason that the very existence of balkanizations, even those intramarkets, is proof that a societal optimum has not been achieved. For *if* exogenously imposed conditions give rise to costs of moving input (professors) among submarkets (e.g., transportation costs among various parts of the country), the cost of moving the input may be greater than the savings in costs resulting from the more desirable distribution. The increased productivity of the more desirably located professor may not be sufficient to offset the cost of getting him there. It is true that balkanizations are bad, but it may be more costly to society to eliminate these divisions than to allow them to stand.

Intermarket divisions give rise to the same types of costs as intramarket ones. But, unlike intramarket movement, the costs to society of moving inputs among markets often outweigh the advantages. To move a man from physics to musicology requires training the physicist to be a musiocologist, a not insignificant allocation of resources, or to allow the musicologist to teach physics inadequately. Moreover, specialization, the basic cause of this type of intermarket division, often gives rise to positive benefits. Through specialization, training time and cost may be reduced, for the expert need not be educated to equal levels of competency in all fields of knowledge. Specialization may allow the concentration of laboratory facilities required by the specialty at a few universities, in preference to partial facilities at many locations. Through disciplinary specialization it may well be possible to reduce the cost of the final educational products and thereby benefit society. Of course, the same benefits will result from other types of specialization which yield the same, or a greater, marginal product at a lower cost. The dividing of professors into teachers and researchers may well be such a specialization.[40]

Thus, from a societal viewpoint, market divisions are both good and bad. In general, the divisions which exist between the labor markets for dissimilar college teachers are beneficial, but the divisions within labor markets, with a few exceptions, are detrimental.

---

[40] There is a danger of too much specialization. A man trained only in physics may not be able to appreciate the social consequences of his work, and the teachers may become sterile without pursuing some research.

5

Corridors of the Academy

Wrote one frustrated job seeker of his experiences in the academic labor market, *In my opinion, there are only two ways to obtain a challenging, interesting teaching position at a university with intellectual atmosphere and cultural opportunities: (1) to know the "right" people; (2) to have published some outstanding books.* His statement borders dogma.

Professional ethic condemns active job seeking, ridicules the use of formal employment liaisons, and accepts only the most diplomatic approaches to the market. Hints in convention conversation, postscripts addended to letters flowing naturally among professional colleagues are the channels of communication, at least for the better schools within academia. Availability is carried circuitously and precariously along partially formalized grapevines.

Yet, as expansion in the number of colleges and professors overloads the informal network and excludes therefore fringe institutions and marginal candidates, the market is responding to the new needs by providing new and more formal mechanisms. Curious blends of tradition and reality, over 2,500 "placement centers" are now in existence. Among them are departmental offices in most of the nation's graduate schools, college placement offices, denominational placement services, public employment agencies, fee-charging private employment agencies, placement operations funded by various types of professional associations, and various specialized agencies. Proof of the usefulness of these liaisons is that over 25 percent of the jobs taken in 1964–65 were found through them.

But even wide use of formal mechanisms does not extinguish the tradition that, for good reason, lives on. Many seek help from a "formalized liaison" with a sense of guilt and a feeling of personal inadequacy. Individuals who can afford it still choose not to use the formal liaisons, and there is a certain amount of snobbery associated with this avoidance. Overt job seeking by formally registering one's availability with an impersonal liaison is still not highly respected.

It is the purpose of this chapter to indicate how market mechanisms are functioning and why, to explain why professors seek jobs by different methods, and to indicate how and why the respected informal placement system and the not-so-respected formal system remain in existence side-by-side.

A Theory of Job Search

Every individual must decide whether to seek a job, and if so, by what methods and how extensively. Since the search process centers around the individual, in developing a theory of job search it is helpful to think in terms of the costs and benefits of the search from his point of view. This theory states that an individual will extend his search as long as his expected gain is positive (expected benefits exceed expected costs), and is summarized in the equation:

Expected gain from search equals probabilistic value of jobs landed as result of search minus cost of search minus value of best job landed prior to search

The probabilistic value of the jobs landed as a result of the search is the sum of the probability that job A will be the best one landed times the value of job A, the probability that job B will be the best landed times its value, and so forth. For example, if a man is certain to land a $7,000 job and 50 percent likely to land a $10,000 job and there are no other options, then the probabilistic value is the sum of one-half of $10,000 and one-half of $7,000 or $8,500.

For each method of job search, and each combination of methods, an individual has a unique expected gain. If any expected gain is positive, he will search. He will use that method for which the expected gain is largest.[1]

[1] A theory of job search is detailed in David G. Brown, *Academic Labor Markets*, A report to the Office of Manpower, Automation and Training, U.S. Department of Labor, 1965, pp. 185–217.

The Extent of Job Search

Using the above equation, it is possible to speculate about what groups of professors will have higher expected gains and, therefore, will search hardest. First are those with very poor original "jobs": students (who have no present job), disinherited professors (who may not return to their previous jobs), and disgruntled professors (who have a very strong desire not to return). In each instance the "value of the best job landed prior to the search" is very low; expected gains are high. Accordingly, these groups search longer and use more methods of search (table 52): for example, compared to the professors leaving desirable jobs, the disgruntled lost three more days of productive time in search and used 25 percent more methods.

52 |
Extent of Search, by Desirability of Original "Job"

Status	Days Lost[a]*	Number of Methods Used*
Undesirable Options		
Disinherited	14.1	4.4
Students	9.7	3.7
Disgruntled	8.5	3.7
Desirable Option		
Satisfied	5.4	2.8

[a] Days of productive time lost looking for a job.

* Means that differences between the desirable option and each of the undesirable options are significantly different by a chi-square test at the .05 level.

Source: survey data.

A second group with high expected gains from job search are the unseen and unsought. They are lost in very large markets where candidates are so numerous that employers only scratch the surface in their search: for example, professors in the larger subject matter specialties such as history and English, and professors seeking appointments at junior ranks. They are also the professors set off in inconspicuous locations such as the smaller and less prestigious schools. Because jobs do not *come to them,* their before-search options are poor, expected gains are high, and searches are extensive (table 53).[2]

[2] Data on "number of methods used" are consistent with "days of productive time lost," except where noted in the text.

53

Extent of Search, by Visibility of Indivdiual

CATEGORY	DAYS OF PRODUCTIVE TIME LOST	
	Least Visible	Most Visible
12 large disciplines vs. 12 small[a]*	9	6
Instructor-assistant professor vs. associate-full professor*	10	7
Faculty leaving bottom 20% institutions vs. top 20%	8	7
Faculty leaving small institutions vs. large[b]	8	7
8 surplus disciplines vs. 8 shortage disciplines	7	8
Students leaving bottom 40% institutions vs. top 20%*	3	9

[a] Size of disciplines are according to COLFACS data.
[b] Under 1,000 students and over 5,000.
* Means that difference is significant by a chi-square test at the .05 level.
Source: survey data.

Paradoxically, over-visible students at the very best graduate schools and over-sought professors in the disciplines of greatest shortage also spend inordinate amounts of time in job search. Sought out by eager employers, these candidates spend little time looking *for* jobs, but a great deal of time looking *at* them. They seek jobs by fewer methods, but spend more time in the entire process. Their higher probability of landing jobs of high value more than offsets the fact that their before-search options are relatively good.

Candidates who anticipate that job search will involve little time or trouble are a third group with high expected gains. Their opposite numbers are discouraged from extensive search because the high costs of search reduce expected gains: for example, new professors reentering academia from the military and other nonacademic endeavors often find it very difficult to get the time off necessary for a comprehensive market search. As a result, their search is less ambitious: they spend only one-half as much time.

Finally, a fourth group with high expected gains from job search consists of those candidates seeking a certain type job, the job where an employer will accept a man who becomes known to him through one of the less respectable intermediaries.

Because overt availability is acceptable in some circles and not in others, the "social" risks of job search differ for various individuals:

for example, where tenured professors are viewed suspiciously and looked down upon when they venture to make their availability known publicly, such behavior of emerging graduate students is accepted. Accordingly, students search more diligently.

There are certain jobs such as those at the tenured ranks in the more prestigious institutions that will not be sought. The man who gets caught chasing such jobs is almost automatically eliminated from consideration. Because the number of persons eligible to fill these jobs is so small, these schools reason that they should be able to identify the candidates for themselves. If a candidate does not naturally come before the selection committee, they argue, he should not be selected. This extreme statement of a prevalent view (a view to be discussed in more detail elsewhere) provides still another explanation of why experienced professors at the more senior ranks in the more prestigious institutions are the least energetic in job search.

The Pattern of Search

Professors, hoping to remain inconspicuous, approach the academic market place sequentially. At first the prospective job changer privately and silently hopes to be tendered an excellent offer out of the blue. This failing, the strategy evolves from casually intimating unhappiness to close friends to informing systematically all acquaintances by all means. As a last resort, help is sought from formal intermediaries.[3] *Formal methods are used only after informal contacts have failed to yield a good job.* Illustrating this pattern is the fact that contracts signed before April 1 account for 38 percent of the jobs located without a search of any kind, 36 percent of the jobs found informally, and only 29 percent of the jobs found through impersonal (formal) intermediaries.

[3] "Formal" and "informal" intermediaries are dichotomized upon the primary relationship between the individual and the liaison. "Informal" refers to all those liaisons with which the individual has relationships which are not primarily for the purpose of finding a job: e.g., a student finding a job through his graduate school office or graduate school professor. When a candidate uses an informal method his primary relationship with the school is to get an education, not a job. "Formal" refers to all liaisons to which the individual relates for the *explicit* purpose of finding a job; the individual has no other relationship with the liaison except as a candidate who is looking for a job and expects the relationship to terminate once a job is found. Advertising in a professional journal and consulting an employment service are formal methods.

Deeply imbedded are professional attitudes against overt job-seeking. The reasoning runs: (1) if Jones is tops or good, Jones will be remembered and asked to do bigger and better things; (2) but if Jones is known to be looking around, he has not been asked, and something must be wrong with him, either professionally or personally; (3) therefore, Jones should not be asked to do bigger and better things, if alternative candidates can be sought out and coaxed to leave perfectly satisfactory jobs. Hence an elaborate but unreliable network of private grapevines has been developed to carry discrete intimations of availability to collegiate recruiters, whose stated purpose is to identify and hire only those who appear satisfied with their current situations.

With good reason, a majority of the most sought-after professors (Ph.D. holders with extensive publications and experience at a top quintile institution) look down upon the formal avenues as "unprofessional," "beneath the dignity of a college professor," and "worthless." Eighty percent of the jobs at top schools are found in the earliest and informal stage of job search (table 54).[4]

54

Method of Finding Current Job, by Desirability of Job

MEASURE OF CURRENT JOB QUALITY	PERCENTAGE FINDING JOB INFORMALLY[a]	
	Good Jobs	Poor Jobs
Top 20% faculty vs. bottom 20%*	80	56
Full professors vs. assistant professors*	77	64
$9,500 and over vs. $8,000 and under[b]*	79	56
Load under 8 hrs. vs. over 16 hrs.*	78	56

[a] The percentage cited subtracted from 100 percent gives the percentage of jobs found formally.
[b] Salary data are for emerging students only.
* Differences in the percentages are significant by a chi-square test at the .05 level.
Source: survey data.

[4] Stecklein and Lathrop note that 33 percent of the jobs at the low prestige Duluth campus of the University of Minnesota are found formally compared to only five percent at the Minneapolis campus. John E. Stecklein and Robert L. Lathrop, *Faculty Attraction and Retention: Factors Affecting Faculty Mobility at the University of Minnesota* (Minneapolis: Bureau of Institutional Research, University of Minnesota, 1960), p. 15. Similarly, Caplow and McGee, who studied only high prestige institutions, stress the importance of informal methods and the unimportance of the formal. Caplow and McGee, *The Academic Marketplace*, pp. 109–10.

THE INFORMAL AVENUES

For most professors, job-seeking is a by-product of more important activities. *Instead of establishing new relationships with specialists in professorial placement, the tendency is to rely upon previous contacts. The result: 65 percent find their jobs through a previous contacts.* Personal friends and professional acquaintances account for 18 percent of the 65 percent (table 55). But the fountainheads of the

55

Role of Market Liaisons

Type of Liaison	Method of Search of All Candidates	Mean Number of Jobs Found Per Candidate	Method of Finding Current Job of All Candidates
	%		%
Informal			
Graduate professor	40	1.41	12
Graduate department office	32	1.72	6
Undergraduate professor	16	0.82	3
Graduate school classmate	17	0.61	3
Faculty colleague	20	1.07	7
Other professional friend	25	1.01	8
Publisher's representative	2	0.86	(a)
Did nothing and was recruited	23	1.82	26
Total	(b)	(b)	**65**
Formal			
Blind letters	46	2.14	19
College placement office	36	2.75	6
Church-related placement service	5	1.30	1
Professional association[c]	14	1.96	2
Ad: "Candidate Available"	3	2.56	(a)
Ad: "Position Available"	9	1.73	2
Convention placement service	14	2.42	2
Public employment service[c]	3	1.65	(a)
Commercial teacher's agency	7	3.05	3
Total	(b)	(b)	35

[a] Less than 0.5 percent.
[b] Totals are not meaningful, for one person could pursue jobs by several methods.
[c] Excluding convention placement service and advertisements in professional journals.
Source: survey data.

network are the thesis advisors at the major graduate schools. Widely known in their fields, inquiries about persons who might fill vacancies in their areas naturally gravitate toward them. Through personal contact, graduate school mentors learn where the vacancies are and refer their protégés to them.

In some large departments placement effort extends beyond the candidate's mentor to the department office which coordinates the entire faculty in scouting vacancies and advertising available candidates. The history department at the University of Wisconsin, for example, asks its staff to carry to conventions vitae on its graduate students who are available for hire and to distribute the vitae among likely employers. When a staff member learns of a job vacancy he is expected to inform a departmental placement coordinator who is responsible for consolidating all such information into a weekly statement of available positions. Although this particular effort is far more extensive than average, many graduate school departments do assume some organizational responsibility for job finding, particularly in the excess supply fields where good jobs are hardest to find. As Logan Wilson pointed out in his book *The Academic Man,* it is in the self-interest of the neophyte's mentor and of the department to place graduates well, for their own reputation stands or falls on the men they educate.[5]

Forty percent of all new faculty members consult their graduate mentors and 32 percent register with a department office. Together graduate institution sources yield, on the average, over three concrete job opportunities. Eighteen percent of the newly hired faculty accept one of them (refer to table 55). Nearly one-fourth of the best jobs (at top 10 percent schools) are found through the graduate school.

Former teachers. The candidates who use their graduate schools most are those who want to teach in institutions known well by graduate school professors: for example, Ph.D. holders, being more likely to locate in a research-emphasizing job at a large university, consult their graduate school more frequently than non-Ph.D.'s (46 percent versus 37 percent). The converse is also true. Professors wanting appointments at institutions outside the university community, such as four-year colleges or junior colleges, shun the graduate school and turn to former undergraduate professors and other sources for help. Both because they do not maintain contacts at the types of schools that would hire them and because they do not have as much self-interest in the placement, graduate schools are less helpful to the marginally qualified.

[5] Wilson, *The Academic Man: A Study in the Sociology of a Profession* (New York: Oxford University Press, 1942), p. 49.

In any case, as time passes, contacts are lost through death and geographic separation, and candidates are decreasingly likely to rely upon their former teachers for job leads. As shown in table 56, after the first five years out of school the use of former teachers diminishes rapidly.

56 | Use of Former Teachers

MEASURE OF SEPARATION	PERCENTAGE CONSULTING
*Age**	
35 and under	69
Over 35	31
*Years since Last Degree**	
None	72
Less than 5 years	66
5–20 years	38
Over 20 years	5

* Differences are significant by a chi-square test at the .05 level.
Source: survey data.

Other studies. The 1964–65 market is not unique. Studies in the 1950's and 1960's all indicate the importance of informal methods: Marshall and Anantaraman on economists, Brown on southeastern social scientists, Stecklein-Lathrop on University of Minnesota faculty, and Poorman, Gleazer, and Brown on junior colleges. Craig, Haggerty-Works, and Hill found the same pattern operating prior to the 1950's (table 57).[6]

[6] For studies of nonprofessors, see, Dorothea De Schweinitz, *How Workers Find Jobs: A Study of Four Thousand Hosiery Workers in Philadelphia* (Philadelphia: University of Pennsylvania Press, 1932), p. 89; Seymour Martin Lipset, *et al.,* "Job Plans and Entry into the Labor Market," *Social Forces,* XXXIII, No. 3 (March 1955), 224–32; Theodore F. Malm, "Recruiting Patterns and the Functioning of Labor Markets," *Industrial and Labor Relations Review,* VII (July 1954), 507–25; William H. Miernyk, *Inter-Industry Labor Mobility: The Case of the Displaced Textile Worker* (Boston: Bureau of Business and Economic Research, Northeastern University, 1955), p. 22; Charles A. Myers, "Labor Mobility in Two Communities," in Bakke, ed., *Labor Mobility and Economic Opportunity,* pp. 68–79; Myers and W. Rupert Maclaurin, *The Movement of Factory Workers* (New York: John Wiley & Sons, 1943), p. 47; Lloyd G. Reynolds and Joseph Shister, *Job Horizons* (New York: Harper & Bros., 1949).

Summary of Thirteen Studies of Methods of Finding Jobs in the Academic Labor Market

Method	A Brown: All College Teachers (1964–65)	B Brown: Southeastern Social Scientists (1962–63)	C Marshall: Economists (1960–64)	D Klugh: Psychologists (1958–63)[a]	E Stecklein-Lathrop: U. of Minn. Faculty (1956–57)	F Anantaraman: "Well-established Economists" (1960)	G Bosley: All College Teachers (1946)	H Haggerty and Works: North Central Assn. Colleges (1936–37)[b]	I Craig: 89 Institutions (1927–28)[c]	J Hill: 7 New England Colleges (1926–27)[d]	K Poorman: California Junior Colleges (1962–63)[e]	L Gleazer: Junior Colleges (1961)[e]	M Brown: Junior Colleges (1964–65)
						(percent)							
Informal													
Former professor	15	11	3[f]	(g)	—	—	23[h]	—	—	28	12	—	6
Graduate department office	6	23	20	—	—	29[i]	2[j]	62	49[k]	8	—	—	2
Professional acquaintance	18	46[l]	26[m]	37[g]	25[n]	29[m]	—	21	22	31	25	—	21
Publisher's representative	*	—	1	—	—	—	—	—	—	—	—	—	1
Did nothing and was recruited	26	—	8	—	33	15[o]	—	—	—	11	—	—	18
Total	65	80	58	37	58	73	25	83	71	78	37	40[p]	48
Formal													
College placement office	6	4	3	13	—	—	28	—	11	4	21	29	16
Convention placement service	2	(l)	26[q]	16	—	—	—	—	—	6	0	0	*
U.S. Employment Service	*	—	4	—	—	—	—	—	—	—	—	—	1
Advertised in a journal	*	—	—	3[r]	—	—	—	—	3[t]	1	—	—	*
Answered a journal ad	2	2	1[s]	12[r]	—	—	—	—	—	2	—	—	2
Church-related bureau	1	—	—	—	—	—	—	2	—	—	—	—	*
Commercial teacher's agency	3	1	*	3	22[v]	13[w]	18	13[u]	5	11	—	10	4
Blind letters	19	7	9	15	10	—	23[x]	1[z]	10[x]	—	38	12	27
Professional association	2	—	—	—	—	—	6[y]	—	—	—	4	9	2
Total	35	20[aa]	42	62	42[bb]	37[cc]	75	16	29	23	63	60	52

[a] The Klugh article reported only the methods used to search for jobs. For purposes of this summary, it is assumed that the methods by which the job was actually found are distributed in the same proportion that the various methods were used.

[b] The data were given as "Percentages of institutions indicating various sources of prospective staff members as most useful." Also see footnote (e).

[c] Sample included only AAUP members. Also see footnote (e).

[d] Sample included responses from faculty of Amherst, Brown, Dartmouth, Harvard, Wesleyan, Williams, and Yale. Also see footnote (e).

[e] Employees were surveyed rather than candidates.

[f] Category was "Other professors."

[g] Category was "Friends or major professor."

[h] Category was "Recommendations of graduate faculty at higher institutions."

[i] Category was "Deans and chairmen of departments."

[j] Category was "Recommendations of our own faculty member."

[k] This includes the categories listed in footnotes (h) and (j).

[l] Convention placement service is included in "Professional acquaintance" category.

[m] Category was "Friends."

[n] This classification was "Known or met Minnesota faculty who indicated opening."

[o] Category was "Outside offers."

[p] Since his survey referred only to "formal methods," it is assumed that the 40 percent not accounted for were informal.

[q] This includes two categories listed as "Informal contacts at annual meetings" and "Regional meetings." Advertisements in the *APA Journal* only.

[r] Advertisements in the *APA Journal* only.

[s] Advertisements were only in the *American Economic Review*.

[t] Category was "Lists from graduate schools."

[u] This includes "Teachers' agency" and "Similar institutions."

[v] Category was "Appointee initiated contact."

[w] Category was "Direct contacts."

[x] Category was "Direct applications."

[y] Category was "Scientific societies."

[z] Category was "Office of AAUP."

[aa] "Other" methods account for six percent.

[bb] "Other" methods account for 10 percent.

[cc] Due to the nature of the report, the 14 percent unaccounted for is assumed to be formal methods

* Less than 0.5 percent.

Sources:

A. Survey data.

B. Brown, *The Market for College Teachers*, pp. 91, 102.

C. Marshall, *The Mobility of College Faculties*, p. 85.

D. H. E. Klugh, "Approaches to the Academic Market," *American Psychologist*, XIX, No. 8 (August 1964), 672.

E. Stecklein and Lathrop, *Faculty Attraction and Retention*, pp. 13, 14.

F. Anantaraman, *Mobility of Professional Economists in the United States*, p. 15.

G. Howard E. Bosley, *The Administration of Faculty Personnel in State Teachers Colleges* (New York: The American Association of Teachers Colleges, 1946), p. 3.

H. William J. Haggerty and George A. Works, "Faculties of Colleges and Universities Accredited by the North Central Association of Colleges and Secondary Schools during 1936–37," *North Central Association Quarterly*, XIII (January 1939), 309–407.

I. Hardin Craig, "Methods of Appointment and Promotion in American Colleges and Universities," *AAUP Bulletin*, XV, 178–9.

J. A. C. C. Hill, Jr., "The Appointment of College Teachers," *Bulletin of the Association of American Colleges*, XIV (February 1928), 523–4.

K. Robert Lewis Poorman, "An Investigation of Selected Staffing Practices Used in Employing Junior College Instructors," (unpublished dissertation, University of California at Los Angeles, 1964), pp. 83–4.

L. Edmund J. Gleazer, Jr., American Association of Junior Colleges (mimeographed).

M. Brown, *The Instructor Exchange*, p. 50.

Hardin Craig in a 1927–28 study involving the sources of faculty supply at 89 colleges and universities concluded:

> It may be said then that the first four headings, which rest to a certain extent on acquaintanceship, at firsthand or secondhand, accounted for 556, or 73 percent of the total number of reported cases. This is so general a policy as to make remarks almost unnecessary. The usual way of filling vacancies in college and university faculties is to recommend a competent person if you know one; or, if you do not, to write to somebody in another institution in whose judgment you have confidence to see if he or she knows anybody who will do.[7]

Similarly, for the period 1885–1937 at Indiana University, A. B. Hollingshead found that 43 percent of all appointees had been alumni, and 20 percent had been members of families connected with the staff. Although he could not statistically measure the influence of friendship, he concluded that:

> we are convinced that these three factors (alumni, friendship, family) account for at least four-fifths of all appointments, and that only a small minority may be attributed to professional competition; i.e., the selection has been largely social rather than competitive.[8]

In a 1942 study Logan Wilson reported that:

> although the candidate with a high record and unqualified recommendations from competent judges stands a better chance than the less meritorious, between eligible individuals of apparently equal ability and training, preferment is always shown for "connections."[9]

THE FORMAL AVENUES[10]

Letters. One of the most surprising results of the study is the frequent and successful use of the direct letter of application, the letter sent cold to a prospective employer. Of all methods, it is used most frequently. Nearly one-half of all newly hired professors have written "blind letters" and, on the average, they have found over two jobs through them. The real success and importance of the letter technique is shown by the fact that 19 percent of all teachers find the job they actually accept by this method.

[7] Craig, *AAUP Bulletin,* XV, 179.

[8] A. B. Hollingshead, "Ingroup Membership and Academic Selection," *American Sociological Review,* III (1938), 831.

[9] Wilson, *The Academic Man,* p. 51.

[10] Formal intermediaries are described and analyzed in detail in Brown, *Placement Services for College Teachers,* pp. 1–240.

Letter writing is a low cost and an efficient means of making one's availability known. It is an indication of willingness to consider seriously a job offer from the institution contacted and, therefore, encourages that institution to make such an offer. In a seller's market, where suppliers may be discriminating about the offers they accept, employers often welcome an early statement of interest. Instead of dissipating hiring effort upon candidates who ultimately reject the offers tendered, employers will often prefer to follow the leads of direct inquiries.

Letters are used throughout the entire spectrum of candidate quality, institutional quality, and academic rank, but the biggest letter writers are, as the theory of job search predicts, those who have the greatest prospect of finding a vacancy and, more generally, those who stand to benefit more from an extensive job search: for example, students write more letters (average = 10.2) than last year's faculty (average = 7.5). Aspirants to junior faculty appointments write more often than persons seeking associate and full professorships. Younger seekers are more prolific than older. Nondoctorate holders send off more leters than those with the Ph.D.

For the very reason that a letter of inquiry is a commitment to consider seriously a job offer, many candidates, especially those who are not actively in the market, do not write such letters. As shown in table 58, which will be referred to frequently, the main reason for not writing blind letters is a reluctance to become too committed to moving. Many persons do not want to be *that* active in job-seeking. Although a small minority (four percent), mostly students emerging from prestigious graduate schools, avoid letter writing because they regard such behavior as "unprofessional" and another slightly larger group (nine percent) view this technique as "worthless," for most the method is respectable and worthwhile.

College placement offices. College placement offices are the most important of the *organized* liaisons in the market. To supplement and support the informal efforts of major professors and department offices, universitywide placement offices provide special services to prospective college teachers. The sophistication of these services varies greatly, from an afterthought of an active industrial placement program or of high school teacher placement efforts, to a full complement of services. In one year at the University of Michigan, which as one of the larger placement offices is more typical of the Mid-

Attitudes toward Formal Placement Liaisons

Types of Liaison	No Reason; Used Method (Percentage)	Reason for Not Using Method (Percentages)[a]						
		(A) Unprofessional	(B) Worthless	(C) Inaccessible	(D) Ignorant	(E) Fear	(F) No Need	(G) Not Looking
Blind letters	46	4	9	3	1	(b)	15	23 (c)
College placement office	36	2	14	2	2	1	18	23
Church-related service	5	4	17	8	20	(b)	19	23
Professional association[d]	14	1	13	5	8	(b)	34	23
Ad: "Candidate available"[d]	3	15	20	3	8	1	27	23
Ad: "Position available"	9	5	19	4	7	(b)	31	23
Convention service	14	2	12	9	11	1	27	23
Public employment service[d]	3	4	21	3	25	(b)	21	23
Private employment agency	7	11	22	2	8	(b)	25	23

[a] Except for the first column, the percentages cited are derived from the answer to the question, "Indicate which of the reasons listed below best explains why you did not use the method." The options given were:
 (A) It is *unprofessional* to use this method. It is beneath the dignity of a college professor.
 (B) Good jobs are rarely found by this method. It takes *more time than it is worth.*
 (C) Good jobs are found by this method but I *did not have the right contacts.*
 (D) I *did not know* that jobs could be found by this method.
 (E) Good jobs are found by this method but I was *afraid my then current employer would find out* that I was looking for another job.
 (F) Good jobs are sometimes found by this method, but there are better ways. I *would have pursued this method if* I had not found a job by other means.
 (G) I was *not looking* for a job in any way.

[b] Less than 0.5 percent.

[c] Rows do not always total 100 due to rounding and because some respondents did not answer the question.

[d] Excluding convention placement service and advertisements in professional journals.

Source: survey data.

west and West than the East and South,[11] over 1,000 candidates were "exposed to" over 12,000 vacancies in college teaching.

That eight percent of all students actually found their jobs through their placement office testifies strongly to their usefulness, but even this statistic understates the overall usefulness of these offices to the market.[12] Besides actually locating jobs, the relatively newly formed placement offices relieve departments and individual professors from the time-consuming tasks of developing credentials on candidates and advising candidates about market conditions and opportunities. In many cases, the credential referral service provided is used and the locator service is not. Asking a person how he first learned about a job is inevitably understating the importance of college placement bureaus. The very valuable services of referring recommendations and credentials to jobs located by other means and of counseling never appear in the statistics.[13]

The primary users of the placement offices are on-campus students, 46 percent of whom seek help from this source. In contrast, only 31 percent of the experienced faculty and 24 percent of the new teachers entering from outside academia consult them. Although

[11] Fifty-three percent of the graduate students in the Great Plains and the West use college placement offices, compared to 39 percent in the Northeast and 46 percent in the Southeast. The distribution of placement offices for these same regions is 63.6 percent in the Great Plains and West, 22.5 percent in the Northeast, and 13.8 percent in the Southeast.

[12] To test the accuracy of our response, 300 questionnaire respondents, all of whom answered that they had *not* consulted their college placement office when seeking new employment, were singled out for intensive study. Their names were sent to the placement offices at their graduate schools in order to learn if they responded correctly to our question. The placement officers were asked to indicate whether the named persons had registered with them during the last recruiting season, and, if so, how they aided the named in finding a job. Almost all placement officers responded. In slightly less than ten percent of the cases, the individuals who failed to check that they had consulted their college placement office had in fact registered. There are indications that most of these individuals had used the office for the credential referral service, but not the locator service. The individuals had interpreted our question to mean help in *finding* jobs, not help in *getting* them. Although there may be some slight understatement of the true significance of college placement offices in our statistics, the understatement is not large.

[13] Placement officers argue, and correctly so, that a permanent record of one's graduate school performance, including letters of recommendations and candid evaluations of potential, can be an asset valuable in finding future jobs as well as the first one, especially since the memories, indeed the lives, of graduate mentors are finite.

some institutions have succeeded in making placement services more accessible and understandable to alumni (for example, the University of Illinois where two-thirds of the registrations are of alumni), successful efforts are rare.

As a rule, the attitude of departmental faculty that placement offices should be avoided because graduate student placement is the time-honored right and responsibility of mentors and that placement specialists are incompetent to advise candidates in substantive disciplines such as history and physics breaks down first in the markets where jobs are least plentiful and for candidates who are least qualified. Tradition is violated first where the needs for placement assistance are the greatest. Accordingly, 43 percent of the candidates in surplus disciplines consult placement offices, compared to 31 percent in shortage disciplines. Whereas 40 percent of the non-Ph.D.'s use placement offices, only 31 percent of the Ph.D.'s do.[14]

Though college placement offices occasionally service high paying, senior positions with low teaching loads at top institutions, the main traffic is in beginning jobs at less visible institutions (table 59). Most of the jobs pay less than $7,000, carry junior rank, require 12 hours or more of teaching, and involve an institution in the bottom 40 percent of the academic hierarchy. Only three percent of placements assisted by college placement offices are in top quintile schools.

Church-related placement offices. To assist and coordinate recruitment, many religious denominations maintain dossier files. The more ambitious efforts involve visits to the major graduate schools for the purpose of soliciting dossier registrations. Typically, a professor expresses interest in teaching at one or several of the related colleges by filing a dossier with a "central office." Upon receiving the dossier, the central office circulates it to the individual colleges (e.g., Methodist colleges) which, if interested, contact the candidate directly. Because they represent candidates with acknowledged sympathy toward their type of institution, the dossiers can be a valuable resource to recruiting administrators in individual colleges.[15]

[14] Occasionally excellent candidates register. Of the students leaving top (decile) graduate schools, 46 percent use placement offices. Overall, 40 percent of the active registrants at college placement offices have their Ph.D.

[15] "Placement Offices," similar in their intent of providing recruiting assistance for one particular group of collegiate employers, are maintained by regional associations such as the Near East College Association which assists institutions in Turkey and Lebanon, and by consolidated systems such as the State University of New York.

Characteristics of Job Found, by the Formal Method Used[a]

				PERCENTAGE USING			
JOB QUALITY	Blind Letters	College Placement Office	Church Placement Services	Professional Association	Ad: Position Available	Convention Service	Private Employment Service
Salary[b]							
$9,500 and above	2	4	0	0	0	9	0
$8,000–$9,000	12	12	18	5	27	13	17
$7,000–$7,999	31	28	18	50	55	26	28
$6,000–$6,999	34	40	18	40	14	43	39
$5,000–$5,999	21	16	45	5	5	9	17
Teaching Load							
7 hrs. or less	13	8	2	17	15	16	6
8–10 hrs.	21	20	25	26	26	29	6
11–16 hrs.	61	65	56	51	55	53	79
17 or more hrs.	4	7	12	6	4	2	9
Rank							
Instructor	47	42	53	38	27	40	41
Assistant professor	43	45	33	40	59	54	26
Associate professor	7	8	13	11	7	6	26
Full professor	3	5	0	11	7	0	7
School Prestige							
Top 20 percent	10	3	0	7	2	13	5
20 to 40 percent	19	15	0	13	16	23	11
40 to 60 percent	16	15	7	21	27	18	9
60 to 80 percent	24	24	50	28	22	29	26
Bottom 20 percent	32	40	43	31	33	18	49

[a] Public employment service and advertised candidates available are not included in this table because the numbers of persons who find jobs by this method, who are also included in our sample, are too small to allow statistically significant inferences.

[b] The salary data are for emerging students only.

Sources: survey data and Prestige Index.

Approximately five percent of all job seekers register their availability with these offices, and one out of five of the registrants actually finds his best alternative by this means. For the persons who have a strong preference for the liberal arts setting, especially one related to a particular church, the church-related placement service is a valuable and efficient means of getting his name before large numbers of prospective employers with a minimum of effort. For the candidate interested in a university appointment at a high prestige school, registering with a denominational placement office is poor strategy as indicated in table 59 by the fact that 93 percent of their traffic is with the 40 percent of vacancies that are least prestigious.

One of the largest problems for church-related placement is visibility. Ignorance of the services provided by denominational bureaus is the reason given for not using these agencies by 19 percent of Protestants, 23 percent of Catholics, and 25 percent of Jews.

Professional associations. The large number of professional associations that provide some type of placement service is indicated by a report of the U.S. Office of Education which listed 112 associations providing placement services in 1961.[16] From the American Nurses Association, which maintains the biographies of over 120,000 nurses and has placement staff at approximately 30 locations throughout the country, to the vest pocket operations of many executive secretaries of professional associations, the extent and nature of the services are quite varied.

Professional association placement services (excluding conventions and journal want ads) are a significant factor in the market for experienced professors (the percentage of jobs filled at full professor is higher for this type of service than for any other type), even though they account for only two percent of all new hires. Because the respectability of professional association sponsorship tempers some of the traditional attitudes that formal intermediaries are "unprofessional," even some of the veteran professors who are thoroughly indoctrinated in the do's and don'ts of academic job-seeking are willing to seek assistance from this source.

Journal advertisements. Although the European tradition of advertising all academic vacancies has not been adopted in the United

[16] U.S. Office of Education, *Placement Services for Personnel in Higher Education,* by Lanora G. Lewis, *et al.,* ("OE–53013"; Washington: Government Printing Office, 1961), pp. 3–15.

States, many disciplinary journals (e.g., *American Sociological Review*) and general journals (e.g., *Bulletin of the American Association of University Professors*) publish partial listings not only of jobs vacant but also of candidates available. Overall, "job available" ads account for nearly two percent of all new hires and "candidate available" ads for 0.5 percent (table 55).

Among members of the profession, the attitude toward "placing" versus "answering" an advertisement differs substantially. Placing an ad about one's self is considered "unprofessional" by 15 percent of college teachers, whereas only five percent consider answering ads about jobs "unprofessional" (table 58). The most common view toward answering an advertised "job available" is that "if I can't find a good job by another method I will certainly try answering these ads." In most instances, however, jobs are found by other methods.

The more established institutions, dreading a flood of under-qualified applicants, tend to leave journal advertising to the less visible institutions. As a result, less than one percent of the hiring at top quintile schools is through advertisements and, among all the professors finding jobs through ads, only two percent locate at these schools (table 59).

The schools that do list vacancies find good candidates. Not only do Ph.D.'s account for 63 percent of the users of ads, but they also represent 64 percent of those finding jobs by answering an ad. Nineteen percent of the students who find jobs by answering ads are trained in the top 10 percent schools. And, 66 percent who find jobs by answering an ad have published.

Convention placement services. The corridors and hotel lobbies at the annual meetings of professional associations are filled with talk about job opportunities, dissatisfaction with present jobs, and available candidates. To facilitate "job talk" in many disciplines more systematic contact networks have been established. Procedural details vary, but the common format is to provide a list of prospective employers and descriptions of the job opportunities they represent, a list of available candidates and their qualifications, and a contact medium. These networks are now used by 14 percent of all job changers. Two percent find their best offer through a convention service (table 55).

The importance of the convention placement service as a force in the market has been steadily increasing in recent years. One of the primary reasons for this is the new role that the United States Employment Service (U.S.E.S.) is taking in the design and financing of such services. In eleven disciplines, the U.S.E.S., upon the invitation of the officials in the discipline, provides a complete placement service. Probably the most extensive and most successful is that provided to the Allied Social Sciences Associations. In 1963 this service helped 100 out of 1,000 registered applicants find their September 1964 jobs.[17] Those who do not use the services often are those who do not attend the convention, or those seeking positions in the very high quality institutions at high ranks.

Professional associations seem most willing to undergo the expense and effort required to provide an effective convention placement service if requested by either employers or association members. The greatest pressures to establish extensive convention placement services are in the disciplines where there are many employment opportunities outside the academic community (chemistry, physics, psychology). Both the candidates, who experience difficulty in identifying likely employers, and the business-government employers, who have very little access to the traditional sources of supply of highly trained personnel, feel that their special needs require such a service.[18]

Once "slave markets" are established, the biggest users (over 50 percent) are students, especially the convention-attending students from the better graduate schools.

Out of all formal methods, the convention placement service is *least* often considered "unprofessional" or "worthless" and is the *most* often not used because of a "lack of contacts" (didn't attend the convention). There is good reason for the least number of teachers considering it a "worthless" method of search. Of all formal methods it turns up the greatest percentage of jobs in the top salary range, the greatest percentage in the top prestige schools, and the second greatest percentage with the lowest teaching load (table 59).

[17] Edwin C. Gooding, "The 7-Year Lag . . . the Market for Economists," *New England Business Review,* December 1964, pp. 11–2.

[18] Even though the candidates in disciplines where opportunities for employment are greatest (as classified by the ranking in table 1 explaining the Shortage Index) represent less than one-half of all new teachers, they account for 71 percent of those persons who find their jobs through the aid of a convention placement service. The difference between the two groups is statistically significant by a chi-square test at the .05 level.

Public employment services. In addition to the convention placement services, the state-related offices of the U.S.E.S. provide year-round placement help to professional workers, among them are college teachers. A nationwide network of over 100 professional placement offices gives aid in counseling and in locating candidates and job vacancies to those who wish to register their needs.

To date, with the notable exception of a few offices such as those in New York City and Washington, D.C., the concept of a public placement service to college teachers lacks realization. Only three percent of all job seekers use this method and, of these, an insignificant number actually find their best jobs. The college teacher labor market is a national one which is not easily adapted to the local and state orientation of these offices. Although some attempts have been made to nationalize the efforts of the professional placement offices, these have not yet been effective.

Private employment agencies. For a fee, usually five percent of the first full year's salary, private employment agencies will provide credential referral and locator service to the candidate seeking a college teaching appointment. At least two such agencies, the College and Specialist Bureau and the American College Bureau, make over 100 college level placements every year. Many other teaching placement agencies, which are primarily servicing teachers below the college level, also have limited traffic in appointments to colleges and universities. Seven percent of those newly hired (roughly 2,300) register with an agency and three percent (1,000) actually locate their current employment through one.[19]

One of the real problems faced by private employment agencies is that most of the jobs listed are average or below average and at the beginning ranks, whereas most of the candidates registered are expe-

[19] The figures cited in this paragraph are based upon the responses of newly hired professors when asked "How did you look for and find your current job?" Of those who stated that they did not consult a private employment agency, eleven out of a randomly selected 300 were active registrants with one of the two agencies listed above. Although it is probable that some of the individuals who had registered with the private employment agencies had done so when seeking a job in previous years and did not view their current registration as active, whereas the private agency still maintains them in the active file, it is also likely that some of these eleven individuals had in fact registered and failed to indicate so on the questionnaire. Thus, the figures cited are probably a slight understatement of the significance of private employment agencies in the academic labor market.

rienced. Generally, the type of school using a private agency must hire at the bottom because of limited financial resources. Yet the inexperienced, mostly students, more often turn to the college placement office. The individuals who need the agencies are typically those who have teaching experience and are ready for a promotion, but have lost contact with informal channels such as their graduate schools.

Agencies rarely list the top notch jobs or the very best candidates. Among all types of liaisons, private agencies account for the greatest percentage of jobs found in the low quality schools and with the heaviest teaching loads (table 59). It is understandable why commercial agencies are considered worthless by the greatest percentage of college teachers. Private employment agencies are usually the last stop in seeking placement help, a stop that is not made until most other placement help has failed. Of the jobs found by this method, 82 percent are finalized between April and September compared to a 71 percent average for all formal methods and a 64 percent average for all informal methods.

Other channels of information. Occasionally still other methods are used to look for and find jobs. For example, retired professors may, and do, register their availability for employment with the Retired Professors' Registry and the American Association of Emeriti. The names of National Defense Education Act fellowship winners, Woodrow Wilson Fellowship holders, and recipients of Danforth Fellowships are circulated as a list of potential college teachers.

Need for Improvement

Any assessment of the network of communications in the academic labor market is insufficient without an evaluation of how well it operates. Voices for reform have been heard from many quarters and for many years: Craig in 1929, Dresden in 1938, Fay in 1943, Wolfle in 1954, Robinson in 1958, and Bolman in 1962 echo the same theme. In Eliot Fay's words: "This service of finding good positions for college teachers and good teachers for college positions has always been performed with deplorable inefficiency."[20]

[20] Eliot G. Fay, "Placement Service for College Teachers," *AAUP Bulletin*, XXXIX (April, 1943), 283–4; Dael Wolfle, *America's Resources of Specialized Talent* (New York: Harper & Bros., 1954), p. 240; Dils, Dolan, and Axt, "What Sources and Techniques Should Be Utilized in the Recruitment of College

If these pleas are well founded, there is good reason for improving communications now rather than later. Some people will not enter the market until they actually know about vacant jobs. Also, the efficiency of a free market is directly dependent on the flow of information. As our economy has become a maze of complexity and the problems of unemployment and underutilization have caused ever increasing concern, the importance of good communication channels has been magnified. Since academia develops human resources, its rank as a primary industry further increases its burden and the necessity of having the best communication liaisons.

AN OVERVIEW: MODEST ADEQUACY

The adequacy of the market mechanism may be judged from several perspectives—that of the demanders, of the suppliers, or of the nation. The national welfare view is undoubtedly the most appropriate. It would be desirable to develop a model of the ideal distribution of college teaching manpower, to contrast the ideal distribution with the actual, and thereby to develop a measure of the extent to which the current market mechanism is not serving the market as well as it might. Unfortunately, opinions of the ideal distribution of teaching manpower differ even more than opinions on the strategies of education. Elementary questions as "should all researchers in a subspecialty be concentrated at one or two institutions so that they might cross-fertilize new ideas, or is it better to distribute the great specialists throughout the nation so that more graduate students may be given exposure to the great minds?" find no general agreement or immediate answers. Vital questions relating to the necessity of being an active researcher as a prerequisite to being a vital teacher lack unanimous or even near-unanimous resolution. If an optimal distribution of teaching manpower *could* be determined, it would be difficult to decide the extent to which the market system per se contributes to the failure to reach the optimum— for the "irrational" actions of employers, the "noneconomic" considerations in job choice, and the misconceived dictates of policy makers might also prevent the optimum from being achieved.

Teachers, and What Methods of Retention Should Be Employed? *Current Issues in Higher Education* (Washington: National Education Association, 1958), p. 187; Frederick deW. Bolman, Jr., "Placing America's Highly Skilled Manpower: College Faculty and Administrators," *Educational Record*, XLIII (Fall 1962), 295.

Rather than wrestle with these many problems and arbitrarily make questionable assumptions, I approached the evaluation of the market mechanism from a very different perspective—that of the persons most vitally concerned with its effectiveness, the suppliers to the market. After answering a series of questions about how they searched for jobs and how they found their current ones, newly hired college teachers were asked, "Which of the following statements best describes, in your opinion, the opportunities for learning about vacant teaching jobs in your field?" The options given, from which they were to check only one, were:

———*Excellent*. Vacancies are well known. There is almost no chance that a candidate will not learn about a vacancy for which he might be qualified.

———*Good*. With some effort, most candidates learn about most vacancies for which they might be qualified.

———*Poor*. Most candidates never learn about many of the jobs for which they might be qualified. New methods of informing candidates of job vacancies should be investigated.

———*Very poor*. A candidate rarely learns about the job vacancy that would interest him the most. New methods of informing candidates must be implemented.

Their answers indicate that the market is satisfactorily serving the majority of suppliers (table 60). With some effort, most candi-

60 | The Adequacy of Placement

Word That Best Describes Opportunities to Find Jobs in Your Field	Percentage of All Newly Hired Professors
Excellent	7.4
Good	57.7
Poor	28.9
Very poor	6.0

Source: survey data.

dates can learn about most appropriate vacancies. Yet, the minority, rating present arrangements as either "poor" or "very poor," is so substantial (10,000 to 28,500) that it presents a major source of concern.[21] Who are these unserved professors? Are there certain pockets that are neglected by current mechanisms? Why are not all professors served well?

AREAS SERVED LEAST ADEQUATELY

By comparing the attitudes of various faculty groups, the effectiveness of the market mechanism in various sectors of the market can be studied (table 61).[22] The market mechanism operates significantly better for good jobs: top schools, high salaried positions, low teaching loads. Researchers find market mechanisms to be more adequate than teachers; students emerging from graduate school rate the market mechanism as more adequate than professors who are already out on their own.

Yet, significant differences do not appear where they might be expected. The non-Ph.D. is no less adequately served than the Ph.D., the nonpublisher no less than the publisher, the small college teacher no less than the large university professor. In spite of the fact that persons aspiring to senior faculty positions do not usually have help from their graduate schools, they view the market as more adequate than persons seeking junior faculty posts.

[21] One of the risks of judging market adequacy from the statements of participants is that the participants may not know what they are talking about. They may be ignorant of excellent mechanisms, and the complaints may simply be a reflection of this ignorance rather than market maladies. By comparing the attitudes of those who confessed ignorance about various liaisons with the attitudes of those who were knowledgeable, it was possible to determine the extent to which ignorance did influence response. The coefficient of determination between ignorance and attitude is only 0.21. This suggests that 79 percent of the complaints are due to factors other than ignorance.

[22] The legitimacy of the complaints can be tested by correlating a teacher's attitude toward liaisons with his position in the market. The difficulty in drawing conclusions from these results is not knowing the direction of influence: for example, data show that teachers in low quality jobs complain more than those in high quality jobs. Do those in low quality jobs complain more because of their poor jobs, or do they complain more because the liaisons which serve them really are inferior to liaisons that serve better quality schools? Without knowing the magnitude of the influence of considerations such as quality, income, and rank, we can still say that at least 86 percent of the complaints are legitimate. This figure is computed by assuming that those well situated in the market (in high rank, a high quality school, or a high income bracket) will report the most accurate evaluation of market intermediaries. In each of the categories above, at least 30 percent of the well situated said intermediaries are "poor" or "very poor." Considering this 30 percent as the minimum proportion of the complainers who are justified in their opinion, we conclude that "at least" 86 percent of the *complaints* are legitimate.

61 |

Inadequacy of Market Mechanism, by Selected Subgroups

Characteristic of Subgroup	Percentage Rating Channels as Very Poor or Poor
Opinion toward Job Accepted	
Excellent, better than I expected	31*
Very poor, unacceptable	64
Orientation	
Spend more time teaching	36
Spend more time researching	32
Prestige of Current School	
Top 20 percent	31*
Bottom 20 percent	39
Prestige of Last School (last year's faculty only)	
Top 20 percent	31*
Bottom 20 percent	39
Size of Current School	
Under 1,000 students	36
Over 5,000 students	35
Highest Degree Held by Individual	
Doctorate	35
Nondoctorate	35
Activity Last Year	
Student	31*
College teacher	39
Current Academic Rank	
Junior faculty	35
Senior faculty	33

* Difference is statistically significant by a chi-square test at .05 level.
Sources: survey data and Prestige Index.

Unexpectedly, it is not always the least visible candidates and the least visible positions that are served least adequately. The attitudes of candidates toward the adequacy of placement suggest that those persons who are originally disadvantaged take action to overcome the liability. The non-Ph.D. holder pursues more methods of search so that, even though the informal market does not serve him, the informal with the formal market serves him well. On the other hand, the more qualified candidate who seeks a more conspicuous appointment fears that formal methods of job search will not help and is frustrated by his inability to make contact with employers. The non-Ph.D. who seeks a position at a small school feels that direct application will not injure his chances of getting such a job, but the Ph.D. aspiring to a prestigious post at an important college or university must make his availability known so circuitously that he comes to believe that the market mechanisms are not adequate.

In certain disciplines, help is needed more than in others. Again, however, as shown in table 62, repeated efforts to identify the types of markets that are not adequately served are to no avail. Patterns are not obvious. Dissatisfaction is equally present in large markets and small, in markets of excess demand and markets of excess supply, in the humanities as well as the sciences, in the fields with extensive outside employment opportunities and those without. There is one pattern, but it is difficult to quantify. In general, individuals in disciplines where the professional associations have taken a larger role in placement, such as French and chemistry, are more satisfied.

62

Inadequacy of Market Mechanism

Discipline	Percentage Rating Channels as Very Poor or Poor
Political science	54
General zoology	53
Civil engineering	51
Physiology	47
Music	46
History	45
Sociology	43
English	41
Biochemistry	41
Economics	39
Education (not elementary or physical)	39
Business and commerce	39
Mechanical engineering	38
Earth sciences	36
Electrical engineering	35
Experimental psychology	33
Elementary education	33
Chemistry	32
Physics	32
Physical education	30
Chemical engineering	29
Fine arts (drama, art)	21
French	21
Mathematics	20

Source: survey data.

EVALUATION OF THE VARIOUS MARKET INTERMEDIARIES

The first column of table 63, "frequency," indicates the popularity of each intermediary. The "46 percent, rank 1," in the "blind letters" row means that 46 percent of all job seekers use this method to search jobs and that this method ranks first in frequency used.

63

Evaluation of Various Market Intermediaries

MARKET INTERMEDIARY	(1) FREQUENCY (PERCENTAGE WHO USED)	(2) EFFICIENCY (NUMBER FOUND/ NUMBER USED)	(3) DESIRABILITY (NUMBER JOBS ACCEPTED/ NUMBER JOBS FOUND)	(4) IMPORTANCE [AVERAGE OF RANKS IN COLUMNS (1)–(3)]
	Percentage (rank in column)	Percentage (rank in column)	Percentage (rank in column)	
Informal				
Faculty colleague	20 (6)	35 (3)	31 (1)	3.3
Other professional friend	25 (5)	32 (4)	30 (2)	3.7
Graduate professor	40 (2)	30 (5)	21 (5)	4.0
Graduate department	32 (4)	19 (8½)	11 (9)	7.1
Undergraduate professor	16 (8)	19 (8½)	25 (4)	6.8
Graduate classmate	17 (7)	18 (10)	29 (3)	6.8
Publisher's representative	2 (16)	10 (14½)	11 (10)	13.5
Formal				
Blind letters	46 (1)	41 (2)	20 (6)	3.0
Commercial agency	7 (12)	43 (1)	13 (7)	6.7
Answered an advertisement	9 (11)	22 (6)	12 (8)	8.3
College placement office	36 (3)	17 (11)	7 (13)	9.0
Church-related service	5 (13)	20 (7)	10 (11)	10.3
Convention placement service	14 (9½)	14 (12½)	6 (14)	12.0
Professional association	14 (9½)	14 (12½)	9 (12)	13.3
Advertised availability	3 (14½)	10 (14½)	4 (16)	15.0
Public employment service	3 (14½)	7 (16)	5 (15)	15.1

Source: survey data.

The second column of table 63 indicates "efficiency." This measure is the quotient of the number of jobs found by a particular method divided by the number of people who use the method.[23] It does not provide an indication of the quality of the various jobs found. The individual who is interested in being exposed to a large number of jobs and is not overly concerned about their quality would be well advised to study the rankings in the "efficiency" col-

[23] A similar measure of efficiency is computed by H. E. Klugh, *American Psychologist,* XIX, No. 8 (1964) 672–3.

umn. Here the real strength of the commercial employment agency is shown by the fact that it, more than any other intermediary, is able to supply the registrant with large numbers of job options. Blind letters are the second most productive technique, whereas individuals who consult publishers' representatives, advertise their availability in professional journals, and register their needs with the public employment service find relatively few jobs—good, bad, or neutral.

The third measure of market media, "desirability," is obtained by dividing the number of people who find their present jobs (which is assumed to be the best one they found because they accepted it in preference to the others) by a given method by the total number of jobs found by that same method. Although this measure tends to bias against those methods that produce a large number of alternatives, its main value is in indicating the quality of jobs found by a method. Whereas column two of table 63 measures quantity, quality is measured by column three. The most obvious conclusion to be reached from the latter column is that informal methods produce much better jobs than formal methods. The five first-ranking methods are informal. A higher percentage of the jobs found by informal methods tends to be accepted. Though formal methods tend to produce large numbers of leads, the best offers result from the jobs found through contemporaries and former professors.

The fourth column shows the unweighted average of the ranks in the first three columns. As such it is a general measure of popularity, efficiency, and desirability. It is quite interesting to note that blind letters are the most important market mechanism, even more so than various informal methods.[24] The great importance of friends, both contemporaries and former teachers, is shown by the relatively low rankings assigned to these methods. The skeptics about commercial placement agencies will be surprised to find them ranking as the second most important formal intermediary. Though their main strength is quantity, for those that use the agency the quality seems to be the best they can find. Also, the relative high rank of "answered an advertisement" among the formal methods indicates that this may be a promising route when devising methods of extending the market mechanism.

[24] Omitted from the entire discussion is "did nothing" to find a job which would probably rank first on all criteria, except number of jobs found.

The low rank assigned to "publisher's representative," the public employment service, and the placing of "candidate available" ads is again another omen against extension of placement services by these means. Whereas the poor ratings given to the convention placement services and the professional associations may be attributed to the fact that in many disciplinary markets these are not possible routes of placement help, the low ratings of publisher's representatives, U.S.E.S., and "candidate available" ads must be attributed to the desire not to pursue jobs by these means and presumably for good reason.

RECENT EFFORTS OF CONSOLIDATION

One of the biggest problems in the academic labor market today is the splintering of market intermediaries. There are so many agencies and organizations willing to extend a helping hand to the candidate-seeking employer and the job-seeking candidate that the employer and the candidate often accept different hands. As a result, the desired and the desirable match may never be made. One placement intermediary is frustrated by not finding the best candidate; and another intermediary fails to provide the best job to his registrant. Yet, plenty exists in the midst of poverty. Even though it is increasingly unlikely that a given intermediary will learn about a particular vacancy (candidate), the number of vacancies (candidates) has been increasing so rapidly that most agencies have more to process than they can handle adequately. So much time must be spent in the routine processing of registration that not enough is left for professional placement.

Recognizing some of the undesirable features of excessive decentralization and some of the economies of scale that may be achieved through cooperative efforts, several organizations have already taken steps to increase cooperation, and other moves toward consolidation are developing. Only four years old, the Cooperative College Registry is a cooperative effort of recruitment by more than 200 colleges sponsored by ten Protestant denominations.[25] The main thrust of the Registry is to register emerging graduate students (and others when possible) who are interested in college teaching in a Christian

[25] Evangelical United Brethren; Lutheran Church in America; United Church of Christ; Presbyterian Church in the U.S.; United Presbyterian Church, U.S.A.; The American Baptist Convention; American Lutheran Church; Disciples of Christ; The Southern Baptist Convention; and Church of the Brethren.

setting. Following the lead of business recruiters, Registry representatives actually visit the campuses of over 120 graduate schools and 25 national conventions to talk with prospective candidates and to gain their registration. Representatives from each of the denominations take the responsibility of visiting an allotted number of graduate schools and subsequently sharing with the other denominations the one-page registration forms that result from the visits. Once the names are collected and distributed to the denominational headquarters of the various church groups, each of the ten offices takes the responsibility of determining how best to inform the administrations at their colleges.

At the time candidates register, they are told that, although it is almost certain that some schools will be contacting them, the Registry offers broad visibility to a large number of employers but it is not a candidate placement agency. The candidate will not receive notices of vacancies. He will not even know when his name has been referred and when inquiries have been made about him until the interested employer makes the contact.

The success of the Cooperative College Registry is attested to by the fact that in its second full year of operation (1964–65) approximately 5,000 registrations were processed and that, since seven charter denominations pioneered the service, three other denominations have seen the advantages of joining in the effort. With less effort and expense, member denominations are finding that they may provide a more meaningful and more inclusive placement service to their related schools.

A second cooperative effort of a very different nature is among the teacher placement offices at the major graduate schools. In addition to the usual amount of sharing of information about the best procedures for running a placement service that one would expect to take place at conventions where the directors of these offices congregate, the professional association of teacher placement offices, ASCUS,[26] has already taken three steps to relate the individual efforts of its members. The first of these is the Reciprocity Agreement.[27] When an individual prefers a type of teaching position in which his home office has very little traffic (openings in a small New Jersey college by the

[26] Association for School, College, and University Staffing, Hershey, Pa.

[27] A copy of the agreement appears as "Reciprocity Policy Review for Old, New ASCUS Members," *ASCUS Newsletter*, XII, No. 2 (October 1964), 8, 11.

placement office at Stanford, for example), the home office may request help from another member of ASCUS. It might, for example, refer the candidate's folder to the placement office at Rutgers which would, for the placement year, treat the candidate as one of its own. The reciprocity agreement was instituted primarily for high school and primary school teachers, where the markets are usually very much oriented by state. In the case of college teaching, where the boundaries of employer search are not usually restricted to the same state or even the same region, the necessity of this type of cooperation is less, as are its benefits. In fact, there are relatively few candidates for college teaching positions that are currently referred across state boundaries. Nevertheless, the reciprocity agreement, and its operation in the lower echelon teaching positions, is a valuable indication of the type of cooperation of which the ASCUS-related offices are capable.

More pertinent to the college teacher labor market is the second phase of cooperation among ASCUS members. At several conventions where employer-administrators congregate (Association for Higher Education, American Association of Colleges for Teacher Education, North Central Association of Colleges and Secondary Schools), the members of ASCUS maintain a "headquarters" where employers may stop by to register their vacancies and staff needs for the next year. At the 1964 convention of the North Central Association in Chicago, for example, representatives from 21 different placement offices manned the headquarters where 54 colleges located in 17 states listed 165 vacancies.[28] Following the convention, a list of the vacancies was distributed to all members of ASCUS.

At its November 1965 convention, ASCUS initiated the development of FILE which becomes operational in the fall of 1967. The candidate using FILE submits a standard job application and résumé form through his college placement office. Candidate forms are processed by a centralized computer center, where basic biographic and career-intent data will be kept on tape for thousands of job seekers.

An employer looking for a new Ph.D. mathematician submits inquiries to the storage center. Access to the storage center is by teletype equipment or letter. The university seeking the mathematician simply

---

[28] "ASCUS Provides Placement Services at Conventions," *ASCUS Newsletter,* XII, No. 2 (October 1964), 9, 11.

places a long-distance call to the computer and requests to be connected with the storage unit. Once connected, he types out questions for the storage unit to answer. The questions are typed on a machine that looks very much like a large electric typewriter on a special table. The computer responds by teletype. A dialogue might run:

Employer: "Do you know of any Ph.D. mathematicians, under age 35, working at salaries less than $12,000 per year, married, willing to locate in North Dakota, moderate publications, and a subspecialty in mathematics for social scientists?"

Computer: "57836, 12580, . . . 48572. More?" (The numbers are identifiers of individuals who have entered the storage.)

Employer: "Add the specification: currently employed in Middle West."

Computer: "57836, 48572."

Employer: "Print out resume of 57836."

Such an interchange will allow an employer instant access to a large segment of the market. Employer cost is considerably less than the conventionally used, high cost methods of locating personnel. The employer pays for the long-distance phone call, about five dollars for the use of the computer, and two dollars for each résumé, plus the one hundred dollars or so per year to rent the teletype machine.

Another computer-based matching service, designed more specifically for college teachers under a special grant from the Esso Education Foundation to the Association for Higher Education of the National Education Association, is reported by George Arnstein.[29] Based upon similar computer technology, MATCH would provide a broader range of options to a more inclusive group of employers and candidates. Still in the developmental stages, it is unclear exactly what services MATCH would provide. Among those considered are: (1) a roster of all persons capable of college teaching which could be consulted by employers; (2) a listing of all persons desirous of new employment (either temporary or permanent) in the academic professions, both in and outside the academic community; and (3) a listing of all job vacancies which could be consulted by job seekers (perhaps even those who do not register their own availability).

Still a third computer-based system is under preliminary consid-

[29] George E. Arnstein, "MATCH: Square Pegs for Square Holes," *Phi Delta Kappan,* November 1965, pp. 122–5; and *Design for an Academic Matching Service* (Washington: National Education Association, 1967).

eration by the United States Employment Service. Discussions are being held throughout the nation with individuals in various disciplines who might want to avail themselves of the possible services. Started in August 1965, a plan for a year-round placement service to be provided by the U.S.E.S. for the American Library Association is in operation. Under this plan, any individual librarian may register availability with the service. By mail the candidate receives a publication which lists the vacancies that have been brought to the attention of the service by employers. From this point forward, all negotiation is between employer and candidate. If this effort proves successful, there is a large probability that the public employment service will cooperate with other professional associations in providing a year-round service. Relationships have already been developed with a large number of professional associations as a result of the excellent services provided by U.S.E.S. at annual meetings, and a number of the associations have expressed interest in the year-round service.

With the exception of the nationwide efforts of certain professional associations,[30] the only other effort that could be construed as a cooperative placement service is the National Register of Scientific and Technical Personnel which is maintained by the National Science Foundation in cooperation with the scientific societies. In 1962, over 215,000 natural scientists had their professional biographies on file with the Register. Since this date, in addition to adding more natural scientists, the Register has expanded its coverage to the social sciences. Here, at one point, is a listing of the scientific manpower resources of a nation.

At the present time, it should be stressed, the Register is in no way involved in placement. Although the Register (then the Roster) was developed to assist in the placement and utilization of scientific manpower during World War II,[31] and is currently being maintained with the thought that it would serve much the same role in another national emergency of major proportions, Register officials at the present time have resisted the temptation of allowing it to be

[30] For example, the cooperation between the state associations and the national association of nurses and the various services provided to the national conventions of professional associations.

[31] "The American Brain Barrel: How Scientists and Specialists Were Mobilized for War Work by Means of a 'National Roster,' " *Fortune* (March 1945).

a resource upon which the recruiters of scientists may draw. The Register officials fear that if they allow the Register to become primarily a placement operation, many scientists will fail to register with them. They would, therefore, not have an accurate and complete inventory of scientific manpower.[32] Thus, although the Register might be called a cooperative effort in placement among various professional associations as coordinated by the National Science Foundation, it would properly be so labeled only in times of national emergency. There has been some limited talk about working directly with the professional associations and capitalizing upon the names they collect for the purposes of the Register in the formation of a placement agency which is independent of the Register. These talks have not, however, proceeded very far.[33]

Although it is tempting at this point to discuss the relative merits of the various plans mentioned above, in order to consolidate all recommendations, this discussion is delayed to chapter 7.

[32] My personal opinions on these and other matters are reserved for the policy implications chapter.

[33] John Caffrey (ACE), George Arnstein (NEA), Marlowe Slater (ASCUS), and I are currently attempting to devise a workable plan for coordinating and centralizing the consolidations.

6

Job Choice in the Academic Labor Market

Before turning to a discussion of the theoretical and policy implications, it is relevant to analyze in detail one final aspect of the market —the decision-making process of the suppliers. With all the commotion that has been made in recent years over professors' salaries, one begins to wonder if the dedicated college professor has turned into some kind of insidious money-grubber. State legislators, reviewing appropriations requests from their public institutions, tire of that annual item providing for yet another raise of faculty salaries. Alumni, perusing the most recent fund-raising literature, wonder why they keep hearing about underpaid professors. With all the publicity devoted to academic salaries through the press, the federal government, and the campaigning of the AAUP, faculty salaries have been steadily climbing over the past decade to the point that college teaching is beginning to become a financially respectable occupation. The national average nine-month compensation was $10,632 in 1965–66, a figure that has doubled in the last decade.[1] Salary scales have become quite competitive, starting in the major league institutions and spreading right down the line.

All the talk of money doesn't coincide with the traditional view of the professor as a man dedicated to the education of young minds, with no goal other than service to his fellow man. Certainly this portrait is a myth. Professors are concerned with salaries, both as a mea-

[1] "The Economic Status of the Profession," *AAUP Bulletin,* LII, No. 2, 141, 159.

sure of prestige and as a means of feeding families. But to what extent have they become concerned with financial rewards? And to what extent are they more concerned with what they will do at their new job than how much they will be paid?

The whole question of job choice is a very complex one, one that deserves to be approached with caution. Job choice is individualistic: factors are rarely given the same weight by different professors. Even for the same individual, the importance assigned to a given job characteristic often changes as he moves from a decision to leave a job, to a judgment about what types of offers to seek, and finally to a choice between the two best job offers received. Motivations for choice are often unclear to the chooser and inconspicuous to the observer. Without depth-interviewing by experienced psychiatrists, the accurate assessment of true motivation in job choice is impossible.

Realizing the dangers involved, yet also recognizing the importance of some assessment of the determinants of job choice, this chapter presents the evidence now available on why professors select and reject certain jobs.

The Deciding Factors

What do job changers say is important? To answer this question, seventeen factors (listed in table 64) were identified as potentially influential in the "select-versus-reject" decision.[2] Newly hired professors were asked: How important were each of these factors in your decision to choose your current job instead of your next best alternative? The results are summarized in table 64.

The typical professor rests his decision upon what he will be doing at his new job (e.g., course assignments, classroom hours, and research facilities). How much he will be paid (salary and rank) is noticeably less important. Academic environment (for example, competency of colleagues) takes clear precedence over geographic location and climatological environment. Preferment is accorded the right assignment at the wrong pay, if the alternative is the wrong assignment at the right pay.

[2] The a priori rationale for selecting each of the factors discussed is presented in David G. Brown, *The Market for College Teachers: An Economic Analysis of Career Patterns Among Southeastern Social Scientists* (Chapel Hill, N.C.: University of North Carolina Press, 1965), Chapter VII, and is not repeated here.

64

Determinants of Job Choice

Choice Variable	Choice Index[a]
Courses taught	3.7
Teaching load	3.4
Research facilities and opportunities	3.3
Competency of colleagues	3.3
Salary	3.2
Future salary prospects	3.2
Reputation of school	3.1
Quality of students	3.1
Administration and administrators	3.0
Cultural opportunities	2.9
Congeniality of colleagues	2.9
Academic rank	2.8
Fringe benefits	2.4
Nearness to graduate school	2.4
Climate	2.1
Nearness to friends and relatives	2.1
Moonlighting opportunities	1.8

[a] In response to the question, "How important were each of these factors in your decision to choose your current job instead of your next best alternative?" three options were given: "very important," "important," and "not important." For each of the seventeen factors, five times the number of very important's, three times the important's, and one times the not important's were summed. By dividing the summed products by the total number of answers, the "Choice Index" was obtained. (For example, if 50 persons were surveyed about the importance of salary, and ten answered "very important," 35 answered "important," and five "not important," then the index would be 3.2.) Thus, the most important variables are assigned the higher Choice Index values.

Source: survey data.

The typical professor of table 64 is, of course, mythic. Hidden in the averages are substantial differences among groups of professors. Consider first the influence of environment.

ENVIRONMENTAL FACTORS

By "environment" is meant the setting in which a job places a professor: cultural opportunities (access to the performing arts, for example), congeniality of colleagues, nearness to graduate school, proximity to friends and relatives, climate and topography, and a way of life and living. For professors in general "environment" isn't important.[3] In the ranking of importance (table 64), such factors crowd the bottom of the list. Moreover, when faced with a decision between their two best job options, over one-fourth of the professors

[3] This statement is true only for five factors mentioned in the previous sentence; it is not true for the environmental factor, congeniality.

chose the *less desirable* environment: that is, over one-fourth of the professors accepted the job that is farther away from friends and relatives (34 percent) and graduate school (26 percent), in a less desirable climate (27 percent), or where culture is less accessible (26 percent). More than *any* other of the seventeen factors, professors were willing to sacrifice their preferred environment in order to attain the other advantages of a given job (table 65).[4]

There are, however, subsets of professors for whom environment is more significant. Some examples may be drawn from table 66—music professors who cherish proximity to cultural opportunities, laboratory scientists who value the congeniality of colleagues because of extensive team research, students leaving graduate school before completing their degree who wish to stay near their graduate school to facilitate consultation, and married women professors who are constrained by their husband's employment.

JOB-RELATED FACTORS

For most professors, the opportunity for meaningful professional activity is the strongest influence upon job choice. In the list of seventeen variables, seven relate to this opportunity; that is, seven define the nature of the work and the work environment. That all seven factors (courses taught, teaching load, research facilities and opportunities, competency of colleagues, reputation of the school, quality of students, and the nature of administrations and administrators) are among the top nine in table 64 indicates their importance. When considered individually, these factors provide the main

---

[4] The above statement of significance of environment in job choice, although it is consistent with both the a priori arguments and the empirical findings of the current study, is a considerable modification of the statements based upon the pilot study alone (*The Market for College Teachers,* pp. 185–92). The pilot study suggests that environment is more important in job choice. The main reason for the necessity of the modification is that in the pilot study the environmental factor was consolidated in one variable, "location," whereas in the nationwide survey, five different environmental factors are considered. The difficulty here is that "location" is more than the sum of the five parts. Although the proximity of culture, friends, and graduate schools as well as the congeniality of colleagues and the desirability of climate make up a portion of the desirability of a given "location," there are also influences such as the "way of life" and the "culture of the region" that are not included in the five specific factors. In the current survey the influence of five particular aspects of location is assessed in greater detail, but the total or aggregate influence of location is not studied.

65

Current Job versus the Next Best Alternative, as Rated by the Individual

CHOICE VARIABLE	JOB ACCEPTED BETTER	TWO JOBS SAME	JOB REJECTED BETTER
	%	%	%
Courses taught	52	31	16
Teaching load	48	33	19
Research facilities and opportunities	50	25	25
Competency of colleagues	51	30	19
Salary	54	25	21
Future salary prospects	58	27	15
Reputation of school	51	23	26
Quality of students	45	30	25
Administration and administrators	50	32	18
Cultural opportunities	49	25	26
Congeniality of colleagues	46	40	14
Academic rank	41	41	18
Fringe benefits	40	38	22
Nearness to graduate school	40	34	26
Climate	36	37	27
Nearness to friends and relatives	38	28	34
Moonlighting opportunities	35	43	22

Source: survey data.

rationale for job choice. Since each one of the factors is significant in job choice, it is desirable to define separate functional relationships.

1. Courses taught. More than any other single factor, college teachers consider competitive job offers in terms of the courses they will be required to teach (table 64). This is the most important determinant of job choice for virtually all professors—the New Englander and the westerner, men and women, young and middle-aged, last year's students as well as last year's professors (table 66). Job offers that promise even slightly more attractive teaching assignments are rarely rejected (table 65).[5]

[5] No attempt was made to specify what the characteristics of the most desirable teaching assignment are. Other studies emphasize the preference toward graduate level courses, courses within a man's special area of interest, and the avoidance of too many different and remotely related assignments. Cf., John E. Stecklein and Ruth E. Eckert, *An Exploratory Study of Factors Influencing Choice of College Teaching as a Career* (Washington: U.S. Office of Education, Government Printing Office, 1961), p. 31; John E. Stecklein and Robert L. Lathrop, *Faculty Attraction and Retention: Factors Affecting Faculty Mobility at the University of Minnesota* (Minneapolis: Bureau of Institutional Research,

66

Importance of Determinants of Job Choice Ranked by Selected Groups

CHOICE VARIABLE	ORIENTA-TION		PUBLICA-TIONS		EDUCA-TION		MILES MOVED		PERMA-NENCY	
	Re-search	Teach-ing	None	Many	Ph.D.	Non-Ph.D.	Less Than 200	Over 1,000	One Year Only	More Than One Year
Courses taught	4	1	1	2	2	1	1	2	1	1
Teaching load	2	2	2	3	3	2	2	3	3	3
Research facilities	1	4	5	1	1	8	3	1	4	5
Competency of colleagues	3	3	3	4	4	6	4	4	2	4
Salary	6	5	4	5	5	5	6	5	6	2
Future salary prospects	8	6	6	8	7	3	5	8	7	7
Reputation of school	5	9	7	6	8	10	7	6	5	6
Quality of students	7	10	10	9	10	7	8	7	10	9
Administration	12	7	9	7	6	4	9	10	9	11
Cultural opportunities	11	11	11	13	12	9	11	12	11	12
Congeniality of colleagues	13	8	8	11	11	11	10	9	12	8
Academic rank	10	12	13	10	9	13	12	13	13	13
Fringe benefits	16	14	15	14	14	14	14	15	14	14
Near graduate school	9	13	12	12	13	12	13	11	8	10
Climate	14	16	16	15	16	17	17	16	16	15
Near friends and relatives	17	15	14	17	15	16	15	14	15	16
Moonlighting opportunities	15	17	17	16	17	15	16	17	17	17

Note: Ranks represent the vertical placing of the percentage rating factor as "very important" taken over the base of all "very important" reasons. The measure is closely related to the Choice Index (table 64). The dash connecting lines are inserted to emphasize rank differences of three or more.

Sources: survey data and Prestige Index.

2. Teaching load. Professors want to know not only "what" they will be teaching but also "how much" (table 64). Variations in load are large: for two-thirds of the professors choosing between their two best options, there is a difference in load (table 65). That over 70 percent opt for the lower load indicates the preference. The desire for lower loads can be misinterpreted as a quest for less task. Actually, the preference stems from a desire to organize one's own time. If fewer assigned classroom hours are required, this increases the

University of Minnesota, 1960), pp. 16–7; and Brown, *The Market for College Teachers,* pp. 196–200. The preference for specialized assignments presents a real recruiting problem for the small colleges who often must expand their course offerings (not always desirably so) in order to make their jobs more attractive to the men they want. Cf., Earl McGrath, *Memo to a College Faculty Member* (New York: Teachers' College Press, 1961), pp. 16–7.

66

Importance of Determinants of Job Choice (continued)

Choice Variable	Disciplines			Prestige of School		Activity Last Year		Control of Current School		
	Mu-sic	Eco-nomics	Phys-ics	Top 20 per-cent	Bot-tom 20 per cent	Stu-dent	Pro-fessor	Pub-lic	Pri-vate	Church-Re-lated
Courses taught	1	1	4	4	1	1	1	1	1	1
Teaching load	10	4	3	5	5	2	2	3	5	2
Research facilities	8	3	1	1	7	4	3	2	2	6
Competency of colleagues	3	7	2	3	6	3	6	4	3	8
Salary	4	2	10	6	4	7	4	6	7	7
Future salary prospects	6	5	11	9	2	8	5	5	13	5
Reputation of school	7	6	6	2	12	5	8	7	4	11
Quality of students	9	8	8	7	11	10	9	12	6	3
Administration	5	11	13	13	3	11	7	8	10	4
Cultural opportunities	2	4	12	12	10	12	12	11	8	10
Congeniality of colleagues	13	12	7	11	8	6	11	9	9	9
Academic rank	12	10	9	10	9	13	10	13	11	12
Fringe benefits	11	13	16	14	13	15	14	14	14	14
Near graduate school	15	9	5	8	14	9	13	10	12	13
Climate	17	15	15	16	16	16	16	16	16	17
Near friends and relatives	16	17	14	15	15	14	15	15	15	15
Moonlighting opportunities	14	16	17	17	17	17	17	17	17	16

Note: Ranks represent the vertical placing of the percentage rating factor as "very important" taken over the base of all "very important" reasons. The measure is closely related to the Choice Index (table 64). The dash connecting lines are inserted to emphasize rank differences of three or more.

Sources: survey data and Prestige Index.

block of discretionary time for which the professor may himself decide whether it will be spent most profitably with students or reading or writing.

3. Research facilities. Of special concern to professors who spend more time researching than teaching is the availability of adequate research facilities (laboratory equipment, well-stocked libraries). For the Ph.D. scholars, the big publishers, the academic scientists, and the professors located at large and prestigious institutions, the availability of research facilities is more important than any other single factor (table 66). The significance of this same factor in the decisions of teaching-oriented, nonpublishers who locate at small, church-related, lower prestige institutions contrasts sharply.

Choice Variable	Region of Current School				Age			Sex and Marital Status Married		Size of Current School		
	NA	GL	SE	W	35 or Less	36–50	51 or More	M	F	S	M	L
Courses taught	1	1	1	1	1	1	2	1	1	1	1	2
Teaching load	3	2	4	3	3	3	5	3	2	2	2	4
Research facilities	2---5---5---2				2	2	3	2---5		7---4---1		
Competency of colleagues	4	4	3	4	4	6	7	4	4	8---5---3		
Salary	6---7---2---6				5	7	4	6---9		10---3---6		
Future salary prospects	8	10	7	5	7	5	9	5--14		5	6	7
Reputation of school	5	6	9	7	6	8	8	7--10		6---9---5		
Quality of students	7	11	11	9	8	12	10	9	8	3	10	11
Administration	10	8	5	8	10---4---1			8	7	4---7--12		
Cultural opportunities	9--12--12--12				12	11	12	13---6		12	11	10
Congeniality of colleagues	11	9	8	11	9--10---6			10	11	9	8	8
Academic rank	12---3--10--14				13	9	11	12	12	11	13	13
Fringe Benefits	14	14	13	16	15	14	13	14	15	15	14	14
Near graduate school	13	12	14	13	11	13	15	13	13	12---9---9		
Climate	16--17--16--10				16	15	16	16	16	16	16	16
Near friends and relatives	15	15	15	15	14	16	14	15---3		14	15	15
Moonlighting opportunities	17	16	17	17	17	17	17	17	17	17	17	17

Note: Ranks represent the vertical placing of the percentage rating factor as "very important" taken over the base of all "very important" reasons. The measure is closely related to the Choice Index (table 64). The dash connecting lines are inserted to emphasize rank differences of three or more.

Sources: survey data and Prestige Index.

4. Competency of colleagues. Ranking within the top four factors considered important in job choice by all professors, the competency of colleagues is of special concern to individuals in the "cooperative" disciplines, such as physics and music, and to young professors who hope to learn from their senior colleagues (tables 64 and 66).

5. Quality of students. Professors moving to small, church-related colleges are predictably more conscious of the quality of the student body. There is a commitment here that does not appear in the professors migrating toward the larger universities. But the split is not, apparently, teaching versus research or high prestige versus low prestige. The research-minded professors, especially the more productive ones, and the professors locating at the most prestigious schools also consider heavily the quality of students in their job choice. What may be happening is that the mediocre professors are forced to choose between a school with good students *or* good research facilities, whereas the top scholars may entertain criteria that contemplate the best of both worlds.

6. Prestige of institution. Reputation for scholarly excellence is a strong magnet (table 64). Among the faculty locating at top quintile institutions, "reputation" was identified as the second most important element in job choice (table 66). "Reputation" is especially attractive to young men on the way up, for they cherish a stimulating, research-publication atmosphere where they may draw upon the talents of established scholars to build their own reputations.

7. Administrations and administrators. Poor administrators repel faculty. At the better institutions, at least a modicum of integrity and competency among administrators is assumed so that these factors rarely figure in the job choice decisions of prospective faculty. But at the poorer institutions, where administrators are more prone to interfere with faculty independence, concern is great. Although the factor "administration and administrators" ranked thirteenth among seventeen for migrants to the top quintile institutions, it was third among seventeen for individuals locating at bottom quinile schools. Migrants to small, church-related colleges expressed greatest concern.

COMPENSATION FACTORS

The tangible rewards connected with job options are defined by the salary, fringe benefits (retirement, insurance), academic rank, opportunities for outside income (summer school teaching, for example), and future salary prospects. In the academic labor market, with the exception of fringe benefits, the terms of employment tend to be set by higgling or individual negotiation sessions. Although there are disciplinary, rank, and other contours—the terms of employment tend to be set for each individual. Even the same individual contemplates widely variant incomes.[6] Over one-third of the professors receiving more than one concrete offer reject college teaching

---

[6] Income refers to the regular academic salary plus consulting and income from part-time jobs. It excludes dividends, interest, gifts, royalties, and the sale of manuscripts because these items would tend to be the same at all jobs.

jobs offering at least $500 lower income per year and over one-third reject jobs offering at least $500 more income per year.[7]

In spite of these differentials, salary and income are not the most important elements in job choice. Overall, salary ranks only fifth according to the Choice Index (table 64). Twelve percent of the professors with two or more offers reject a teaching job paying $1,000 more. When considering their two best job options, 21 percent choose not to accept the offer carrying the better pay (table 65).

As a rule with exceptions, the relationship between salary importance in job choice and the salary level is inverse. Individuals with low salaries place more stress upon this factor in job choice: e.g., the music professors more than the physics professors, those at the lower echelon schools in contrast to those at the top 20 percent, and professors in the Southeast more than those in other regions.

The evidence of the present study tends to verify the theory put forward in the pilot study that salary is an important factor up to a point but beyond that the incremental changes in net advantage tend to be relatively small.[8] Two modifications are appropriate, however. In the pilot study it was hypothesized that professors virtually never move to a job with lower monetary rewards. This is not exactly the case. Although 57 percent of the professors moving between two teaching positions increase their income by the move, 23 percent actually take a pay cut. Small cuts in income are acceptable, although less than one percent lose more than $500 by the move.[9]

The second modification relates to the significance of very high salaries. The present evidence suggests that the lure of money never diminishes to zero: the services of most professors will be sold to "any" institution if the price paid is sufficiently high. Admitting that salary differentials of the magnitude typical of today's market are rarely influential in job choice decisions, an attempt was made to learn if much higher salary differences *might be* influential. The fact that increasing salaries by magnitudes of $25,000, $10,000, and even $2,000 is, for most schools, completely infeasible, was ignored.

---

[7] These statistics do not include nonteaching jobs.

[8] Brown, *The Market for College Teachers,* pp. 181–5.

[9] This suggests that the minimum factor theory developed in the pilot study still applies but that the minimum level is approximately $500 below current salary.

To test the hypothesis that big money might redirect mobility, last year's college teachers who said "my old job was *unacceptable* and I had a strong desire to move" were asked, "Approximately how much higher (than the amount actually offered) would your annual income have to have been in order to have induced you to stay at your previous job?" Ninety-five percent of them would have stayed if their salary had been increased sufficiently. Only five percent said it would take more than a $25,000 increase to keep them (table 67).

67 |

Dollar Income Increase Necessary to Keep Professors at Unacceptable Jobs[a]

Amount	Percentage
Less than $500	11
$ 500 to $ 999	14
$ 1,000 to $ 1,999	25
$ 2,000 to $ 4,999	26
$10,000 to $24,999	8
More than $25,000	5

[a] Eleven percent did not answer.
Source: survey data.

From the data it is apparent that the salary that influences job choice is long-run more than short-run. The choice indexes for "salary" and "future salary prospects" are identical, suggesting that respondents tend to think of salary and salary prospects in the same terms. Not only are the choice indexes the same—but so also are the groups that tend to stress salary on the one hand and future salary on the other. Though there are some differences among one-year appointees versus others and between age groups, the general similarities suggest that professors are long-run rather than short-run men.

Neither of two other aspects of compensation, fringe benefits and opportunities for outside income, have a great deal of influence upon job choice, even when only selected subgroups are studied (tables 64 and 65).[10] In fact, "opportunities for moonlighting" is consistently rated as the least important of seventeen factors.

[10] Fringe benefits are discussed in more detail on pages 53–5.

Nor is academic rank very important. Among the seventeen factors rated by the Choice Index, academic rank is only twelfth most important. There is amazingly little resistance to accepting decreases in rank, as shown by the fact that over 25 percent of professors moving between two jobs actually accept a lower rank (table 65).

The Reliability of the Choice Index Measure

Any statement about motivations for job choice which is based upon the post hoc reflections of the choosers is immediately suspect, and rightly so. There are at least two sources of error in information collected by these means. First, the choosers may not know themselves why they chose the job they did. Or, secondly, they may know but be unwilling to admit that they did not follow a rational or an "acceptable" pattern. They may know, for example, that salary was crucial in their decision but hide the fact so that the monastic image of the college teaching profession may be preserved.

WORDS AND ACTIONS

To assess the extent to which the responses on which the Choice Index is based are unreliable, words and actions were compared. Did the man who said that "research facilities" are "very important" in job choice actually move to the job with better "research facilities"? An index of comparative merit of the job accepted and the next best alternative (the Merit Index) was computed from the answer to "Compare your current job with the one at which you would probably be working had you not obtained this one."[11] The options "much better," "slightly better," "about the same," "slightly worse," and "much worse" were weighted as 5, 4, 3, 2, and 1, respectively, in order to obtain an overall index. The Merit Index values were then ranked over the 17 variables.[12] Correlating these ranks with the ranks of the Choice Index (table 64), a high relationship is seen (Spear-

[11] This question was answered only by persons whose next best alternative was another college teaching position.

[12] By asking the individuals themselves to rank the comparative merits of the two jobs considered most seriously, many thorny problems of interpersonal comparisons and of rating the comparative merits of two jobs could be avoided. Each individual could decide, for example, whether he preferred Fort Lauderdale to San Francisco. We did not have to decide for him. Moreover, it was possible for one individual to prefer the East whereas another the West.

man's $= .89$), an indication that the jobs chosen are most often better in the ways that individuals say they should be.[13] This test tended to strengthen our confidence in the Choice Index measure.

LIMITATIONS OF MEASURE

The major limitation of the Choice Index is not that it inadequately describes why the best job offer is chosen instead of the second best one, but that it considers only this one decision and no others. Prior to the "finals" there are usually many choices made: for example, to follow up job A rather than B, to eliminate job C because it is in an undesirable climate, not to seek information about jobs at D because it is not a church-related school. The criteria used to make these decisions, though they may be much the same as those used in the "finals," may be quite different. In short, the present discussion of the choice process does not define the minimal characteristics necessary in a job.

Secondly, the Choice Index rates the importance of factors "actually considered," not those "desired to be considered." It may be

---

[13] The actual differences in ranks (Choice Index rank minus Merit Index rank) are:

Courses taught	−1	Cultural opportunities	−1
Teaching load	−1	Congeniality of colleagues	4
Research facilities	−5	Academic rank	0
Competency	0	Fringe benefits	−1
Salary	0	Nearness to graduate school	1
Future salary prospects	5	Climate	0
Quality of school	−2	Nearness to friends	−1
Quality of students	−2	Moonlighting opportunities	1
Administration	3		

Note that the largest variations between actions and words occur with respect to the factors hardest to rate before actually taking the job. When they answered our questionnaire, some months after serving on their new jobs, the newly hired professors were able to rate with some accuracy the relative merits of their present jobs versus their next best alternatives. They state that their colleagues are more congenial, the future prospects for salary increases are greater, and the administration-administrators are superior. These same factors, however, are not so influential in the actual choice process because they cannot be accurately estimated before the fact. The data are consistent with the interpretation that at the point that the choice decision had to be made these factors would have been more important if they could have been more definite. Evidently, the advance rateability of research facilities has exactly the opposite effect upon the decision-making process. Since research facilities can be assessed accurately before taking a job, even small differences are influential in the decision-making process.

that in a substantial number of instances individuals would have liked to base their decisions upon other factors—but neither the best nor the second-best job offer promised as much of the factor as would have been desired: for example, a professor might reply, when asked why he accepted the job at Siberia College rather than Outer Mongolia College, that the decision was made on the basis of the courses to be taught at the two schools. In his answer he does not indicate that he would have preferred to make the decision on the basis of the prestige of the institutions but was unable to do so because neither school offered any. In short, the Choice Index measures the importance of factors when choosing between two real world alternatives, not the factors desired in a dream job.

Finally, the Choice Index is limited because it considers only reasons for job choice and ignores reasons for job switch. The Choice Index rates the importance of factors when deciding among two competitive offers; it does not consider the factors stressed when deciding whether or not to leave a previously held job.[14]

To compensate for these shortcomings of the Choice Index, it is desirable to extend the discussion.

THE MINIMALLY ACCEPTABLE JOB

To determine the factors that make jobs unacceptable, the persons who left their last college teaching position because it was "unacceptable and I had a strong desire to move" were asked to check the one or two most important reasons for their wanting to leave. The list of options, and distribution of checks, is given in table 68.

Four of the first five factors in the list are the same as the five most important factors according to the Choice Index. The courses to be taught, teaching load required, research facilities offered, and salary paid are factors taken into consideration at all stages of the choice-making process. Not only are they important determinants when choosing between the two best job options but they are also important factors in determining the most marginally acceptable (and unacceptable) jobs. These four factors not only provide the basis for decision-making in the final round, but also in preliminary stages.

Similarly, environmental factors such as nearness to friends and relatives, cultural opportunities, and climate—factors which are

[14] Unless the previously held job is the next best alternative.

rarely determinative at the final stages of choice-making—tend to be equally insignificant when determining criteria for the minimally acceptable job. Likewise, fringe benefits and opportunities for outside income are equally inconsequential at both the beginning and the final stages of decision-making.

68

Reasons for Leaving Unacceptable Jobs

Reason	Percentage Checking[a]
Administration and administrators not competent	35
Research facilities and opportunities poor	16
Teaching hours excessive	16
Salary too low	15
Courses assigned undesirable	14
Advancement prospects in academic rank poor	13
Colleagues not competent	12
Colleagues not congenial	9
Reputation of school among scholars poor	7
Quality of students poor	7
Future salary prospects poor	6
Cultural opportunities poor	6
Climate undesirable	6
Fringe benefits poor	3
Friends and relatives too far away	0
Opportunities for outside income poor	0

[a] Percentages exceed 100 because one individual could check two factors.
Source: survey data.

In fact, the lists in table 64 and 68 are very much the same throughout, except for one factor, administrators and administration. Only ninth in importance in the final stages of decision-making, the attitudes and abilities of top management are *by far* the most important element in defining the minimally acceptable job. This factor is mentioned by more than one-third of all professors leaving jobs that they rate as unacceptable and is mentioned more than twice as frequently as any other single factor.

The implications are clear. Though professors will consider jobs where the teaching hours are excessive, the salaries are low, and so forth—they will not give a second thought to job opportunities where the administrators are viewed as incompetent, misdirected, or improperly constrained. It is at the very beginning stages of the de-

cision-making process that the professorial insistence upon independence of action and academic freedom is effected. The conviction
that every college teacher must have the freedom to decide how and
what he teaches and researches is so strongly imbedded in the professorial psyche that the right of independence of action is the *primary*
determinant of job choice. This one factor is so important that jobs
not promising independence are eliminated without further consideration. Academic freedom is a minimum requirement for all jobs.

It is most deceptive to conclude on the basis of the Choice Index
that the attitude and ability of administrators is the ninth most important factor in job choice. In fact, it is the most important. It is so
important that virtually all jobs that do not offer acceptable top
management never reach the "finals."

THE IDEAL JOB: EL DORADO

To compensate for another limitation of the Choice Index rating,
an attempt was made to identify the factors present in ideal jobs by
asking, "If you could teach at any school in the United States, where
would you like to teach most?" By analyzing the prestige, the size,
and other characteristics of the institutions listed, a vision of the
ideal job can be developed.

Unfortunately, the picture of the "ideal" job cannot be as complete as that of the minimally acceptable one. Sole reliance must be
placed upon the information available from knowledge of only the
name of the school (location, quality, control, highest degree offered,
size). Although these general characteristics will allow a limited
number of inferences about the importance of other factors (at the
larger schools teaching loads tend to be lower, for example), it is impossible to judge job characteristics that depend upon individual situations such as salary, rank, and nearness to friends and relatives.
Even so, an analysis of the ideal job can provide a valuable supplement to the Choice Index rating of factors.

In response to the "El Dorado" question, professors tended to
identify three distinct sets of institutions: (a) their present employers
(20 percent); (b) an alma mater (25 percent); or (c) a large, northeastern (or western), public (or nondenominational private), first-
quality university.[15] The salient characteristics of the institutions

---

[15] Because special factors undoubtedly influence the selection of institutions of
previous attendance and present employment, the subsequent discussion is based

chosen by the 55 percent who chose an institution other than an alma mater or their current employer are summarized in table 69. Separating out which characteristics of these institutions most attract individuals is extremely difficult, for the large institutions which have the advantage in prestige and in research facilities also have better than average student bodies and more attractive teaching assignments. Strong multicollinearities exist.

The size of the institution, for example, can indicate a host of conclusions about the ideal position. Size is a reliable estimate of research possibilities. Economies of scale, whereby several faculty members use the same facilities without getting in each other's way, and the generally large budgets of the big schools enable them to supply their faculties with better laboratories and larger libraries. Larger departments allow more specialization and greater cross-fertilization of research ideas among department members. It may be possible to give examples of large schools with minimal research facilities and small schools with excellent ones, but such examples are exceptions. That almost all of the research-minded college teachers are currently locating in the larger schools and envision the larger schools as El Dorado is another indication of the positive relationship between size and research opportunities.[16]

The larger schools, with some exceptions, offer graduate degrees. This is important because certain prerequisites, making teaching positions more desirable, are usually paired with graduate-level teaching. In addition to better research facilities and opportunities, these

---

upon only that 55 percent of all El Dorado's with which individuals have no obvious connection. Before leaving behind the group of professors who identified their current jobs as their El Dorado's, it is pertinent to mention one piece of evidence that reaffirms the conclusion of the earlier section, "words and actions." In this section, evidence was presented to show that professors tend to choose the job offers that promise more of the very variables that they rate as most important. Spearman's rank correlation coefficient run between the Choice Index and the Merit Index was .89. This same test, when run on that group of professors who have just moved to their El Dorado, yields a slightly higher correlation coefficient, an indication that when an individual actually has the option of choosing his "ideal job" his actions are even more in conformity with his words.

[16] Of all newly hired professors who state that they spend more time researching than teaching, 60 percent are currently located in large schools (student bodies over 5,000), and 76 percent envision their ideal jobs in a large school. The comparable percentages for those who spend more time teaching are 31 percent and 59 percent.

69

Characteristics of El Dorado's Other Than Institutions of Current Employment or of Previous Attendance[a]

CHARACTERISTIC	PERCENTAGE
Control	
Public	48
Private nondenominational	40
Protestant	9
Roman Catholic	3
Quality	
Top 20 percent	51
20 to 40 percent	16
40 to 60 percent	15
Bottom 40 percent	17
Size	
Over 5,000 students	63
1,000 to 5,000 students	27
Under 1,000 students	10
Level	
University	73
College	24
Junior college	3
Location	
North Atlantic	33
West and Southwest	33
Great Lakes and Plains	21
Southeast	13

[a] The El Dorado school is that given in response to the question: "If you could teach at any school in the United States, where would you like to teach most?"

Source: survey data.

include graduate student protégés, lower teaching loads, and more prestige. For comparably qualified individuals, the weighted average of hours of teaching required is nine at the university level and twelve in the four-year college.

The link between "prestige" and the "presence of a graduate school" is less measurable but nevertheless significant. For the teaching-oriented professor, the presence of a graduate school often means better students and greater challenges. To the research-oriented professor, the graduate school situation offers greater possibilities for publishing, greater potential for research grants,[17] and superior facilities to carry out research projects.

Academic freedom is a dear and precious element of the teaching

[17] In 1965, 100 institutions received 77 percent of all federal support to higher education. (*Higher Education and National Affairs,* December 16, 1966, p. 5.)

profession.[18] For virtually all prospective faculty members it is an essential characteristic of all jobs considered. As a rule with notable and tragic exceptions, faculty at the larger institutions, especially the ones which are privately financed and beyond the control of a religious sect, are less bound by constraints placed upon the ideas and issues aired in higher education settings. The greatest number of problems about academic freedom arise in the public institutions of conservative states and privately financed, denominationally related schools where misguided outsiders, failing to understand the meaning and method of liberal education, regard sponsorship as a license to maintain the school as their private preserve for propaganda dissemination and one-sided "education."[19] These same schools, limited by inadequate financing, are rarely large. Accordingly, of all the El Dorado institutions, 47 percent are under private nondenominational control and another 39 percent are under public control in a nonsoutheastern state. Less than 50 percent of all institutions, these more loosely controlled schools account for a total of 87 percent of all El Dorado choices. When an individual chooses his El Dorado from the more tightly controlled categories of schools, he overwhelmingly chooses a school under the control of his own religion or denomination.

Summary

From all of these attempts to ascertain the determinants of job choice, a reasonably accurate vision of the choice-making process evolves. Setting the standards by which individual jobs are judged are the background influences, especially the schools attended. Although some individuals are more deeply impressed by the attitudes and objectives of their undergraduate alma maters, the average college teacher comes to believe that the best teaching jobs are in large, prestigious universities—probably while in graduate school. For

[18] Paul F. Lazarsfeld and Wagner Thielens, Jr. *The Academic Mind* (Glencoe, Ill.: The Free Press, 1958).

[19] An analysis of the "censured administrations" listed by the American Association of University Professors (*AAUP Bulletin,* December 1964, p. 310) shows that of the 17 institutions listed—eight of the eleven public schools are in the conservative Southeast and Texas and only two of the schools are nondenominational and private. The University of Illinois, which is conspicuously atypical of the list, is the only institution on the list that was cited as an El Dorado.

many, however, this ideal is not realistic. They must choose among the jobs that are actually offered to them.

The first criterion on which choices are made is the attitude and ability of the institution's top management. Job offers that fail to offer independence of action and competent leadership are usually rejected at the very beginning stages of the search-choice procedure. As the field of job options narrows to the two best, the decision to accept one offer and reject the other is usually based upon the characteristics of the job itself—especially the courses to be taught, the teaching load, and the competency of the colleagues. Environmental factors such as the availability of cultural opportunities and climate play an insignificant role. Although large salary differentials influence the direction of mobility, especially when the salaries considered are quite low in terms of the average earnings of academicians, this factor is rarely the primary determinant of job choice. Other aspects of compensation such as opportunities for outside income, rank, and fringe benefits rarely influence decisions in the final stages of choice-making. Professors appear to be most concerned about what, how, and how much they work. Of less concern are where and under what terms.

7

Recommendations

This study was designed with twin objectives—one theoretical and the other practical. Since the major implications for economic theory are not of general interest to noneconomists, they are treated summarily in the next section. Economists wishing more detail should consult *Academic Labor Markets*.[1] The main burden of this chapter is to suggest how the enterprise of higher education might be improved as a result of this study. Although the policy implications of the foregoing analysis have been alluded to throughout, it is desirable to take a step toward a summary by consolidating them in one chapter.

Implications for Wage and Employment Theory

A wage and employment theory that is meaningful for professional workers must incorporate the following elements:

1. A concept of "net advantage" that transcends salary alone. Job attractions are work environment and duties, living situation and research facilities—not only salary. The "utility" gained from work exceeds the satisfaction from consuming the goods bought by the paycheck and includes satisfaction from performing a socially useful and enjoyable mission.

2. A concept of a "unit of labor" that accounts for the widely varied productivity of different men in an hour's time. The freedom of

[1] David G. Brown, *Academic Labor Markets,* A Report to the Office of Manpower, Automation and Training, U.S. Department of Labor, 1965.

professional jobs, which allows men both to succeed magnificently and fail drastically, contributes to widely varied productivity and accentuates the inappropriateness of the assumption that all units of labor are equal. A meaningful theory must, it seems, measure units of labor in terms of tasks accomplished (output efficiency) instead of hours contributed.

3. A concept of a labor market that is bounded by skill differences instead of miles. Whereas the local labor market concept has meaning for occupations where retraining workers is cheaper and faster than relocating, in the professions the costs of training and the benefits of experience dictate that employers draw boundaries that are related to what a man can do instead of how convenient is it for him to come.

4. A concept of labor demand that is derived from the consumer desire for professional services and is immensely complicated by the immeasurability of output.

5. A concept of labor supply that is, in the view of an individual college, responsive to salary changes and is, in the view of all colleges, responsive to modifications of employment requirements (a new willingness to hire non-Ph.D.'s where before only Ph.D.'s were acceptable, for example).

6. A concept of market equilibrium that is dynamic.

Implications for Public Policy

It is tempting to leave the reader with a series of guarded generalizations—the labor market should be improved; candidates and employers should approach the market more intelligently and rationally; the overall supply of manpower to the nation's colleges should be increased. Though relevant, such statements have limited value; they fail to advance suggestions as to how markets may be improved, what more rational approaches to the market might be taken, and how supply can be increased. At the risk of raising criticism and controversy, I have decided to make recommendations that are specific and concrete. Presented below are plans of action that, after analyzing the information available, I believe should be taken as steps toward improving the flow of manpower in academic labor markets. The recommendations are presented in three sections according to which group might best take the step suggested. In the case of "the society," any number of groups might act as "society's agent."

FOR SOCIETY

Recommendation 1. Two major steps should be taken to increase the flow of information in the academic labor market: (1) *a "Journal of Academic Vacancies" should be published, and* (2) *"The Academic Register" should be established.* These two recommendations represent the major suggestions growing out of this study.

Journal of Academic Vacancies. This publication would list and briefly describe openings in four-year colleges and universities. Any institution of higher education could list as many vacancies as desired without charge. Vacancies would be arranged by subject matter specialty (discipline) and, within each discipline, ordered by salary. The Journal would be published monthly, except July, September, and October.

The Journal would be published in two forms. The complete edition of the Journal would be published for use by college placement offices, commercial placement agencies, other placement intermediaries, and potential employers. This might be sold for an annual fee of between $50 and $100. The Journal could be made available on punch cards if desired. Summary statistics on the salaries offered to Ph.D.'s in various disciplines, the average beginning ranks offered, and so forth, would be included to assist employers in framing job specifications and counselors working with job-seeking candidates. Separate "discipline issues" would be prepared and mailed to individuals who subscribed for, say, $3 per year, or sold (at a large discount) to professional associations who could distribute them as supplements to their scholarly journals.

The main problem with any published list of vacancies is obtaining the interested cooperation of institutions. If the suggestion of a journal is a good one—and I believe it is—there will be no problem once it gets started. To begin, however, it will be essential to wage a concerted, personalized campaign and to elicit the cooperation of the placement intermediaries. The larger of the college placement offices, for example, receive over 10,000 vacancy notices per year. Upon receiving a notice they might return a note to the notifying employer asking him to "check here and return" if he would not object to his vacancy being publicized in the newly established journal.

The Academic Register. A nationwide inventory of manpower capable of teaching at the college level, the Register would list not only those currently looking for jobs and those currently employed by academic institutions but *all* persons who have the graduate-level training that might allow them to teach in college. The Register would be similar to the National Science Foundation's Technical and Scientific Manpower Register.

Individuals would be encouraged to complete forms for the Register by their professional association, and their college placement office, their graduate school, and other appropriate organizations and individuals. Registration would be free of charge. Only one leaf, the form would ask for basic information about the individual, his activities and accomplishments, degrees obtained and granting institution, disciplinary specialties and subspecialties, extent and character of publications and other career-related accomplishments, courses taught, age, and employment experience relevant to academic employment. At the bottom of the form would be a question such as "are you interested in relocation?"

The information would be transferred to punch cards at the central office. An employer could then request a "search of the cards" for the most appropriate candidates, defining his needs as specifically as he might desire. The employers requesting such service might be charged $10 per search. At the time of registration individuals would be given the option of requesting to be notified of suitable vacancies for a fee of, say, $5.

The issues involved. There are many details to both plans that could be specified, but these skeleton descriptions are sufficient to indicate a position on the major issues involved. Let us look in detail at each of these.

1. Is a centralized "placement facilities" necessary and desirable? My answer obviously is "yes." But why? Thirty-five percent of the newly hired college teachers rate the current opportunities to learn about vacancies as "poor" or "very poor." Employers are continually calling for more and better channels of communication. Candidates and employers are seeking help from different intermediaries and neither is as satisfied as he might have been if the two had gone to the same intermediary.

In addition, I am convinced that the excessive proliferation of intermediaries is weakening all of them. There are so many that in order to reach even a majority of the job-seeking candidates an employer must mail hundreds of notices. Intermediaries throughout the country—college placement offices as well as commercial employment agencies—complain that too much of their time is spent in merely processing these requests. Each is doing essentially the same thing—translating these into a standard form and cataloguing for future reference. Much work and effort would be spared if this clerical task were done only once, and the results were shared by all. Centralization of the processing would reduce the workload of the hiring institutions. Most importantly, it would tend to increase the chances that candidate and vacancy are placed in "pools" that come in contact one with the other to better insure that all vacancies and all candidates have an opportunity to be paired.

2. To what extent should the centralization be pursued? My answer is "limited." Many aspects of effective placement assistance cannot be centralized. A computerized locator service is no better than the instructions fed into the computer. As proposed, the Journal and the Register would probably increase rather than decrease the need for assistance in decision-making. The present placement intermediaries would need to continue in their work as "instruction experts" who define the parameters for the individuals and institutions with whom they have personal contact. In the case of the Journal, all candidates are exposed to all jobs. There is no preselection. Jobs are not rated, openings are not referred. The Journal is simply a resource instrument. In the case of the Register, the preselection role played by the central office is greater, but still leaves a great deal of discretion to the user. Instead of attempting to identify the one best candidate for a given job, the Register would provide names of twenty-five or so candidates. From these, either the employer or his agent would necessarily have to make further cuts. If the employer was not satisfied with the names he received, he could request a computer rerun with slightly different parameters. It is important that at no point should the Register "ration" names of available candidates.

3. Should a centralized system be entirely new or should it be tied in with the existing placement system? I am convinced that the success of any consolidated system rests upon the enthusiastic cooperation of existing placement intermediaries. There are a number of services essential in the placement process that neither the Journal

nor the Register offer. First, there are no provisions for the collection of recommendations and the mailing of dossiers. It would be hoped that college placement offices, or the graduate school offices, would continue to assume responsibility for maintaining these credentials.

Second, and most important, there are no provisions for counseling. The very nature of the two proposals is such that counseling is almost impossible. Yet, many individuals need advice on what to look for in jobs and how to approach the market. The professional association, the college placement office, the graduate school department, and the advisor of the Ph.D. thesis would still be an essential element in the placement process.

Third, at least in the transition stages, both candidates and employers would need to be urged to use the Journal and the Register. The success of these innovations will be enhanced if the existing placement intermediaries will distribute application forms and encourage registration. Many of the intermediaries may prefer not to suggest direct registration but to register the candidates who come to them, or the job vacancies, themselves.

Completely centralized placement is neither necessary nor desirable. There are strengths in pluralism which must not be lost. Uniformity would be tragic. The existing network capitalizes upon special interests. Most of the more active placement liaisons serve two needs simultaneously: their own needs and the needs of the market; for example, college placement offices, the departmental offices of graduate schools, and the professional mentors of graduate students work to place their products and, in the process, enhance their own reputations as well as that of the candidate. Well-placed protégés serve as appropriate advertisements and thereby enhance the school's prestige and the individual's prestige as well.

Each type of placement organization has a special role to fill. The consolidation that occurs must be cognizant of these special roles. What might be gained through economies of scale, by decreasing the obscurity of liaisons, and by widening the scope of any given labor pool, must not be lost by losing the strength that diversity affords. The consolidation must unify but not destroy. The solution is to consolidate some functions of placement services while strengthening other functions within the current organizational structures.

4. By whom should the Journal and the Register be managed and

financed? The answer is "they should be managed by an independently organized, private, nonprofit corporation and financed by whoever is willing."

The most crucial element in the success of the Journal and the Register is gaining the acceptance of the academic community. Any placement effort is sure to fail without a strong and enthusiastic endorsement by the community of scholars and the endorsement of organizations such as the American Council on Education; the Association of American Colleges; the regional accrediting associations; the Association for School, College, and University Staffing; the College Placement Council; the American Association of University Professors; the church-related boards of education; the Association for Higher Education; the American Association of University Women; and the many disciplinary professional associations. Only if a large number of these organizations are willing to have their names associated with the effort will the Journal and Register be guaranteed the respectability and acceptance that is crucial. For this reason I suggest that an independent corporation be established for the sole purpose of publishing the Journal and maintaining the Register, a corporation similar to the National Merit Scholarship Corporation.

As for financing, at least in the beginning when the Register is becoming established and when the Journal must be given extensive publicity, the small fees proposed will not cover expenses. Funding will be necessary. Hopefully, the effort will be sponsored by a major five-year grant from a large, private foundation. If, however, funds are not available from this source, the feasibility of financing with government funds should be investigated. Although the current study gives many strong indications that a publicly controlled, centralized placement facility will not be accepted by the academic community, it may be that a privately controlled and publicly financed effort could be devised that would gain acceptance.

Although I have not developed specific cost estimates, there is no doubt that the sums involved would be substantial. If the scientific professional associations would cooperate by releasing the forms which most of their members have completed for the Technical and Scientific Manpower Register, the total expense would be reduced considerably but still would be sizeable.

5. Should registration by candidates and employers be compulsory or optional? In both instances, my answer would be "optional." The

aim would be to provide a service so valuable that few candidates and employers could afford not to register their needs. Although a complete listing of candidates and vacancies would definitely be desirable, the "manpower control" overtones and the enforcement problems of compulsory registration speak in favor of allowing individuals and employers not to register. Moreover, any attempt at compulsory registration would so alienate the academic community that the efforts would be sure to fail.

"Optional" does not mean, however, that strenuous efforts should not be made to elicit complete registration. In all instances, individual graduate schools should be encouraged to advise strongly their emerging students to place their name in the Register and consult the Journal. Educational associations such as the American Council on Education, the Association of American Colleges, and the regional accrediting associations should be encouraged to urge their members to list vacancies. Several of the more prestigious institutions should probably be approached about including their vacancies in the initial issues of the Journal so as to increase its acceptance and respectability. Pressure should be applied, but the option of not listing should be allowed.

6. Should employers be exposed to candidates, or should candidates be exposed to employers? Here the question is a matter of ordering. One technique that might be pursued by a placement intermediary would be to collect information on many candidates and distribute it to prospective employers. The opposite technique would be to develop a list of job vacancies and distribute it to candidates.

As the proposals imply, I believe that both techniques are necessary. In a shortage market, such as that which exists today, candidates may be particular about the jobs they select. Employers understandably resent expending a great deal of effort pursuing candidates who will not accept the jobs offered. The publicizing of vacancies allows candidates to preselect employers. In most instances candidates will contact only those employers for whom they would be willing to work (under certain realistic terms). At the same time, the traditions of the academic labor market are such that many candidates are timid about active job-seeking. They are only on the fringes of the labor market. They are not even sure that they are interested in pursuing alternative employment unless and until a specific opportunity comes along. These individuals will never respond to advertised jobs available; many will never read them. Only an employment register, one that includes candidates who are not actively in the market, can provide a solution to the marginal nature of participation of individuals in the academic labor market.

7. Should individuals and institutions be allowed to remain anonymous? My answer: "No" in both cases. The name of an institution can be very helpful in evaluating the job opportunity. At the same time, there seems to be little value to the school of withholding its name. It is true that if an obviously underqualified candidate replies to a "box number," the school may forever remain anonymous and does not need to reply. At the present time it is also true that there may be a certain "unrespectability" about advertising in professional journals and that the withholding of a name must be done to "save face." But both of these disadvantages may be easily overcome. In the first instance, the Journal may, perhaps at the top of each page, include a brief statement to the effect that if an employer does not respond within two weeks it may be expected that he is not interested. Or, a standard form letter may be developed by institutions. As for "unrespectability," this will be overcome by the very publication of names. Already there are some quite respectable academic institutions that are advertising vacancies in professional journals. When newly solicited vacancies from very respectable institutions are added to these most administrators will realize that the sanctions that at one time may have been placed upon those who advertise no longer prevail.

As for individuals, there is little need for anonymity. Listing with the Register is not a statement that the individual is looking for a job. It is simply a statement that he is a chemist, a historian, a mathematician. The only safeguard that seems necessary under the presently proposed Register is not to refer the names of persons currently teaching at college A to the administration of college A.

8. Should the Journal and the Register be extended to include junior college teachers and high school teachers? At this time our answer is "no." Again, the major concern is gaining the acceptance of the academic community. At least until the Register and the Journal are firmly established as respectable instruments it is important not to dilute their respectability with large numbers of underqualified applicants and professionally less respectable jobs. Once established, it may be feasible to enlarge coverage.

At the beginning, a minimum requirement for membership in the Registry should probably be either a master's degree or the holding of a teaching assignment at a four-year college or university. At the beginning nonacademic employers, junior colleges, and other noncollegiate employers should probably be denied participation.

Recommendation 2. An inexpensive pocketbook or pamphlet on "How to Find a College Teaching Job" should be written and distributed widely. Included should be brief statements about the qualifications normally required of individuals who teach in various types of institutions of higher learning and in various disciplines, the types of placement assistance that are available and the names and addresses of these intermediaries, the "ethics of job-seeking" such as the May 15 deadline on resigning appointments, the average salary levels and rank attainments of beginning Ph.D.'s in various disciplines, and a pertinent bibliography. A checklist of the factors that might be considered when choosing a job, such as the 17 factors discussed in chapter 6, would be valuable. By thus providing information that will allow individuals to make more intelligent marketing decisions, the efficiency of the labor market should be increased and the frequency of incorrect moves should be reduced.

Recommendation 3. Market information should be more widely publicized. For example, current information on the salaries being offered by other schools would be generally helpful to prospective employers. (It may be that the Journal of Academic Vacancies proposed above could make such general data available to collegiate employers.) General information on methodologies of approaching the market might also be helpful to academic employers. In many institutions the employment process is delegated to department heads, the turnover of which is such that no one man has a great deal of experience in hiring. Although much of what needs to be known is transmitted by the chairman's superior and predecessor, the distribution of a booklet similar to that prepared for candidates would probably be helpful. One suggestion might be simply to orient a section of the pocketbook for candidates toward employers.

Recommendation 4. Professional associations should be encouraged to offer placement services at their annual meetings. The annual meetings in many disciplines are involving increasing numbers of individuals so that the previously informal methods of communication are no longer adequate. More formal structures are needed.

Convention placement services have earned the respect and attention of many members of the academic community. In many disciplines they are currently providing a valuable and needed service, proving that such formal structures are possible. Innovations—advance registration, the provision of adequate interviewing space, the process of self-selecting of candidates and of jobs, and the flexible provisions allowing anonymity—have advanced the art of convention placement service to a degree that most disciplines would find it helpful. The United States Employment Service is often willing to take on both the mangement and financing of such services. Professional associations should be encouraged to inquire.

The associations not already doing so might consider scheduling their annual meetings during the recruiting season, between November and May. Few will deny that one of the main contributions of the professional association meeting is the provision of an opportunity to talk about jobs. Summer and early fall meetings are poorly timed; most institutions and individuals have not yet assessed their situation for the year ahead.

Recommendation 5. Graduate school departments should appoint a faculty member as liaison with the college placement office. The college placement office has valuable services to offer prospective college teachers and their professors. Even if the department desires to maintain control of the matching of candidates and jobs in the time-honored tradition of informal placement, it behooves the departmental faculty to delegate some of the more routine chores to an office that has the facilities and staff to handle them and unburden the department of the responsibility of processing large numbers of job vacancies and of developing and distributing candidate credentials.

Recommendation 6. Graduate schools should consider the possibility of requiring candidates for graduate degrees to develop a credential file with the placement office. The file should include an official grade transcript, at least three letters of recommendation from graduate school professors written at a time when the candidate is still well remembered by the writers, and a form on which standard information, such as age, publications, and job experience, are entered. Once developed, this credential file serves as a lifelong reference. (The advantages of having a credential file are developed under recommendation 24.)

FOR HIRERS OF COLLEGE TEACHERS

Recommendation 7. Recruitment strategy should be based on extensive knowledge of the market and varied according to the type of man sought. Much effort is dissipated in unnecessary activity while, at the same time, recruitment efforts are not sufficiently extensive. As the search commences, it is important to identify the object of the hunt; to specify the type of person the institution would like to hire (rank, research versus teaching emphasis, subspecialty) and would be able to attract. Realistic terms should be attached to the job and expectations should be properly framed in the light of these terms. Too often a recruiter goes to the market looking for a well-trained Ph.D. without the wherewithal to attract him. Naturally he returns home without his catch which gives rise to still another round of recruitment in which either the terms of employment must be made more attractive or quality standards lowered.

Each institution should know the "hunting grounds" in which it is most likely to be successful. College teachers have definite preferences for and against teaching in a church-related setting, in a large university, in a particular region. Recruiters should recognize these contours and take advantage of them. By narrowing the field, the search becomes more surmountable.

Recruiters could avoid a great deal of wasted effort if they would educate themselves about the major sources of supply and the characteristics of the faculty found at these sources. To state the obvious it is unwise to be looking for a department chairman in the high schools just as it is poor strategy to seek someone to teach 15 hours of elementary-level courses from the faculty of major graduate schools. As much, if not more effort may be saved by developing the type of knowledge that the University of Michigan is a major producer of Ph.D.'s in music, that the University of North Carolina has one of the top-rated sociology departments, that Harvard University offers no doctorate in geography.

Finally, it is important for recruiters to know the traditions in various disciplines and in various graduate schools. Whereas it is usual for a person to leave graduate school before receiving his degree if his field is English, the non-Ph.D. in chemistry should be regarded with suspicion. Similarly, even within the same discipline individual graduate schools differ in their desires for their students to have a full-time teaching experience before getting their degree.

I would not suggest that one recruiter may be expected to develop all of this information and still maintain his regular faculty appointment. All that would be hoped is that recruiters recognize the relevancy of such information when approaching the market and do the best they can to use the information they do have.

Recommendation 8. Well-planned recruiting trips to the campuses should be considered. Similar to the descent of industrial recruiters upon the graduating seniors, the campus visit is becoming increasingly popular with academic recruiters. An efficient means of contacting a large number of candidates with a minimum amount of effort and expense, the success of these trips is heavily dependent upon advance planning.

It is important, of course, that the recruiter alert officials well in advance so that prospective candidates may be lined up. But it must be realized that 25 percent of newly hired college faculty *do nothing* to seek their jobs. Professors remain timid, reluctant to make known their availability. Many of the best qualified never enter the market and must be sought out. It is the recruiter's responsibility to identify methods for contacting these individuals.

The academic labor market is still primarily an informal one. If at all possible, it is best to visit campuses where entrees into the informal market exist: for example, the college dean contemplating a recruitment trip might check with his faculty to learn if anyone knows personally a faculty member at the school he is to visit and, if so, urge a letter of introduction.

If planning well, the recruiter will get a chance to talk with far more candidates than would consider actually visiting his campus. Moreover, during these visits it is often possible to talk with persons who know of candidates at other schools who might be qualified and interested. If the recruiter is convincing, he may actually influence the choice process of prospective faculty so that they do not eliminate his institution from consideration without at least a visit to his campus.

Recommendation 9. Department chairmen should nurture professional contracts. The predominance of grapevine placement suggests that the maintenance of informal contacts is extremely important for a recruiting department. To nourish such relationships, it is important to pay expenses to professional meetings and encourage attendance, to encourage participation in professional association government, to urge membership on national commissions, and to understand some of the side benefits of certain types of consulting. Adequate telephone budgets and secretarial assistance also aid recruitment.

Recommendation 10. Curricula flexibility should be maintained. Considering only the implication for the staffing problem, there is strong evidence in favor of maintaining sufficient flexibility in curriculum to enable the addition of a new course in the subspecialty of a prospective new faculty member or the deletion of an old one that he does not want to teach. With the possible exception of the attitude and ability of administrators, the courses that a prospective professor would be asked to teach are the most important determinant of job choice. When staffing problems become acute, an individual institution may be able to attract faculty by letting them, within limits, "write their own tickets."

Almost as important in job choice is the number of hours of classroom teaching required by two competitive job offers. The institution that wishes to attract the higher qualified man might well consider allowing experimentation in class size and teaching technology (for example, educational television) to reduce, at least somewhat, teaching loads.

Recommendation 11. Above all, an institution must establish and maintain a confidence in the academic community. If it is to be successful in recruitment, an institution must have a reputation for freedom of thought and action. If such a reputation does not exist, a substantial majority of prospective college faculty will not even consider a vacancy at that school, no matter how attractive the offer might otherwise be.

Recommendation 12. Smaller colleges should, whenever possible, cooperate with nearby institutions in developing research facilities for their faculties. This may involve working out an arrangement for library permits for college faculty at a nearby university, access to a large computer, or shared professorships. In some cases, it may be advisable for several smaller schools to bind together in a cooperative effort to coordinate their library purchases and to purchase jointly a computer.

The importance of developing such facilities is indicated by the consistent statements of academic scientists (and to a lesser extent social scientists) that among seventeen factors the most important determinant of job choice is the research facilities provided. Without providing these facilities the smaller institutions cannot expect to compete for faculty with the larger colleges and universities, at least not in the more research-oriented disciplines, and for the better qualified staff.

Recommendation 13. The nonequalitarian salary structures currently existing should not be substantially altered. The argument that it is best to pay the physicst, musicologist, historian, and electrical engineer approximately the same salary because all have undergone extensive and costly training, all contribute to the vitality of the academic community, all are college professors and may be expected to maintain similar social circles, all are specialists in their field, is dangerously fallacious. The salary of a professor is not dictated by inherent worth or training expense. Salary is determined by scarcity value.

If five top-notch theologians are willing to supply themselves to a small Methodist college for $7,000 per year and not even a mediocre chemist can be found and attracted at that price, the institution must decide whether it wants another religion course or a course in chemistry. If it wants the chemistry course it must pay the price the chemist demands. By dividing its markets and paying high salaries to professors in scarcity disciplines and low salaries to ones in surplus disciplines an institution is able to maximize the value of limited funds.

An analogous situation arises even within the same discipline when the institution must "capitalize" on the noneconomic ties of its longer-service faculty by paying them less than it would have to pay for equivalent talent on the open market to free funds to compete with more wealthy institutions at the beginning ranks. Few would deny that penalizing those who have been most loyal is undesirable. But I think that many will agree with me that, when faced with the choice of hiring second-rate faculty to pay old faculty equitable salaries, remaining competitive may be most important. There is a breaking point, the point at which the old faculty rebel, morale is broken, and the teaching-learning process ceases. Within this limit, however, the policy of paying different salaries according to scarcity value is well conceived and should be continued.

However, given the low rating of rank in job choice, it may be that arguing for the granting of promotions at an earlier stage in the scarcity disciplines is not justified. I am inclined to believe that it might be wise for individual institutions to offer rank on an egalitarian basis to preserve an intracampus, interdisciplinary measure of worth and experience—and to allow the salary differentials *only* to be dictated by the markets exogenous to the individual campus.

Recommendation 14. New appointments should be made without tenure. Usually ranks of associate and full professor automatically carry with them the right of tenure, of lifetime job security. For the institutions with such tenure provisions, hiring at the associate and full professor levels involves substantial risks. There is no opportunity to correct misjudgments. These risks do not need to be taken. Evidence strongly suggests that moves are made for motives different than rank and security in the vast majority of instances. Most movers are sufficiently well qualified not to worry. Since the immediate granting of tenure does involve risks and since the job-changing professors are not particularly concerned about tenure, it would seem wise for schools to consider a policy whereby all new faculty, regardless of the "hiring in" rank, are on probation for at least one year.

Recommendation 15. Employers should recruit more actively and advertise more openly. The current balance of the supply of and demand for college faculty is such that the recruiter cannot be complacent and expect to hire the best people. The imperfect academic labor market often hides the best qualified candidate. Moreover, it is the very best qualified candidates who are on the market for the least amount of time and who often never reach the market.

Although the advertising of vacancies cannot be so overt that it violates the prospective faculty member's vision of "acceptable behavior" for a reputable academic institution (newspaper want ads and the like), publicity efforts can be widened considerably without endangering this limit. Surprisingly few methods are generally regarded by college teachers as "unprofessional."

The fear that a well-advertised job will bring avalanches of applications, though partially valid, is substantially unfounded. Evidence suggests that the candidates themselves have relatively accurate self-images that allow them to discriminate the jobs for which they will be seriously considered from those for which many better qualified candidates will be available.

There is a large segment of supply on the fringes of the academic labor market that cannot be drawn to a job by any means other than advertising. At all times there are a number of college teachers who are susceptible to job offers but hardly realize it themselves. If they hear about the right opportunity, they will apply. But if they do not hear, no one will know they would have been available. This type of relationship to the market is particularly frequent among many individuals who are not currently teaching at the college level but are qualified to do so. Unusually large numbers of these "nonacademics" must be drawn out of business, government, and the high schools by specific and concrete job offers. These potential sources of supply will be lost to the employer who chooses not to advertise and recruit.

Recommendation 16. Employers with accession rates substantially different from the norm (about 18 percent) should investigate and determine why. High turnover rates may indicate frequent administrative blunders, unusually low faculty morale, or a large number of other problems which might be subject to correction. The continuance of high turnover is costly both in terms of the instability imposed on the students and research as well as the not inconsiderable cost of finding and attracting new staff. However, on the other hand, high accession rates may indicate a program of rapid expansion.

Low rates of turnover may indicate lack of vitality and a complacency in the faculty. Too much stability may mean new staff is not being added to advance new ideas and question old ones. It may mean that the staff is so poorly regarded by other colleges that no one is willing to make an offer. However, low accession rates may be the successful result of a concerted effort toward faculty retention.

There is nothing wrong per se with accession rates considerably different from the norm. The cause of the variance should however be examined.

For Individuals Seeking New Jobs

Recommendation 17. Individuals should recognize that a price must be paid for remaining at one job and being unwilling to consider seriously alternative offers. With few exceptions, academic institutions have been forced to follow expeditiously the policy of paying high salaries and scheduling low teaching loads where competitive pressures are greatest. This means they must offer premium terms to the newly hired and compensate that portion of their present staff which allows itself to become isolated from competitive markets at less than their competitive value. For the professor who is willing to relocate, almost every move represents an increase in salary and often a higher rank. There is, of course, the point when a work history of too much mobility will make employers suspicious, and they will refuse to offer the usual premiums.

Recommendation 18. Individuals should realize that after age 45 mobility is less acceptable and less possible. Job-shopping in the early years of an academic career is accepted, indeed expected. The market is a large one for the services of the young junior faculty member. As he switches from job to job he develops breadth, exposure, and avoids becoming tied down by large amounts of immobile job capital. He is ready to assume an associate or full professorship, yet many institutions fill these positions by promotion from within. Where before his desire to move about was unquestioned, prospective employers now start to wonder and to ask why he has not as yet settled down.

Recommendation 19. Individuals should be aware of the premiums placed upon different abilities in the academic labor market. Hopefully, the differential scarcity values of various types of college professors will be recognized before the field of graduate study is chosen, but at any stage of a career this knowledge is important for intelligent market behavior. College teachers should know, for example, that engineers are more scarce than mathematicians, research-publishers than teacher-counselors, and Ph.D.'s than non-Ph.D.'s. The importance of obtaining a Ph.D. before entering teaching varies greatly according to discipline specialty. In most of the scientific fields, few persons leave graduate school without the doctorate and those who do are second-class citizens in the academic community. Though the Ph.D. is important for those in English and music, its importance is considerably less than in the data-oriented disciplines.

Recommendation 20. Individuals should realize that decisions made in the early stages of their careers will largely determine their future available courses of action. Although beginning positions at highly prestigious institutions, as contrasted to those at the poorer schools, pay no more, often offer a lower academic rank, give less promise of promotion and of permanent assignment, and demand greater research productivity, these institutions facilitate research by scheduling lower teaching loads, provide better resources, and generate a highly competitive atmosphere conducive to research productivity, and are ports of entry to a wider range of job opportunities.

One primary advantage of an appointment at a highly prestigious institution is the opportunities to which it may lead.

Although it is *always possible* to move up the ladder of academic prestige and although confinement to "scholar's Siberia" is the product of the individual's abilities and ambitions (not artificial barriers between academic institutions of different qualities), resistance to movement down the ladder is more easily accomplished than movement up. It is best to start as an undergraduate at a highly prestigious institution, move to an equally prestigious graduate school, and accept the initial job at an institution of high prestige.

Recommendation 21. Individuals should recognize that starting salaries are not always a valid index of the monetary value of various job options. Competition has forced all academic institutions to pay approximately the same salary to beginning Ph.D.'s. Yet, large salary differentials are common at the associate and full professor levels where competitive pressures are less binding. Moreover, fringe benefits vary widely among schools. In general private schools offer more attractive packages than public ones. There are differences not only in the level of benefits but also in their transferability and vesting that should be considered when choosing among jobs.

Recommendation 22. Checklists of the factors to be considered in job choice should be developed and used. Job choice decisions are complex. There are a large number of influences upon the desirability of competitive job offers. To aid the individual in his decision, a list including factors such as those listed in table 66 should be used to place the various attributes and drawbacks of each job offer on an objective and comprehensive scale.

Recommendation 23. Individuals should educate themselves on the modes of behavior and various methods of finding jobs in the academic market. The individual should know the ethics of behavior required in the various submarkets. He should learn, for example, that the rules for finding senior positions at top prestige institutions do not always apply when seeking appointment at a less well-known and less prestigious school.

Schools, too, having hiring preferences: church-related colleges prefer individuals of the same denomination; women's schools prefer (or at least do not discriminate against) women; top prestige schools demand a record of strong publications for senior positions.

It is important to realize that many intermediaries provide placement help that, in spite of traditional beliefs to the contrary, are used often. Blind letters are an especially productive method of locating job vacancies. Unsolicited letters of inquiry often receive serious consideration and result in good offers. Although the poorer institutions who must hire more because they have higher than average turnover and expansion rates are more prone to follow up blind letters, some of the better employers also consult them.

Individuals should learn about the possibilities of registering with church-related placement services and understand the importance of the professional meeting as a time of placement, especially if an organized placement service has been established.

The importance of nurturing friendships and acquaintances as channels to knowledge about job opportunities should also be appreciated. Responding to this knowledge, individuals should strive to develop professional contacts and to maintain them.

Recommendation 24. A credential file should be developed. Such a dossier is usually requested by employers as an aid in the initial stages of evaluating candidates. Additionally, the dossier is a permanent record useful whenever an individual decides to change jobs. Although the dossier gathered several years prior to the time of job search will certainly need to be updated, it may well include letters of recommendation which cannot be reproduced at a later date.

If, considering a large number of job options, it is unrealistic to ask recommenders to send individual letters of recommendation to all prospective jobs. Instead, a "cooperative dossier" should be developed at a college placement office, a commercial teachers' bureau, or some other placement intermediary, that may be sent to many prospective employers. Even if an individual will not need a dossier when seeking his first job, it is good standard procedure to develop such a record when leaving graduate school.

Recommendation 25. Women should not be discouraged from pursuing careers in college teaching. To some degree the lower salaries paid to women professors, the lesser academic appointments in terms of both academic rank and institutional prestige, and the higher teaching loads reflect the fact that, on the average, women are not as qualified and as committed to an academic career as are men. The woman who is willing not to place constraints such as "I must confine the jobs I consider to within commuting distance of my husband" may expect to receive virtually the same recognition as a man.

A

Methodology

In determining the universe of professors relevant in a mobility study, and the nature of the sample to be drawn from the universe, several important methodological questions need to be resolved.

Definition of the Universe

My intent was to study behavior in the academic labor market. Because theirs is the most recent contact with the market, and therefore the most likely to be remembered, the experiences of professors who have newly arrived at their jobs were collected through questionnaires. The universe is all professors newly hired for the academic year, 1964–65.

By "professors" is meant "all full-time faculty who are responsible for teaching at least one hour of degree credit courses per term." Part-time faculty (persons receiving fractional compensation) are not included, though temporary faculty (persons receiving full pay who are on one-year or terminal appointments) are. Since they are more graduate students than faculty, a special exclusion is full-time faculty who are teaching at the same institution where they are currently working on a degree. Academic administrators (who have no teaching responsibilities) and full-time researchers are not included.

"Newly hired" means all persons added to the payroll of a particular institution. Thus, a man who moves from the University of Missouri to the University of Maine is "newly hired," though he is not a new college teacher in the sense that he has never taught in college before; a man's previous job is irrelevant to his inclusion in the universe.

Realizing that their methods and motives in mobility are not always self-initiated, two groups of persons are arbitrarily excluded: professors who are on active military duty, such as R.O.T.C. professors, and unsalaried members of a religious order.

The universe is further restricted to professors in accredited four-year institutions of higher education in the United States, as listed in the *Education Directory, Part III, 1963–64* of the U.S. Office of Education. Professors in certain professional schools (law, medicine, dentistry, nursing, and pharmacy) are excluded from the universe in the belief that behavior in the markets for these personnel differs substantially from behavior in the markets for arts and sciences faculty.

So limited, the universe includes 28,700. This is approximately one-sixth of all professors. That is, one-sixth of all professors are serving their first year at a new job. The 28,700 figure is derived by counting the names of all newly hired faculty as they were returned by college presidents in response to our request. Actually, the 28,700 figure is an estimate. Ninety-five percent of the college presidents responded to our letter requesting a list of the names of new appointees. To estimate the number of new professors hired by the nonresponding schools, the name count was increased by 3.7 percent, for the total number of students in the nonresponding schools is 3.7 percent of all students in the responding schools (as listed by the American Council on Education in *American Universities and Colleges,* 9th edition, 1964). This estimating procedure rests upon the implicit assumptions that the ratio of the faculty to students is similar in the two groups of schools (responding versus nonresponding) and that turnover rates are also similar.

Sampling Procedure

Each name was placed in a subset, the subsets being defined by the professors' type of employer and field of specialization. Stratified sampling was used. In fact, two different samples were drawn. The first was "balanced" (by discipline) and is used by far the most frequently. It was drawn by mailing a questionnaire to every sixth name appearing on the lists of new appointments from four-year *college* presidents and to every fifth name from the lists submitted by *university presidents.* The larger sampling ratio for university faculty was necessitated by the smaller size of the group when professional school faculty were excluded. The relative size of the faculty at colleges (four-year institutions without graduate programs) versus universities was estimated from COLFACS data.

The second sample was an extension of the first. All persons included in the first sample were also included in the second. But the first sample was too small to allow rigorous analyses in disciplinary detail. There were too few economists, too few electrical engineers, and so forth. Therefore it was necessary to draw supplementary samples for selected disciplines.

As a result of the receipt of a special grant from the National Science

Foundation, questionnaires were sent to all members of the universe in the natural and social sciences (excluding the 3.7 percent of all faculty whose college presidents did not reveal their new appointments). For the other disciplines, supplementary sampling was pursued for English, history, French, elementary education, physical education, and music—disciplines chosen because the number that naturally fell within the balanced sample was already large and the supplementary need was small. With the supplementary sampling, questionnaires were sent to 40 percent of English professors; 60 percent of the professors in music, history, and physical education; and 100 percent in French and elementary education. Again, the variations in sampling percentages reflect size differences in the discipline-specific universes, as estimated from data on all full-time faculty from COLFACS.

Rate of Return and Response Error

Two questionnaires were sent out: the first to college presidents requesting the names of new appointees, and the second to the new appointees asking about their experiences in the academic labor market.

The response to the presidential questionnaire was very high, roughly 95 percent. Moreover, the nonresponse was rather evenly distributed throughout the system of higher education, as shown by table 70. There are no statistically significant variations in the rate of response when the

70

Response by Presidents, by the Characteristics of Their Institutions

Characteristics[a]	Number Responding	Number Not Responding	Percentage Response[*]
Control of School			
Public	358	19	95.0
Private	1,029	49	95.5
Region of School			
North Atlantic	439	15	96.7
Great Lakes and Plains	403	22	94.8
Southeast	285	18	94.1
West and Southwest	264	12	95.7
Level of School[b]			
College	1,171	61	95.0
University	215	8	96.4

[a] Two factors included in table 71 are not included here because the size distribution of schools and the quality ratings of schools could not be identified without considerable effort.
[b] Junior college: 92 percent.
[*] Chi-square tests (0.5) indicate no significant differences by control, region, or level.
Source: survey data.

institutions represented by the presidents are divided by method of financing, region, or level. Because of the originally very high response rate, and the substantial similarity between the group of nonresponding institutions and responding ones, I am reasonably confident that there is little bias because of an atypical list of names of new appointees.

Although over 70 percent of the sampled new appointees returned questionnaires, the response was neither as high nor as balanced as that of the college presidents (see table 71). On the basis of information supplied by the presidents it is possible to identify the nonrespondents by field of specialization and certain employer characteristics and compare them to the respondents. When grouped by control of employer (public versus private), region of employer, size of employer, and disciplinary

71

Response by Individuals, by the Characteristics of Their Employers, and by Their Specialties[a]

CHARACTERISTICS	NUMBER RESPONDING	NUMBER NOT RESPONDING	PERCENTAGE RESPONSE
Control of School			
Public	4,435	1,191	71.2
Private	2,860	1,131	71.7
Region of School			
North Atlantic	2,082	945	68.8
Great Lakes and Plains	2,197	814	73.0
Southeast	1,475	558	72.6
West and Southwest	1,642	599	73.3
Level of School *			
College	3,474	1,266	73.1
University	3,727	5,384	69.2
Size of School			
Under 1,000 students	1,049	425	71.2
1,000–5,000 students	3,216	1,248	72.0
Over 5,000 students	2,595	1,088	70.5
Prestige of School *			
Top 20 percent	509	272	65.2
20 to 40 percent	1,234	493	71.5
40 to 60 percent	1,420	508	73.7
60 to 80 percent	1,513	629	70.6
Bottom 20 percent	1,823	702	72.2
Discipline of Individual			
Sciences	3,630	1,142	76.1
Humanities	2,387	684	77.7
Social sciences	1,167	437	72.8

[a] The numbers in blocks do not always add to the same totals because it was easier to identify, for example, the region of the school of an individual than the prestige of the school.

* Means significant difference by a chi-square test at the .05 level.

Sources: survey data and Prestige Index.

specialty, the respondents and nonrespondents are not significantly different. The response was equally high from small schools and large, public schools and private, scientists and humanists. There is one point, however, where results may be slightly biased by the nature of the response: professors from the high prestige universities were slightly more reluctant to respond than others. For example, the rate of response from institutions in the top 20 percent of the prestige hierarchy was only 65.2 percent, compared to slightly over 70 percent in all other categories. In order to allow compensation for bias along these lines, the results throughout the volume are often broken down according to the prestige of the professors' employers. With one exception noted in the above paragraph, the sample of questionnaire response appears to be typical of the universe.

B

The Prestige or Quality Per Student Index

Not all of the four-year colleges and universities in the United States hold equal stature. Quality differences are substantial. There are a few, such as Harvard and Yale and the University of Chicago, which stand above all others in their ability to command respect. Caplow and McGee have dubbed these "major league" institutions. Beyond these, another 25 or 30 schools are very highly respected and generally reputed to produce the highest quality of students and research. The names of these schools are recognized by all and respected by most. Following Berelson, we might think of these schools as roughly approximating that portion of the membership of the Association of Graduate Schools that are not included in the first-mentioned group, though for our purposes it would be necessary to add some high quality schools which are solely undergraduate.[1] There are another 100 or so institutions whose reputations are widely known and which are viewed with respect. Beyond this there are many institutions which enjoy good reputations locally, but which rarely reach national eminence. And, finally, there are large numbers of marginal and submarginal institutions which, rightly or wrongly, are thought to be staffed by underqualified faculty and attended by students who cannot get in better schools.

The American system of higher education is eclectic. No attempt has been made to equalize the merit of the various units of the system. Each type of school, each quality level, is thought to have its place in the system; and all levels are thriving at the present time.

That institutions vary in quality is commonly agreed. But when one is faced with the task of identifying the good and the bad, as I was, disagreements are sure to arise. No matter what basis is used for rating

[1] Bernard Berelson, *Graduate Education in the United States* (New York: McGraw-Hill Book Co., Inc., 1960), p. 280.

193

institutions, a substantial group will argue for the inappropriateness of the measure used, and rightly so. Harvard does not want to be rated on its success in providing a place to go to school for young people within a 50-mile radius of the campus, whereas a city-owned community college would regard this statistic as an important index of the school's "success." And rating the community college on the basis of the number of scholarly publications by its faculty would be inappropriate, though Harvard would feel this index to be far more appropriate than the first. One of the major problems in rating institutions is that their objectives vary and that a rating system that is appropriate for schools with one set of objectives is almost certain to be inappropriate for another set of schools.

The index that I have chosen to use, which undoubtedly does not place all institutions in their best light, is meant to be a measure of "quality per student" and the stature of institutions in the eyes of the scholarly community. Stature is most relevant to this study. Professors seek out prestigious institutions. For many professors, institutional prestige takes on a significance in job choice that is reserved for monetary reward in most other professions. Even when recognizing the risks involved, it is extremely desirable to have an "objective" measure of institutional prestige. How good an institution is thought to be by candidates qualified to teach at the college level is the rating thought to be most appropriate for this study.

The ideal measure of "institutional prestige in the eyes of scholars" would be to ask all scholars to rate all schools in the country. Because the various departments within universities and colleges are likely to vary, it would probably be desirable to divide all answers on the basis of each discipline. Unfortunately, to have undertaken such a survey would have been well beyond the scope of this study.[2] A close approximation of such a rating can be achieved by studying the factors that determine institutional prestige, that allow a school to become prestigious. Although not all of these factors are identifiable, and some of those which can be identified cannot be quantified, many are subject to measurement.

The index used herein is based upon up to eight such factors.[3] The overall prestige rating represents the unweighted mean of the ratings received on each of the eight factors. Each institution is ranked against all other institutions on each of the factors; thus, for each variable an institution may receive a rank between 1 and 1,121, with the lower rank

[2] For schools with graduate departments, the American Council of Education under the supervision of Allan Cartter has recently completed such a survey (Allen M. Cartter, *An Assessment of Graduate Education in the United States*. Washington, D.C.: ACE, 1966).

[3] An average rank, or composite rating, was computed where at least four of the eight factors were known.

representing the better school. By averaging these eight individual ranks, an overall rank, or composite rating, is obtained for each school. The schools with the lowest average ranks are the top-rated.

According to their average ranks, the colleges and universities are divided into six groups. The total number of faculty employed by the schools in each group represents a certain percentage of all faculty in all groups. The schools in group A employ ten percent of all faculty. The 28 schools with the lowest average ranks account for ten percent of all faculty appointments, even though they represent only about 2.5 percent of all colleges and universities. The schools in group B also account for ten percent of all faculty. These schools have average ranks which are not quite low enough to place them in group A but are not so high as to place them in group C. Groups C, D, E, and F each account for 20 percent of all faculty positions. These data are summarized in table 72.

72

Groupings, by Prestige Index

Group Number	Number of Institutions in Group	Percentage of All Faculty in Group[a]	Percentage of All Institutions in Group	Range of Average Rank for Group
A	28	10 (top 10)	2.4	22–142
B	47	10 (next 10)	4.2	142–233
C	134	20 (20–40)	12.1	233–372
D	201	20 (40–60)	17.9	372–509
E	283	20 (60–80)	25.2	509–639
F	428	20 (80–100)	38.2	639–1,009
Total	1,121	100	100.0	

[a] "All faculty" refers to the total number of persons on the faculty, not the number of those newly hired.

Source: Computed from data published by the American Council on Education, *American Universities and Colleges* (9th Edition; Washington: ACE, 1964), and by the American Association of University Professors, "The Economic Status of the Profession, 1962–63: Report on the Self-grading Compensation Survey," *AAUP Bulletin,* XLIX, No. 2 (Summer 1963).

The eight factors on which institutions are ranked are the following:

1. Percentage of faculty with Ph.D.'s

2. Average compensation (salary and fringe benefits) per faculty member,

3. Percentage of students continuing to graduate school,

4. Percentage of students studying at the graduate level,

5. Number of volumes in library per full-time student,

6. Total number of full-time faculty members,

7. Faculty-student ratio,

8. Total current income per student.

A priori there is reason to believe that each of these factors influences the quality and therefore the stature of an institution. The Ph.D. is a widely accepted measure of faculty quality which is used by many accrediting agencies. Though it is not a guarantee, the Ph.D. is a conspicuous sign that a man has been exposed to and absorbed the substantive material of a given discipline. The Ph.D. also indicates that a man has shown some ability to pursue original research and to communicate the results of this research to other members of his chosen profession. The man who has earned the Ph.D. has been exposed to the content of his field on the graduate level and, it is usually safe to assume, knows the material that he is to teach.[4]

Now that the AAUP has given wide publicity to academic salaries, there is prestige per se in paying well. Also, to the extent that salaries influence mobility by attracting faculty, the better paying schools will be able to draw more candidates to a given job and may, therefore, make more discriminating judgments on noneconomic bases. Other things equal, the better paying schools will attract better faculty.[5]

A conspicuous indication of the quality and orientation of the student body is the percentage of students continuing into graduate school.[6] This

[4] Measure 1 is computed as number of Ph.D. holders divided by total number of faculty. Numerator and denominator include part-time faculty and weight them equally with full-time faculty. All data are from American Council on Education, *American Universities and Colleges,* 9th Edition (Washington: ACE) 1964.

Unfortunately, some very good schools received unjustifiably low ranks on this variable because in the report to ACE they included graduate student instructors (who do not have Ph.D.'s) as full-fledged faculty. Perhaps the worst case of this is the University of California at Berkeley, where virtually all full-fledged faculty members must have Ph.D.'s in hand before being hired. By including graduate student instructors, the percentage of Ph.D.'s on the faculty reported to the ACE is only 77.1 percent, which places Berkeley 52nd. In contrast, at Harvard the Ph.D. is a necessary prerequisite to being reported as faculty to the ACE so that 100 percent of Harvard's faculty have Ph.D.'s

A second, though less serious, limitation of the Ph.D. measure is that some men are not teaching in the field where they received their Ph.D.'s This is especially true of doctorates received in education. An Ed.D. might be teaching physics even though his training is in general science.

[5] Measure 2, average compensation for full-time faculty 1962-63, includes for all ranks both salaries (adjusted to nine-month basis when necessary) and fringe benefits. The statistics are taken from AAUP, "The Economic Status of the Profession, 1962-63: Report on the Self-grading Compensation Survey," *AAUP Bulletin,* XLIX, No. 2 (Summer 1963). Compensation data were available for 598 schools. An adjustment was made so that this ranking scale had the same range as the others.

[6] Measure 3 is a statistic quoted by each school's top administrators as reported in ACE, *American Universities and Colleges,* 1964.

statistic is especially significant for scholars, for some portion of the impression one gains about a school comes from who the students are and what they do. A school which produces a high percentage of its products for the graduate schools, where the opinion-influencing scholars tend to be located, is almost certain to enhance its image in the eyes of these scholars, and thereby increase its own stature.

The presence of a graduate school and graduate students almost certainly augments the stature of an institution of higher learning. Regardless of actual fact, the presence of a graduate program is usually regarded as an indication that a school has the staff qualified to teach in such a program, which means a relatively well-qualified staff. Also, the institution which grants graduate degrees has an opportunity to influence the people voting in the opinion polls. Some of the scholars who form opinions on the relative stature of the various schools are home-products. Again, most graduate faculties are expected to publish, and publications increase the prestige of both the publisher and the institution which employs him.[7]

A commonly regarded prerequisite to good education and good research is adequate facilities, and the most important facility, in most disciplines, is the college library. Stature-producing research is unlikely without a good library. It is for this reason that a measure of the size of the library was included in the determination of the composite prestige index.[8]

Sheer size also may be expected to be a determinant of stature. The larger universities have more faculty members, more students, and more chances for fame. Other things equal, more publications will come out of large schools because there are more people to publish. Also, at a

[7] Measure 4 is computed as the ratio of graduate students to undergraduate students. Counted as students are all full-time students and 40 percent of all part-time students. The statistic is taken from ACE, *American Universities and Colleges,* 1964.

[8] Measure 5 is computed as the ratio of volumes in the school library to number of students. Students are here measured in full-time equivalents. Data are from ACE, *American Universities and Colleges,* 1964.

Proximity to a good library would have been a better measure, but these data were not used for obvious reasons.

The decision to divide the total volumes in the library by the number of students cannot be justified when one thinks of measure 5 alone. Clearly, it is the total number of volumes in the library, not the volumes per student, that is most important to the researcher; and to the student also total volumes are probably more important than volumes per. By the measure used, most of the top-ranking libraries are respectable libraries in institutions with small student bodies, though Yale and Harvard rank fifth and sixth.

The division by the number of students was made as a mechanical adjustment to insure that not all of the top-rated schools would be the large multiversities, that good liberal arts colleges such as Amherst and Williams would not automatically be eliminated from the possibility of gaining the top composite rating because of their small size.

large school specialization is more possible and more probable. And specialization has academic respectability; generalization of interest does not.[9]

Because it is commonly believed to influence the overall quality of the educational service, the faculty-student ratio has also been included in the composite index of quality-stature. When there are relatively few students per faculty member, this allows both for the closer contact between students and their mentors and for greater time for faculty research. When faculty members are relatively numerous, it is usually more feasible to free the faculty for research leaves and the like.[10]

Income per student, the last element in the composite index is included as a general indication of the extent to which a college can afford the luxuries that often enhance stature. Besides a library, low teaching loads, high faculty compensation, and low faculty-student ratios, money can buy captive journals, monograph series, outside lecturers, laboratory facilities, secretarial staff, computer facilities, and many other items which may influence both directly and indirectly the stature of an institution.[11]

Each of the above factors is thought to influence stature, each in a slightly different manner. When taken alone, no one of the factors adequately reflects the complex entity, stature. But when taken together, the factors, as summarized in the composite index present a reasonably accurate picture. Injustices occur, but they are not frequent enough to destroy the usefulness of the measure.

[9] Measure 6 is computed as the number of full-time faculty and their equivalents. Data are from ACE, *American Universities and Colleges,* 1964.

[10] Measure 7 is computed as full-time equivalent faculty divided by full-time equivalent student enrollment. Data are from ACE, *American Universities and Colleges,* 1964.

[11] Measure 8 is computed as educational and general income divided by the full-time equivalent student enrollment. Data are from ACE, *American Universities and Colleges,* 1964.

C

Academic Labor Market Study

Dear Newly Appointed Faculty Member:

This is a study of college professors who moved to a new institution in 1964. The study is financed by the National Science Foundation and the U.S. Department of Labor, Office of Manpower, Automation and Training, and conducted by the Department of Economics of the University of North Carolina.

We are interested in learning how and why college professors find and select new jobs. Our intent is to appraise the role currently played by placement and referral agencies and to evaluate various proposals for improving the flow of manpower through academic markets. Your cooperation is requested.

Thousands of newly appointed professors are being asked to fill out this questionnaire and return it to us for statistical analysis. Information obtained from this questionnaire will be kept strictly confidential.

We are asking *everyone* to fill in the first four questions. You can aid research and save follow-up costs by responding promptly. An addressed envelope requiring no postage is provided for your convenience. Note that an answer is expected for every part of each item. We appreciate your help in making this study a success.

Sincerely yours,
David G. Brown
Associate Professor of Economics
University of North Carolina

PART I. PRELIMINARY QUESTIONS

1. Are you now working toward a degree at the *same* institution at which you are teaching?
   ☐ Yes   ☐ No

2. Are you on active military duty?
   ☐ Yes   ☐ No

3. Do you teach as an unsalaried member of a religious order?   ☐ Yes   ☐ No

4. Are your primary teaching responsibilities in a school of law, medicine, dentistry, nursing, or pharmacy?   ☐ Yes   ☐ No

IF YOU ANSWERED "YES" TO ANY OF THE ABOVE QUESTIONS, PLEASE STOP AND RETURN THIS QUESTIONNAIRE IN THE ENCLOSED STAMPED ENVELOPE.

5. Are you a full-time employee of the institution listed above for at least 9 months of the academic year 1964–65?   ☐ Yes   ☐ No

IF YOU ANSWERED "NO" TO QUESTION 5, PLEASE STOP AND RETURN THIS QUESTIONNAIRE IN THE ENCLOSED STAMPED ENVELOPE.

PART II. PERSONAL DATA

6. When were you born?
   ☐ Before 1899   ☐ 1914–1918   ☐ 1929–1933
   ☐ 1899–1903   ☐ 1919–1923   ☐ 1934–1938
   ☐ 1904–1908   ☐ 1924–1928   ☐ After 1938
   ☐ 1909–1913

7. Sex: ☐ Male   ☐ Female

8. How many credit hours are you teaching this term? (Check the number nearest the actual.)
   ☐ None   ☐ 9   ☐ 18
   ☐ 3   ☐ 12   ☐ 21
   ☐ 6   ☐ 15   ☐ 24

IF "NONE" STOP AND RETURN QUESTIONNAIRE.

9. Please provide the information requested below concerning your education. (Include post-doctoral training.)

Name and Location (State) of School Attended	Name of Degree	Date of Degree
High school last attended:		
Higher education:		

IF MORE SPACE IS NEEDED, PLEASE ATTACH A SEPARATE SHEET.

10. In what field is your highest degree? _____

11. What is your principal teaching field in your present position? _____

12. In what other field are you teaching? If none, put "0." _____

13. What is your primary field of scholarship, research, or creativity? _____

PART III. PREVIOUS JOB

14. What was your primary activity during the academic year 1963–64? (Check only one.)

    ☐ Check here and skip to Question 15 if you were on leave from an institution of higher education last year. Answer questions 15 through 21 as if you had not been on leave.
    ☐ Student (Include "student and part-time teacher" and "student and research assistant.")
    ☐ Teacher in higher education
    ☐ Administrator in higher education
    ☐ Teacher or administrator in primary or secondary school
    ☐ Business employee
    ☐ Government employee (exclude military)
    ☐ Military service
    ☐ Foundation employee
    ☐ Other. Please specify:

QUESTIONS 15 THROUGH 20 ARE ABOUT YOUR PREVIOUS TEACHING JOB. IF YOU WERE NOT PRIMARILY A "TEACHER IN HIGHER EDUCATION" LAST YEAR, CHECK HERE ☐ AND SKIP TO QUESTION 21. OTHERWISE, ANSWER THE FOLLOWING QUESTIONS.

15. In the space below, write in the name of the school where you were employed last year.

16. What was your academic rank last year?

    ☐ Instructor   ☐ Institution has no
    ☐ Assistant Professor   ranking system
    ☐ Associate Professor   ☐ Other
    ☐ Full Professor

17. Which of the following words best explains the urgency of your desire to locate a new job for 1964–65?
    (Check one.)

    ☐ My old job was *unacceptable* and I had a strong desire to move.
    ☐ My old job was *unavailable* and I had to move.
    ☐ My old job was acceptable, yet I felt I could do better and was looking around.
    ☐ My old job was acceptable, yet I was keeping my ears open and remaining available.
    ☐ I was quite satisfied with my previous job and had not seriously thought about moving.

IF "UNAVAILABLE" (i.e., OPTION 2), SKIP TO QUESTION 21. OTHERWISE, GO ON TO QUESTION 18.

18. What was wrong with your previous job that caused you to want to leave? (Check *one or two* of the most important factors.)

    ☐ Friends and relatives too far away
    ☐ Climate undesirable
    ☐ Cultural opportunities poor
    ☐ Colleagues not congenial
    ☐ Colleagues not competent
    ☐ Reputation of school among scholars poor
    ☐ Administration or administrators not competent
    ☐ Research facilities and opportunities poor
    ☐ Courses assigned undesirable
    ☐ Teaching hours excessive
    ☐ Quality of students poor
    ☐ Advancement prospects in academic rank poor
    ☐ Salary too low
    ☐ Fringe benefits poor
    ☐ Opportunities for outside income poor
    ☐ Future salary prospects poor
    ☐ Other. Please specify:

19. In the space below, write your best estimate of what your *annual income* would have been in 1964–65 (Sept. to Sept.) if you had remained at your previous job. (Include salary, extra teaching, honoraria, and income from part-time jobs. Exclude dividends, gifts, interest, royalties, and sales of manuscripts.)

    $_____

20. Approximately how much higher than the amount noted in Question 19 would your annual income had to have been in order to induce you to stay at your previous job? (Check one. Assume that nothing else about the previous job changed.)

- [ ] $0–$499
- [ ] $500–$999
- [ ] $1000–$1999
- [ ] $2000–$4999
- [ ] $5000–$9999
- [ ] $10,000–$24,999
- [ ] More than $25,000

PART IV. METHODS OF LOCATING JOB

21. Listed below are some of the methods used to learn about jobs. (See instructions at Questions 21a, 21b, 21c and 21d.)

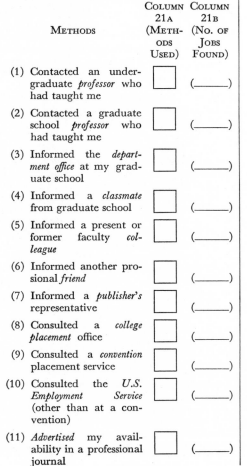

METHODS	COLUMN 21A (METHODS USED)	COLUMN 21B (NO. OF JOBS FOUND)
(1) Contacted an under-graduate *professor* who had taught me		(_____)
(2) Contacted a graduate school *professor* who had taught me		(_____)
(3) Informed the *depart-ment office* at my graduate school		(_____)
(4) Informed a *classmate* from graduate school		(_____)
(5) Informed a present or former faculty *col-league*		(_____)
(6) Informed another pro-sional *friend*		(_____)
(7) Informed a *publisher's* representative		(_____)
(8) Consulted a *college placement* office		(_____)
(9) Consulted a *convention* placement service		(_____)
(10) Consulted the *U.S. Employment Service* (other than at a con-vention)		(_____)
(11) *Advertised* my avail-ability in a professional journal		(_____)

	21A	21B
(12) *Answered an adver-tised* "job available" in a professional journal		(_____)
(13) Consulted *denomina-tional* placement bureau or board		(_____)
(14) Consulted a *commer-cial* teachers' agency		(_____)
(15) Sent *letters* of inquiry directly to potential employers		(_____)
(16) Consulted placement service of *professional or educational* associ-ation		(_____)
(17) Did *nothing* and was recruited		(_____)
(18) Used *another* method. Specify.		(_____)

21a. In COLUMN 21a (in the appropriate squares) check *each* of the methods you used to inform others of your willingness to move or to learn about job vacancies. Consider the period from June 1963 to September 1964.

21b. In COLUMN 21b (on the appropriate lines) write the number of job offers that you first learned about by each method. (Interpret "job offers" to mean "I'm certain or almost certain that I could have had the job if I wanted it.")

21c. For each of the methods that you *did not use* (i.e., did not check in COLUMN 21a), indicate which of the reasons listed below best explains why you did not use the method *by placing the appropriate letter code* in the *empty squares* in COLUMN 21a.

LETTER CODE (Use in answering Question 21c):
(A) It is *unprofessional* to use this method. It is beneath the dignity of a college professor.
(B) Good jobs are rarely found by this method. It takes *more time than it is worth.*
(C) Good jobs are sometimes found by this method, but there are better ways. *I would have pursued this method if* I had not found a job by other means.
(D) Good jobs are found by this method but I *did not have the right contacts.*
(E) Good jobs are found by this method but I was *afraid my then current employer would find out* that I was looking for another job.
(F) *I did not know* that jobs could be found by this method.

(G) I was *not looking* for a job in any way.

EVERY SQUARE IN COLUMN 21A SHOULD HAVE EITHER
A CHECK OR A LETTER IN IT. IF NOT, PLEASE RE-
ANSWER QUESTIONS 21A AND 21C.

21d. Indicate how you first learned about your
current job by placing the appropriate number
from the left margin of this page (i.e., 1
through 18) in the space below.

Method Number: _____

IF YOU WERE NOT PRIMARILY TEACHING IN HIGHER
EDUCATION LAST YEAR, CHECK HERE ☐ AND SKIP TO
QUESTION 23. OTHERWISE, GO ON TO QUESTION 22.

22. Indicate how you first learned about your *previous* job by writing the appropriate number
from the left margin of this page in the space
below.

Method Number: _____

23. How many letters of inquiry sent directly to
potential employers did you write (between
June 1963 and September 1964)?

☐ None   ☐ 11–15
☐ 1   ☐ 16–30
☐ 2–5   ☐ 31–60
☐ 6–10   ☐ More than 60

24. How many professional conventions did you attend between September 1, 1963, and September 1, 1964?

☐ None   ☐ 5
☐ 1   ☐ 6
☐ 2   ☐ 7
☐ 3   ☐ 8
☐ 4   ☐ 9 or more

25. You are a member of how many professional
associations? (e.g., American Historical Association)

☐ None   ☐ 5
☐ 1   ☐ 6
☐ 2   ☐ 7
☐ 3   ☐ 8 or more
☐ 4

26. Which of the following statements best describes, in your opinion, the opportunities for
learning about vacant teaching jobs in your field?
(Check only one.)

☐ *Excellent.* Vacancies are well known. There
is almost no chance that a candidate will not
learn about a vacancy for which he might
be qualified.

☐ *Good.* With some effort, most candidates
learn about most vacancies for which they
might be qualified.

☐ *Poor.* Most candidates never learn about
many of the jobs for which they might be
qualified. New methods of informing candidates of job vacancies should be investigated.

☐ *Very poor.* A candidate rarely learns about
the job vacancy that would interest him the
most. New methods of informing candidates
must be implemented.

PART V. JOB OFFERS

27. Approximately how many different jobs, starting about the same time as your present job,
were you considering and how seriously were
you considering them? (Write the total number
of jobs on each line. Do not count any job
twice. Include the job offer that you accepted.)

NUMBER OF JOBS

(_____) Investigated, but did not have a
personal interview with employer

(_____) Had personal interview, but either
did not pursue or did not receive a
concrete offer

(_____) Received concrete offer (i.e., I
was told that if I wanted the job it
was mine.)

28. Please list the *concrete offers* you received and estimate the annual incomes involved. (List your
current job first, other teaching jobs next, and
non-teaching jobs last.)

NAME OF EMPLOYER	LOCA-TION (STATE)	JOB TITLE	APPROXI-MATE ANNUAL INCOME *
Current job:			
Other job offers:			

* Includes salary, consulting, and income from part-time jobs.
Exclude dividends, interest, gifts, royalties, and sale of manuscripts.

(IF YOU NEED MORE ROOM, PLEASE ATTACH A SEPA-RATE SHEET.)

29. If you had not accepted your current job, what would your *probably* be doing this year?

- ☐ Retired
- ☐ Student
- ☐ Teacher in higher education
- ☐ Administrator in higher education
- ☐ Teacher or administrator in primary or secondary school
- ☐ Business employee
- ☐ Government employee
- ☐ Military service
- ☐ Foundation employee
- ☐ Other

IF ABOVE ANSWER WAS *NOT* "TEACHER IN HIGHER EDUCATION," SKIP TO QUESTION 34. OTHERWISE, GO ON TO THE NEXT QUESTION.

30. Please name the institution of higher education where you would *probably* be working this year if you had not accepted your current job.

Name: _____

31. On the following items, compare your current job with the one which you would probably be working at had you not obtained this one (i.e., the job listed in Question 30.). *Check once in each row.*

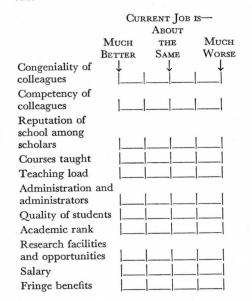

CURRENT JOB IS—
ABOUT
MUCH — THE — MUCH
BETTER — SAME — WORSE

Congeniality of colleagues
Competency of colleagues
Reputation of school among scholars
Courses taught
Teaching load
Administration and administrators
Quality of students
Academic rank
Research facilities and opportunities
Salary
Fringe benefits

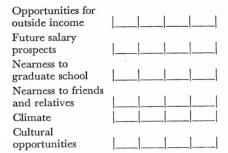

Opportunities for outside income
Future salary prospects
Nearness to graduate school
Nearness to friends and relatives
Climate
Cultural opportunities

32. How important were each of these factors in your decision to choose your current job instead of the job listed in Question 30? *Check once in each row.*

JOB CHARACTERISTICS	VERY IMPOR-TANT	IMPOR-TANT	NOT IMPOR-TANT
Congeniality of colleagues	☐	☐	☐
Competency of colleagues	☐	☐	☐
Reputation of school among scholars	☐	☐	☐
Courses taught	☐	☐	☐
Teaching load	☐	☐	☐
Administration and administrators	☐	☐	☐
Quality of students	☐	☐	☐
Academic rank	☐	☐	☐
Research facilities and opportunities	☐	☐	☐
Salary	☐	☐	☐
Fringe benefits	☐	☐	☐
Opportunities for outside income	☐	☐	☐
Future salary prospects	☐	☐	☐
Nearness to graduate school	☐	☐	☐
Nearness to friends and relatives	☐	☐	☐
Climate	☐	☐	☐
Cultural opportunities	☐	☐	☐

IF YOU RATED *FRINGE BENEFITS* AS "NOT IMPOR-TANT" SKIP TO QUESTION 34. OTHERWISE, GO ON TO QUESTION 33.

33. Check the one or two fringe benefits most im-portant in your decision.

☐ Retirement plan   ☐ Medical package
☐ Leave with pay   ☐ Secretarial and
☐ Tuition for faculty   other assistance
   children   ☐ Other.
              Specify:

34. If you could work at any school in the United States, name the one (or one among several) where you would like to teach most.

Name of school: _____

PART VI. CURRENT JOB

35. When did you assume duties at your current job?
☐ Fall, 1964   ☐ Spring, 1964
☐ Summer, 1964 ☐ Other. Specify:

35a. When did you make your final, binding commitment to accept your present position? (Check one. Estimate if you don't remember the exact date.)
☐ Before Sept., 1963 ☐ April–May, 1964
☐ Sept.–Dec., 1963   ☐ June–July, 1964
☐ Jan.–March, 1964 ☐ August–Sept., 1964

35b. When did you first learn that a position might be available at your current institution? (Check one. Estimate if you don't remember the exact date.)
☐ Before Sept., 1963 ☐ April–May, 1964
☐ Sept.–Dec., 1963   ☐ June–July, 1964
☐ Jan.–March, 1964 ☐ Aug.–Sept., 1964

36. With whom did you have the most dealings about securing your present job? (Check one.)
☐ Department (division) chairman
☐ Dean
☐ President
☐ Other. Please specify:

IF YOU DID *NOT* ANSWER "DEPARTMENT (DIVISION) CHAIRMAN," CHECK ☐ AND SKIP TO QUESTION 38. OTHERWISE, GO ON TO QUESTION 37.

37. How many new faculty has your department (division) chairman hired to start in 1964? (Check one.)
☐ Only myself   ☐ 3 or 4 others
☐ 1 other   ☐ 5 or more others
☐ 2 others   ☐ Don't know

38. Did you have a personal interview before you accepted the job? (Check the *first one* that applies.)
☐ Campus interview at school's expense
☐ Campus interview at own expense

☐ Personal interview, not at campus
☐ Telephone interview
☐ No interview

39. What is the person whom you replaced doing this year? (Check one only.)
☐ Check here and skip to Question 40 if the person is on leave (e.g., sabbatical, government, research, visiting professor at another institution)
☐ Had no predecessor
☐ Working at another academic institution
☐ Working at the same institution as an administrator
☐ Working in government
☐ Working in business
☐ Attending graduate school
☐ Retired
☐ Deceased
☐ Don't know
☐ Other. Please specify:

40. How long do you think you will remain at your current institution? (Check one only.)
☐ Until retirement
☐ This year only
☐ Probably 2–3 years
☐ Probably 4–10 years

41. At the present time, how do you rate your current job?
☐ Excellent, better than I expected
☐ Good, about the best I could expect
☐ Poor, not as good as it should be
☐ Very poor, unacceptable

42. What is your basic salary for the regular academic year? (Exclude "other income" such as summer school teaching.)
$_____

43. How many months are you expected to work for this salary?
☐ 9 or 10 months
☐ 11 or 12 months
☐ Less than 9 months

PART VII. BACKGROUND INFORMATION

44. About how many days of productive time did you lose looking for and at jobs?
☐ Less than 1 day
☐ 2 days–1 week
☐ 1–2 weeks
☐ 2–4 weeks
☐ More than 4 weeks
☐ Don't know

45. About how many days of productive time did you lose when moving?
    - ☐ Less than 1 day
    - ☐ 2 days–1 week
    - ☐ 1–2 weeks
    - ☐ 2–4 weeks
    - ☐ More than 4 weeks
    - ☐ Don't know

46. Who paid the moving costs?
    - ☐ I paid most of them
    - ☐ The school paid most or all
    - ☐ The school and I split the cost
    - ☐ Moving costs were paid by a third party
    - ☐ I didn't move the location of my residence

47. How many miles did you move?
    - ☐ None
    - ☐ Less than 50
    - ☐ 51–200
    - ☐ 200–500
    - ☐ 500–1000
    - ☐ Over 1000

48. Did you own your home at your previous job?
    - ☐ Did not have previous job
    - ☐ Yes
    - ☐ No

49. What is your religious preference?
    - ☐ Protestant. Please specify denomination: _____
    - ☐ Roman Catholic
    - ☐ Jewish
    - ☐ Other. Please specify:
    - ☐ No religious preference

50. What have you published in the last five years? (In each of the spaces below write in the appropriate number. If "none," write "0." Include co-authorship.)

(_____) Books

(_____) Monographs and articles in professional journals. (Do not include newspaper articles, instructional material published only for your classes, book reviews, and short notes of less than one page.)

(_____) Art pieces, patents, and other creative works of a major nature, especially if exhibited or sold for large sums.

51. What is your race?
    - ☐ Caucasian
    - ☐ Negroid
    - ☐ Oriental
    - ☐ Other. Please specify:

52. What is your marital status?
    - ☐ Single
    - ☐ Married, living with husband or wife
    - ☐ Separated, divorced, or widowed

53. Number of dependent children under 21 years of age:
    - ☐ None
    - ☐ 1
    - ☐ 2
    - ☐ 3
    - ☐ 4
    - ☐ 5
    - ☐ 6
    - ☐ 7
    - ☐ 8
    - ☐ 9 or more

54. During a typical week do you spend more time "teaching and counseling" or more time "researching and writing"?
    - ☐ Teaching and counseling
    - ☐ Researching and writing
    - ☐ Equal time spent

Index